The Book of Chord Tones

Book 1 • Major Chords • Bass Clef

ISBN 978-1-105-01679-0

Table of Contents

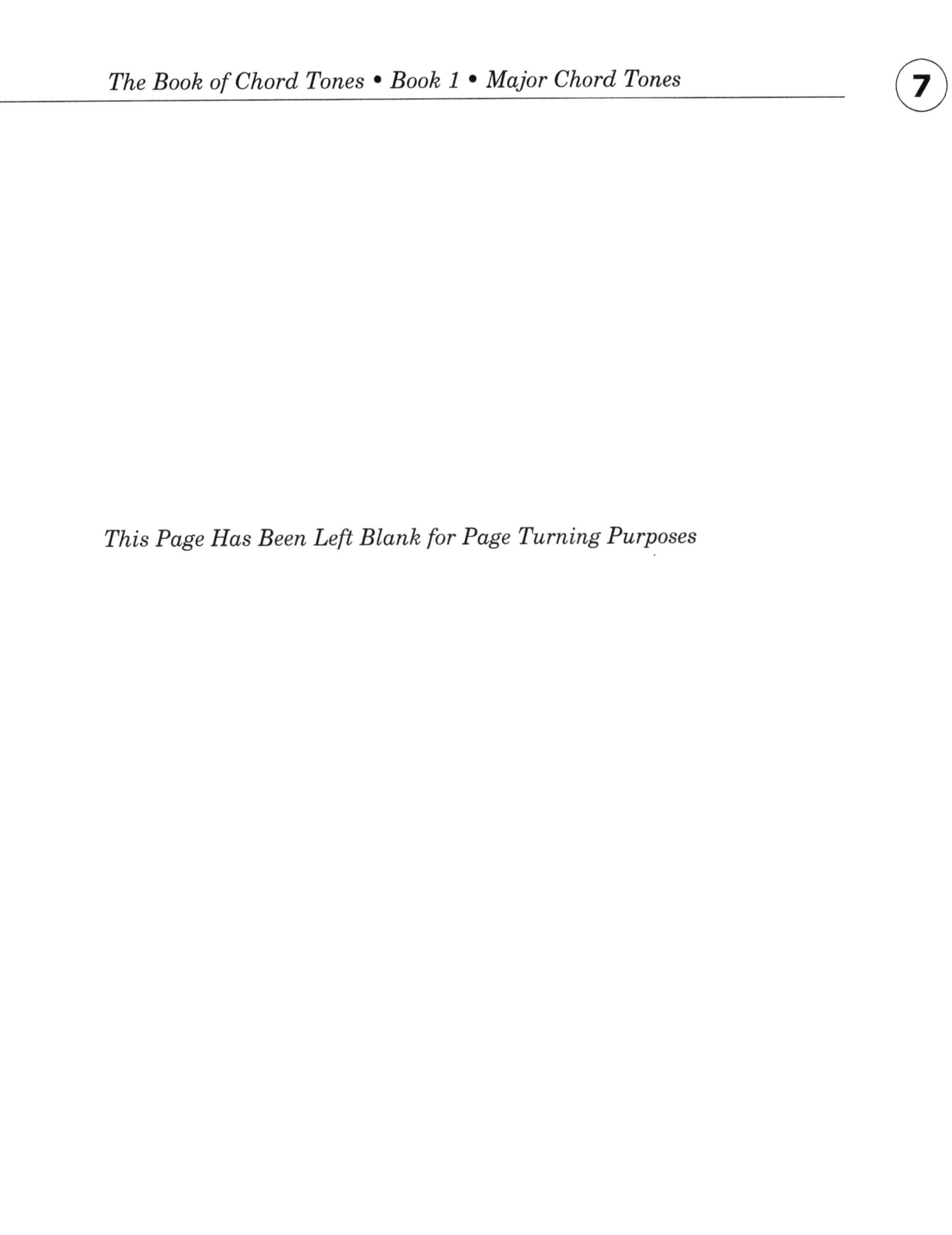

This Page Has Been Left Blank for Page Turning Purposes

Forward

Chord tones are the notes that make up and define a chord.

For instance, for the chord *C Maj7,* the chord tones are:

C E G B

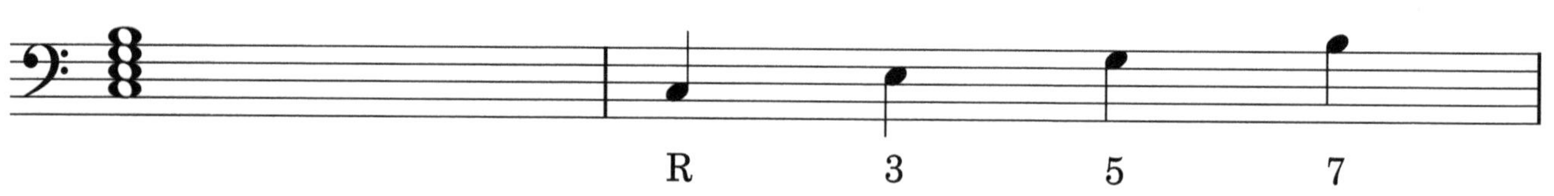

With any four-note set of chord tones there are 24 different permutations.

Using *C Maj7* as an example, the 24 combinations are:

C E G B	E C G B	G C E B	B C E G
C E B G	E C B G	G C B E	B C G E
C G E B	E G C B	G E C B	B E C G
C G B E	E G B C	G E B C	B E G C
C B E G	E B C G	G B C E	B G C E
C B G E	E B G C	G B E C	B G E C

This book contains each of these 24 patterns for all 12 of the Major 7 chords.

Performance Notes

The exercises are arranged so that they can be played on a standard four string bass with at least 22 frets. If you run out of frets for an exercise, just go up as high as you can. If your instrument has five, six, (or even more!) strings, feel free to continue the exercise in either direction as far as possible on your bass.

The exercises can be played in either 4/4 or 12/8 time. They are written out in 4/4, but if you feel adventurous, phrase the notes in groups of three.

Start slow and strive for full tone and exact rhythmic definition. Precision, good tone and solid time are much more important than velocity.

The tablature shows basic suggestions, however there are many possible fingerings for each exercise. Explore them based on how many strings you have and what is comfortable.

Many other great books are out there for exploring various musical patterns and chord tones together. Check out books by Jerry Bergonzi, Gary Campbell, Jeff Berlin, Chuck Sher, Hal Galper, Jerry Coker, Raymond Richter, Wayne Krantz and George Garzone, to name only a few.

For more articles about bass playing, including transcriptions and other exercises, check out Basso Ridiculoso on the web at:

http://BassoRidiculoso.blogspot.com

Keep Practicing!

Basso Ridiculoso
BassoRidiculoso@gmail.com
August 2011

C Major - Root Pattern 1

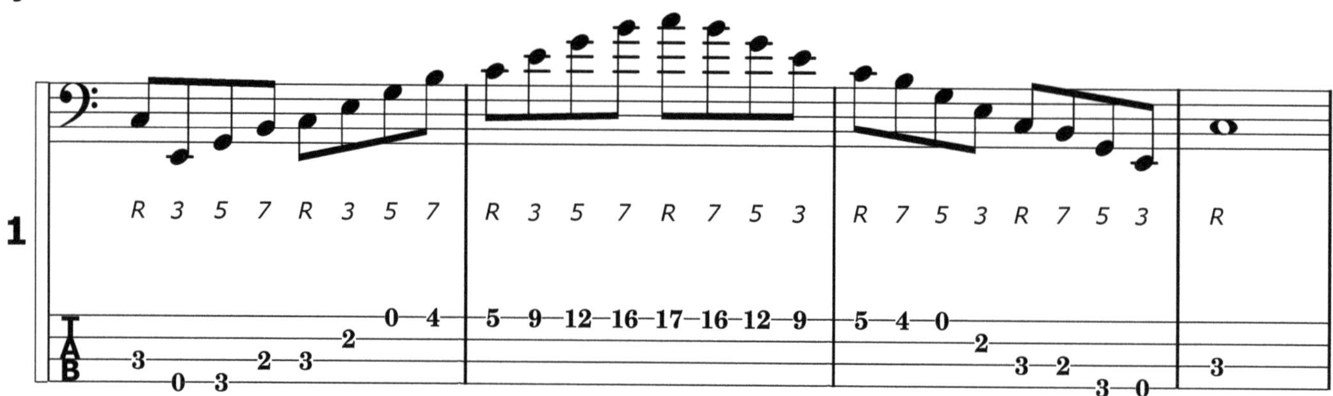

C Major - Root Pattern 2

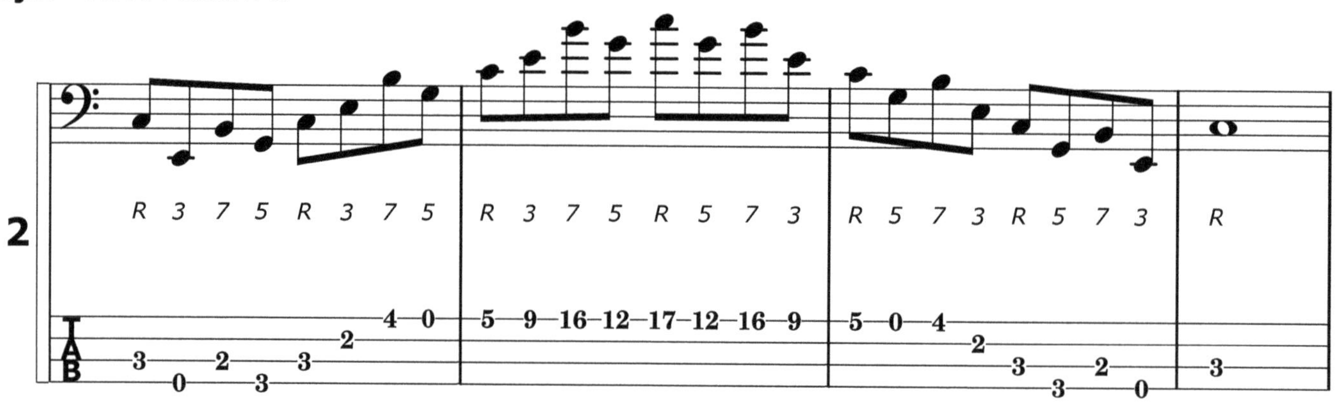

C Major - Root Pattern 3

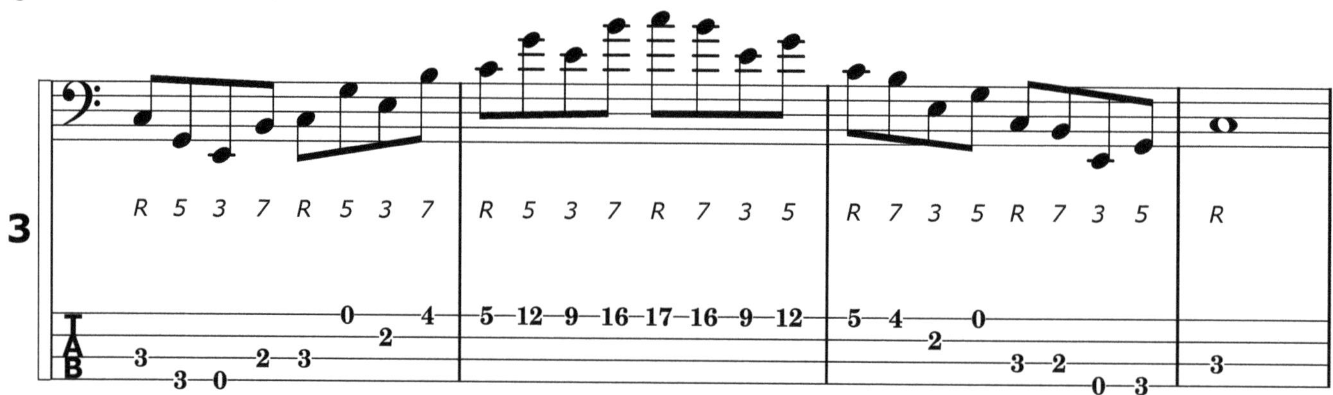

C Major - Root Pattern 4

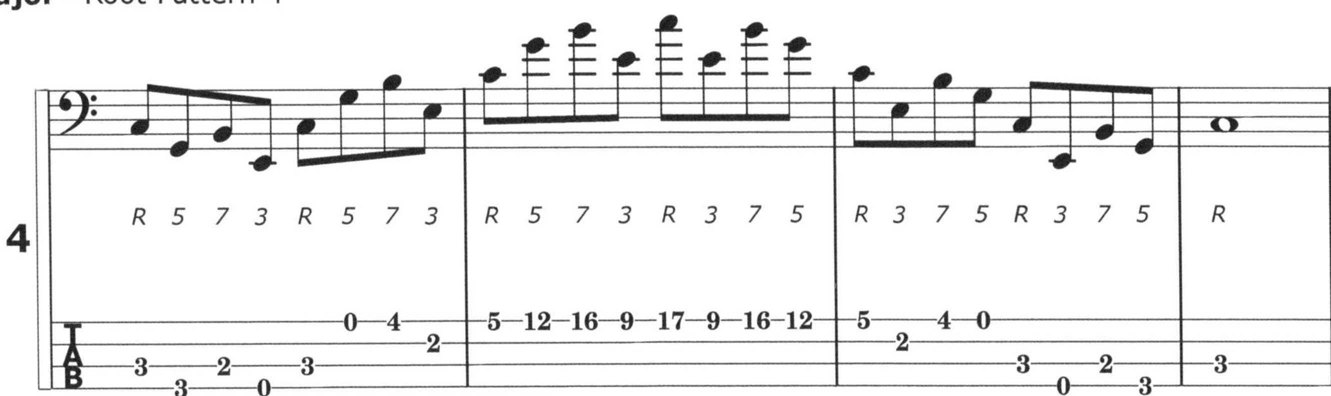

C Major - Root Pattern 5

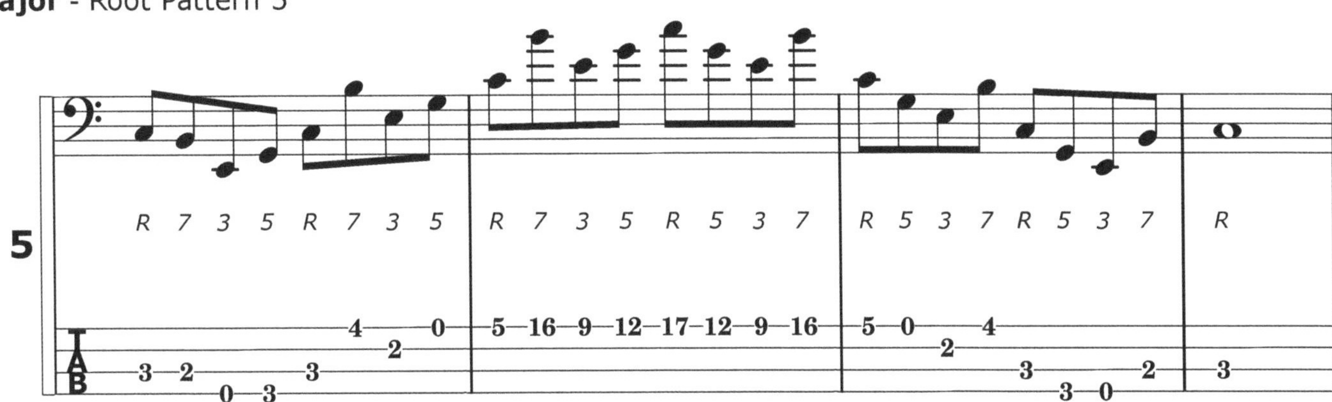

C Major - Root Pattern 6

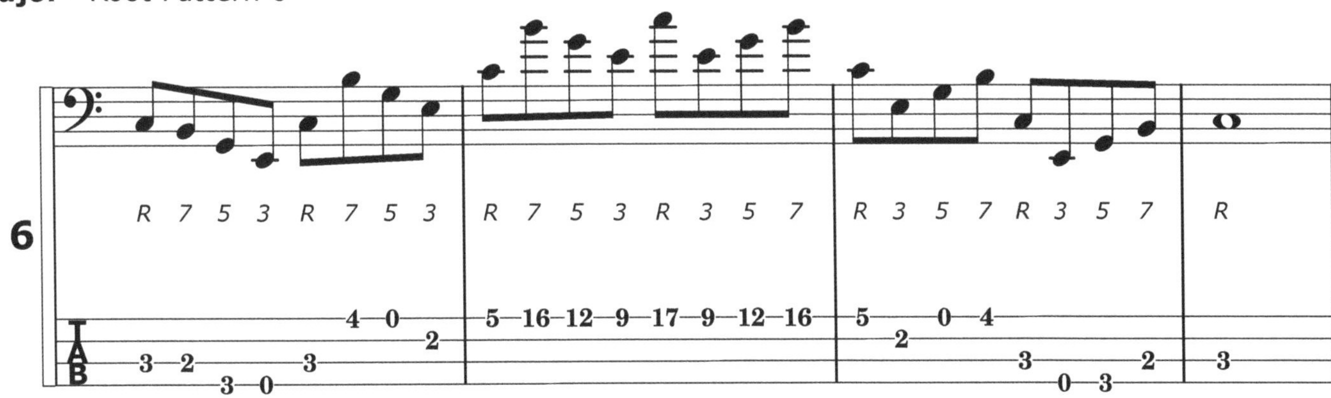

C Major - Third Pattern 1

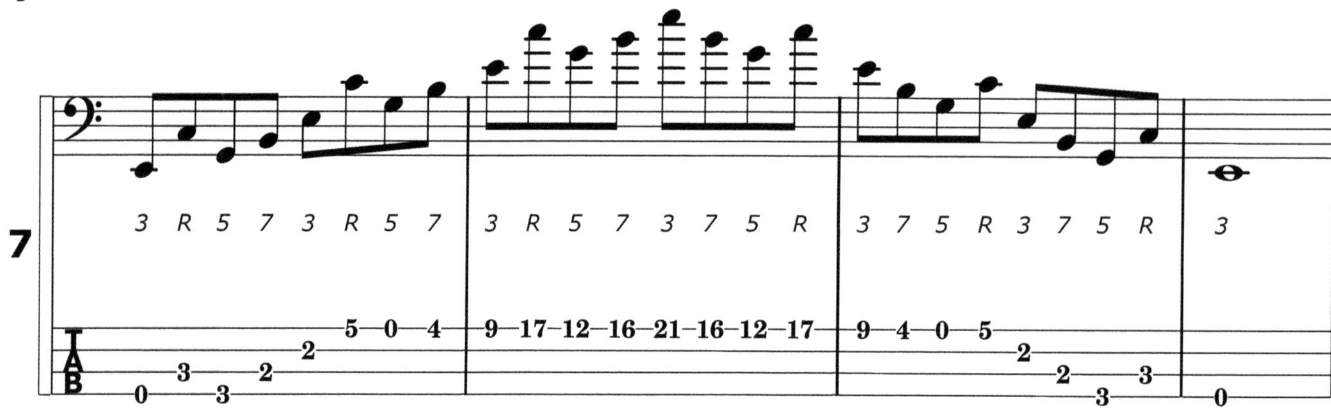

C Major - Third Pattern 2

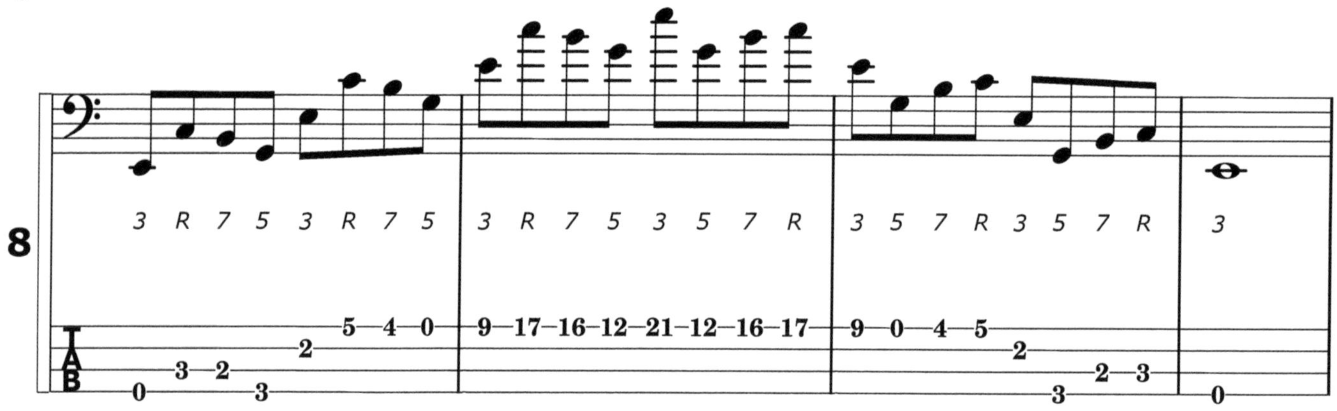

C Major - Third Pattern 3

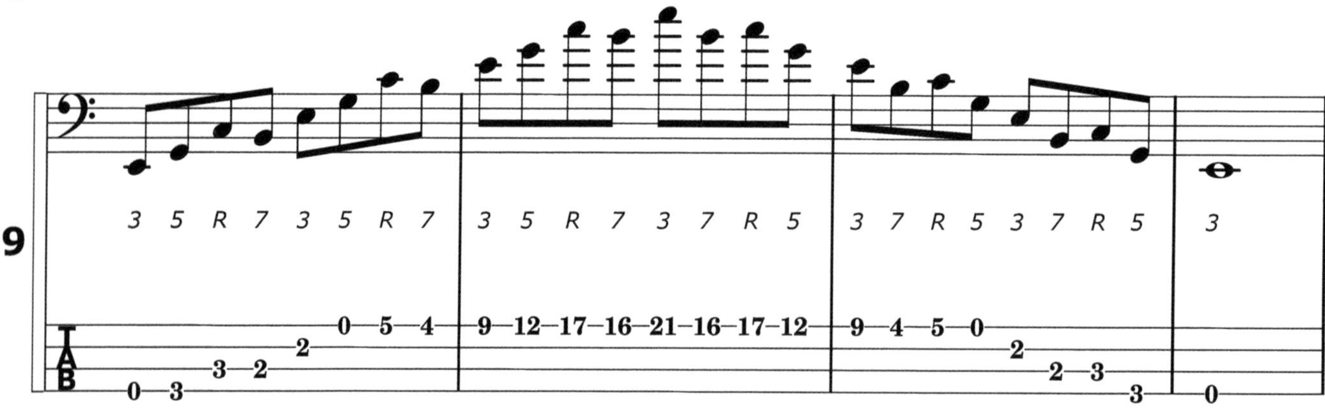

C Major - Third Pattern 4

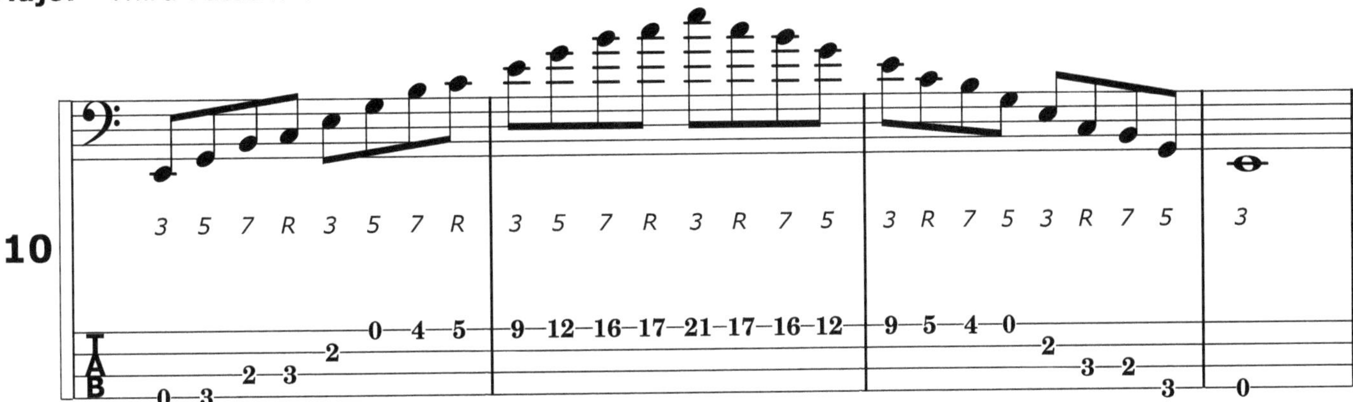

C Major - Third Pattern 5

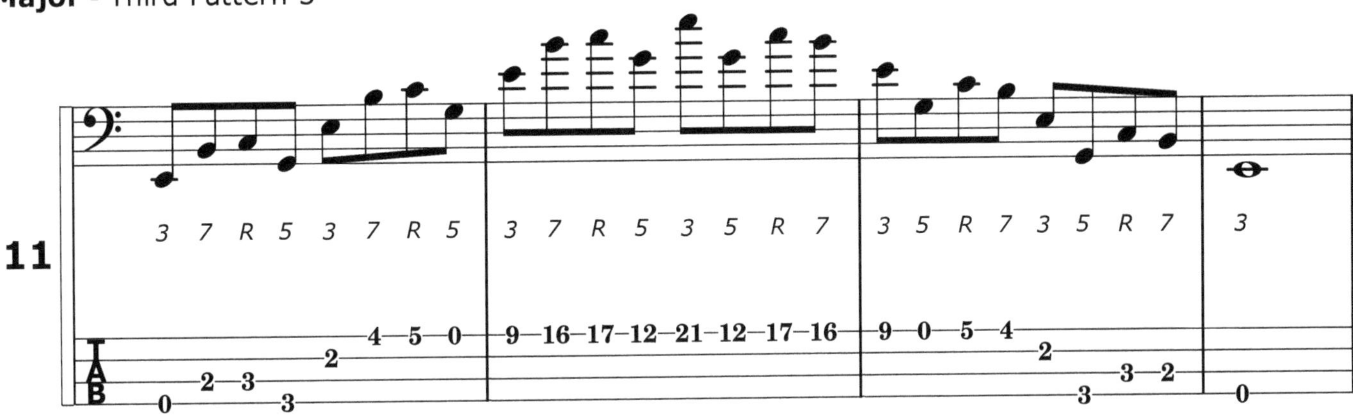

C Major - Third Pattern 6

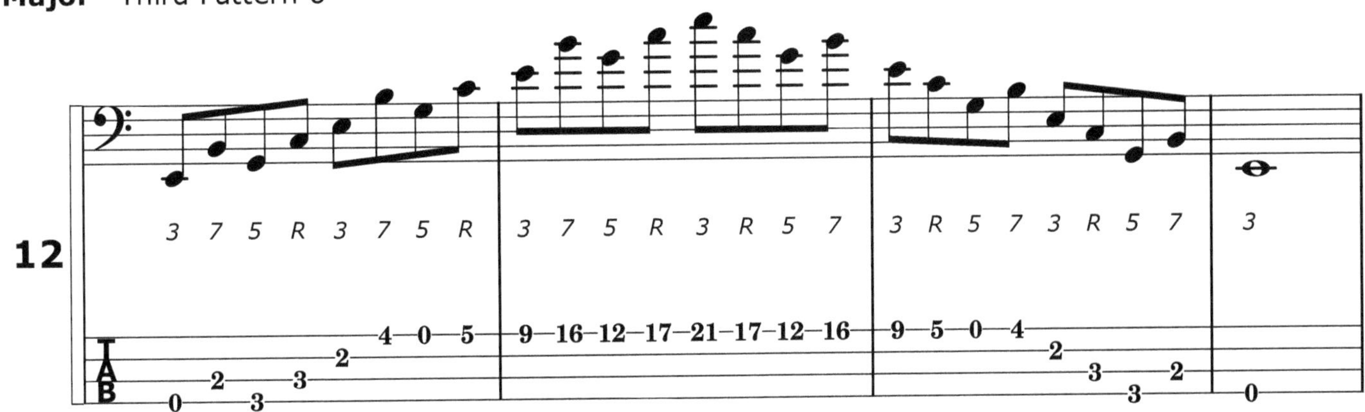

C Major - Fifth Pattern 1

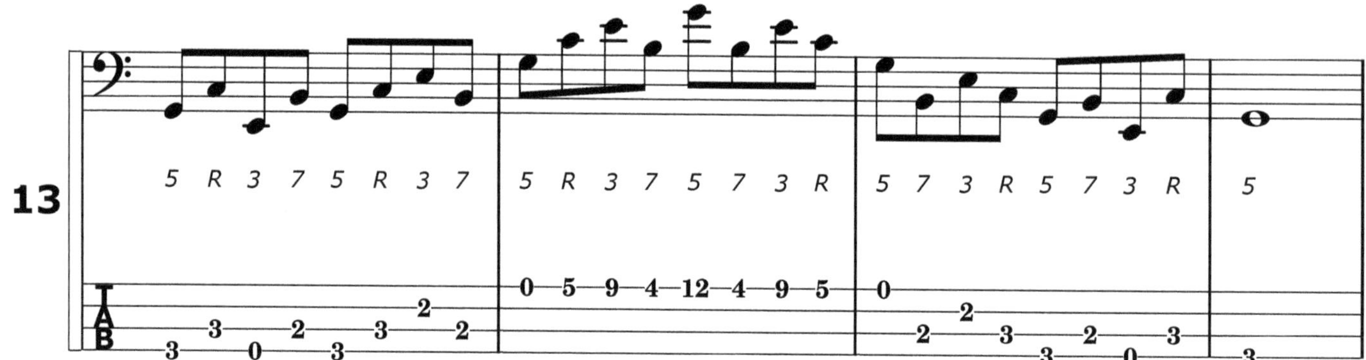

C Major - Fifth Pattern 2

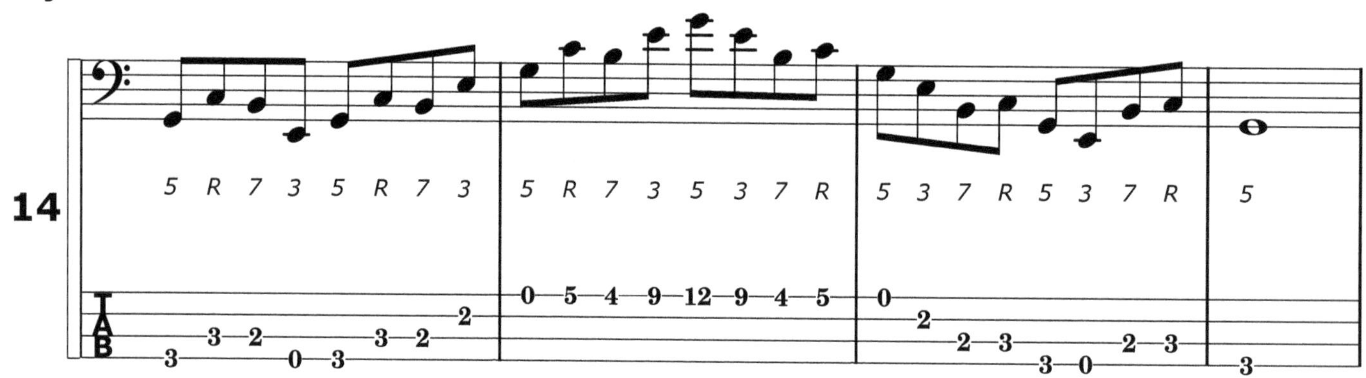

C Major - Fifth Pattern 3

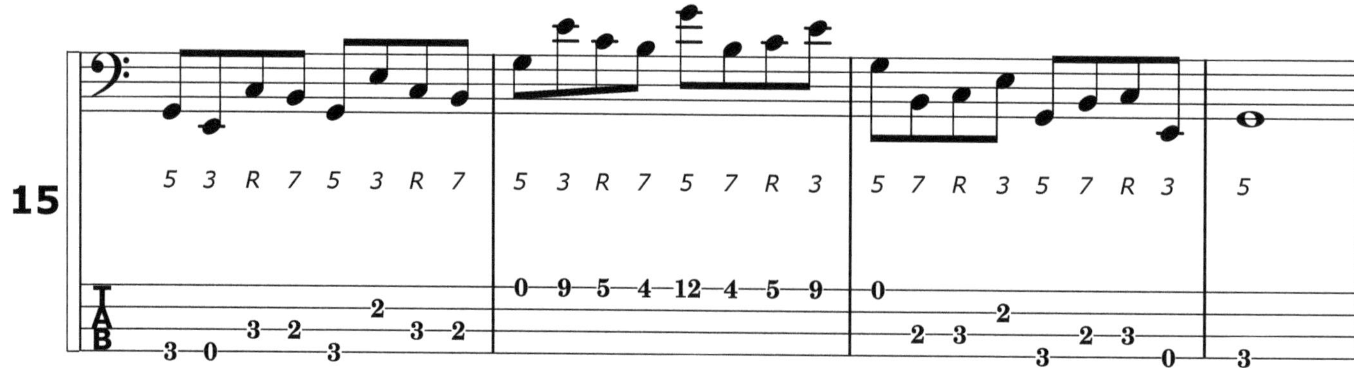

C Major - Fifth Pattern 4

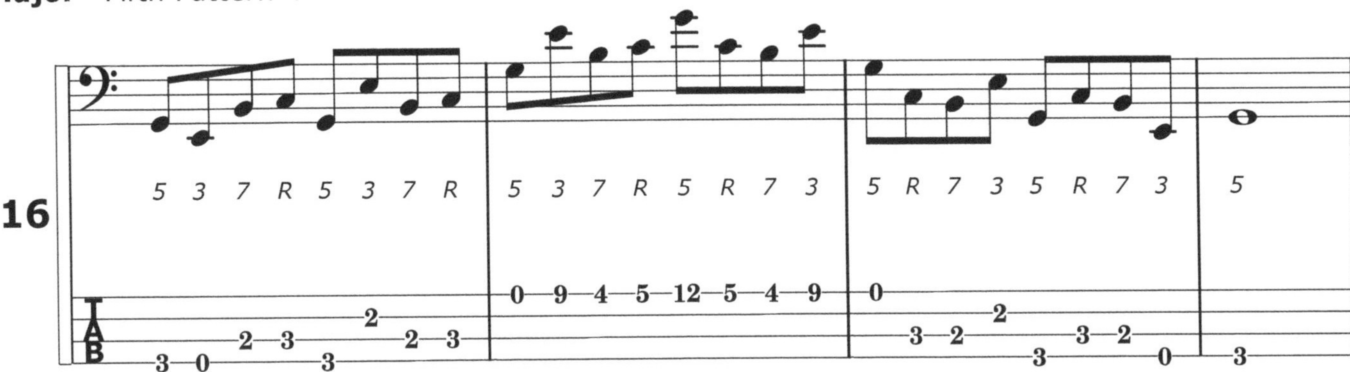

C Major - Fifth Pattern 5

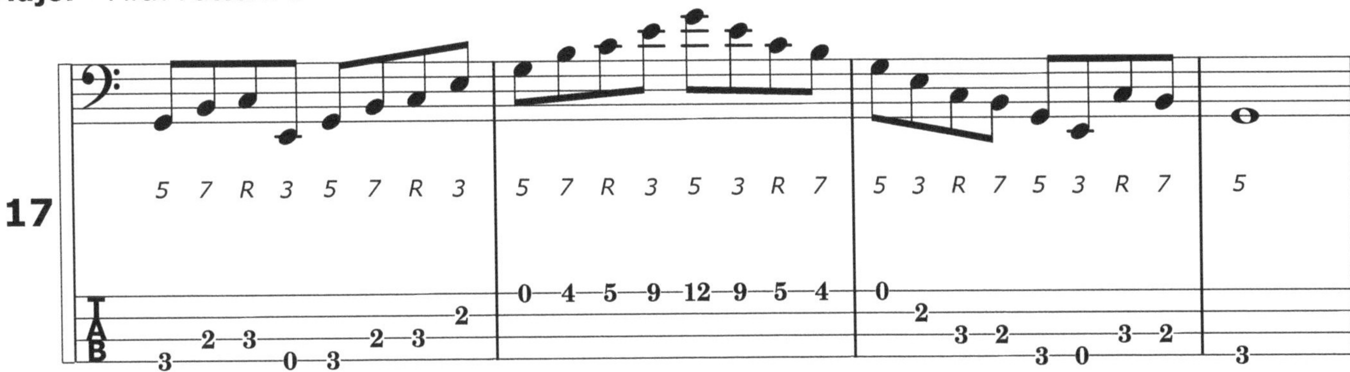

C Major - Fifth Pattern 6

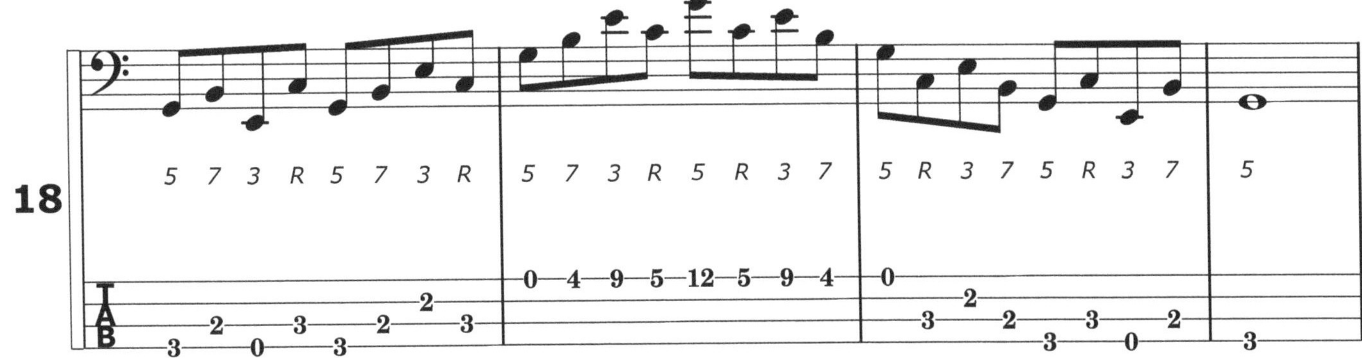

C Major - Seventh Pattern 1

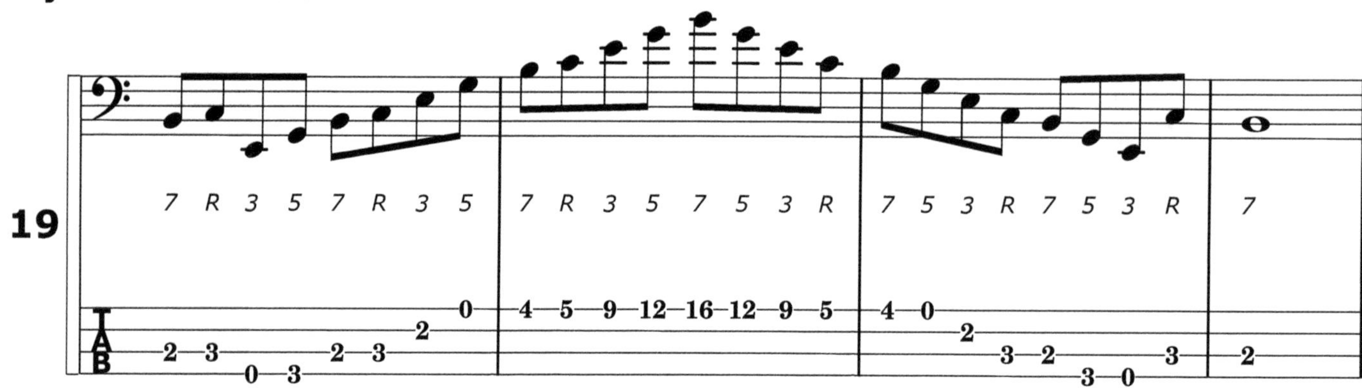

C Major - Seventh Pattern 2

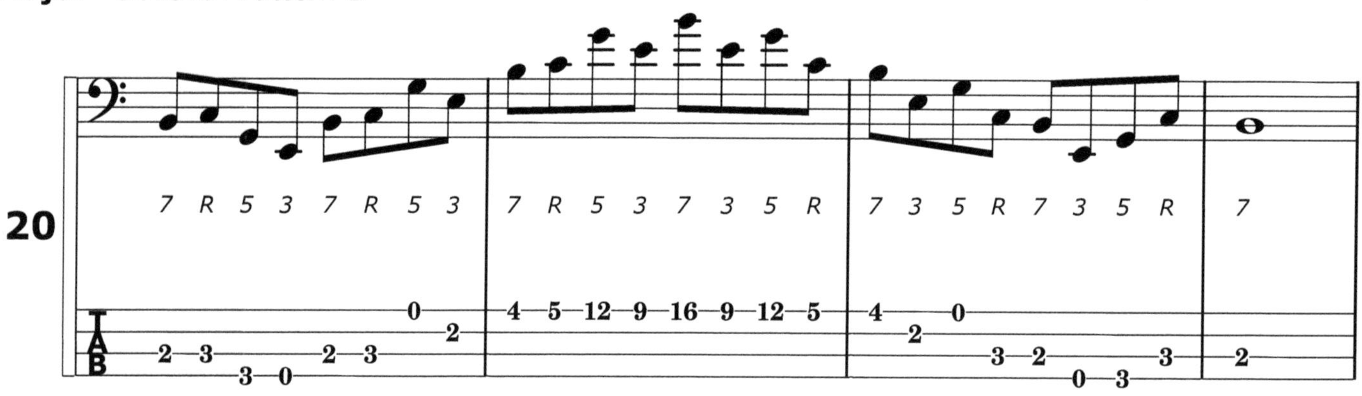

C Major - Seventh Pattern 3

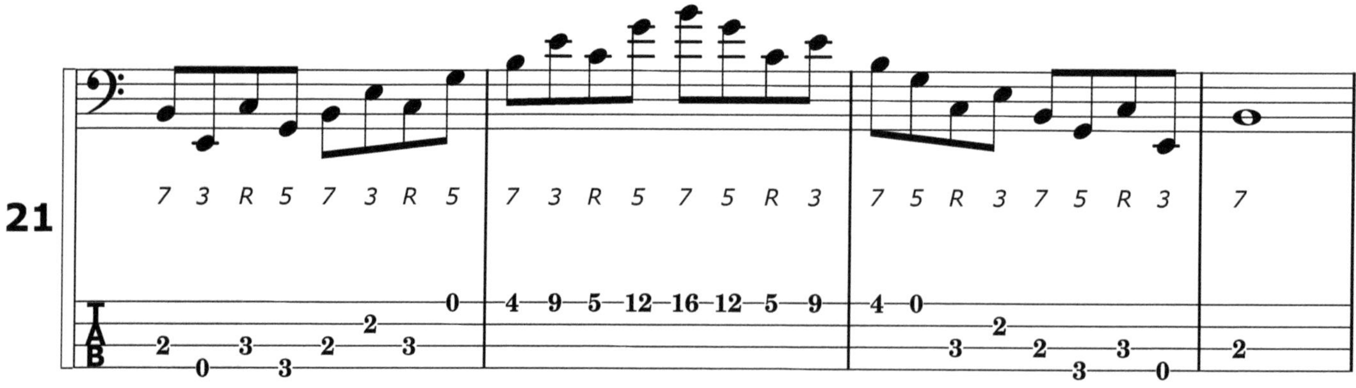

C Major - Seventh Pattern 4

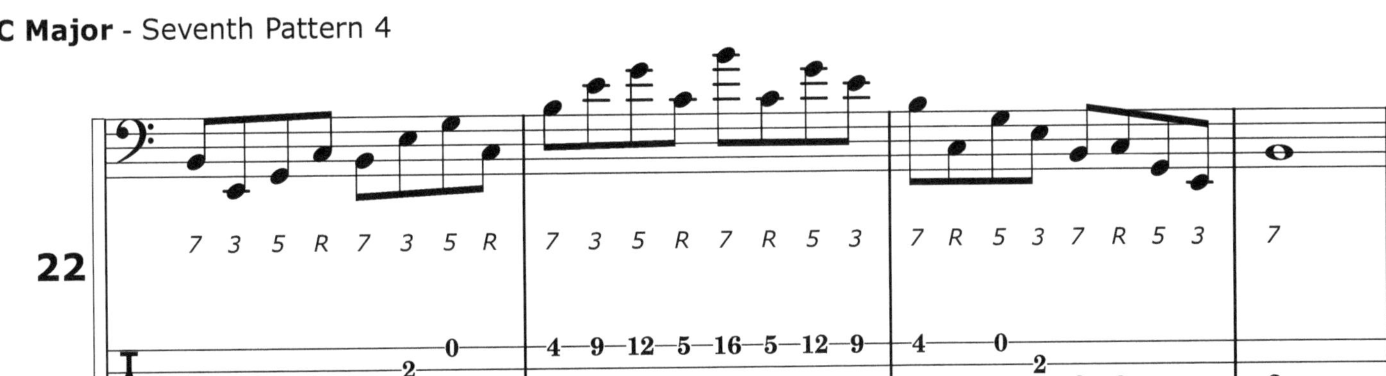

C Major - Seventh Pattern 5

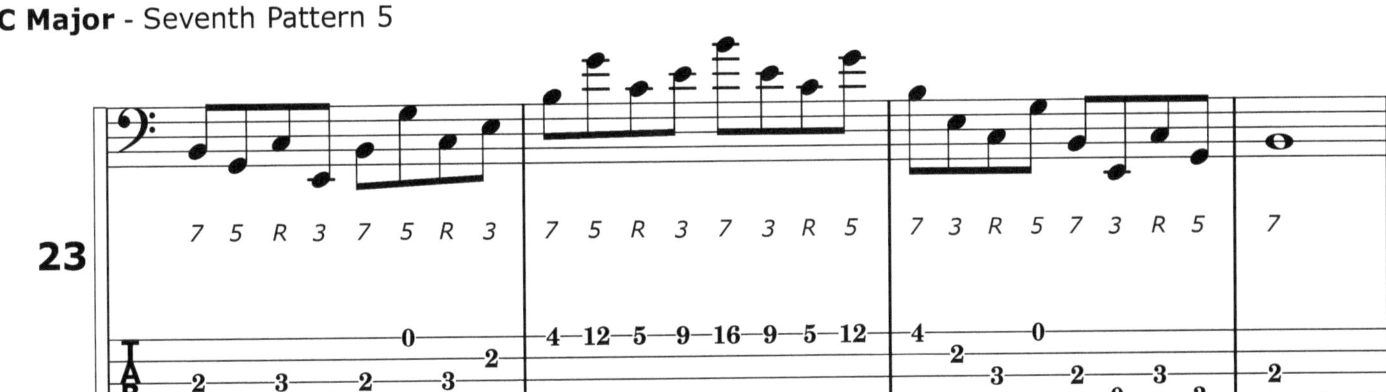

C Major - Seventh Pattern 6

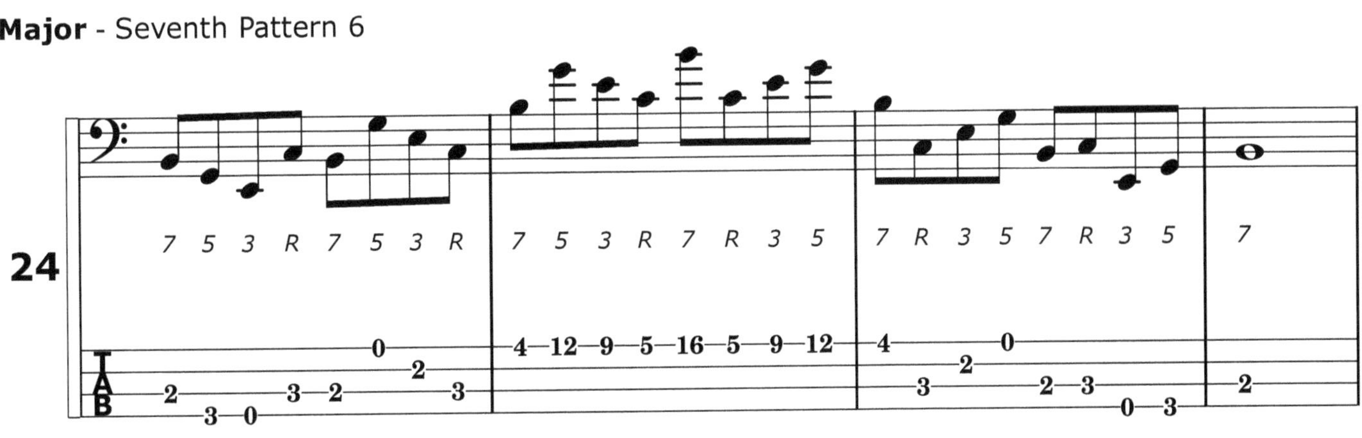

F Major - Root Pattern 1

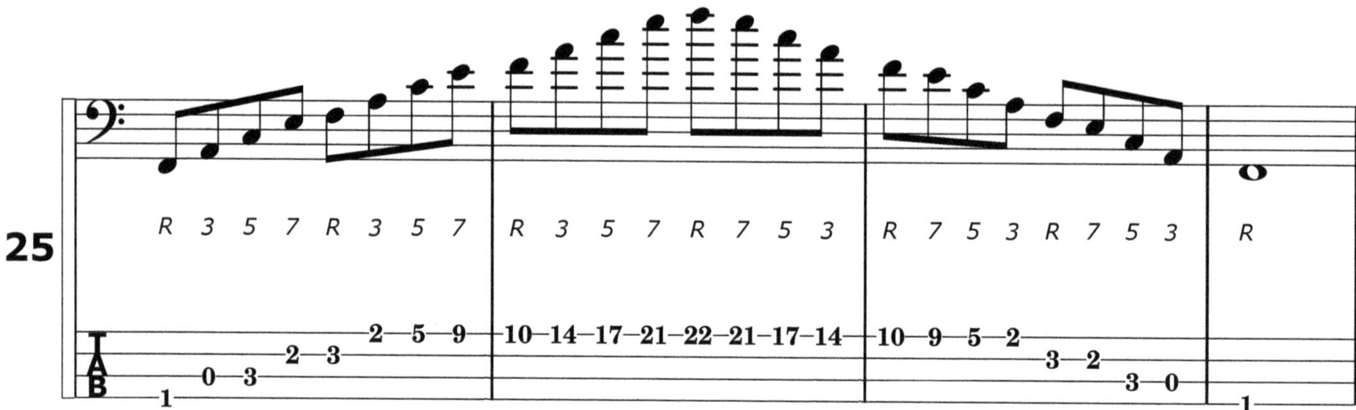

F Major - Root Pattern 2

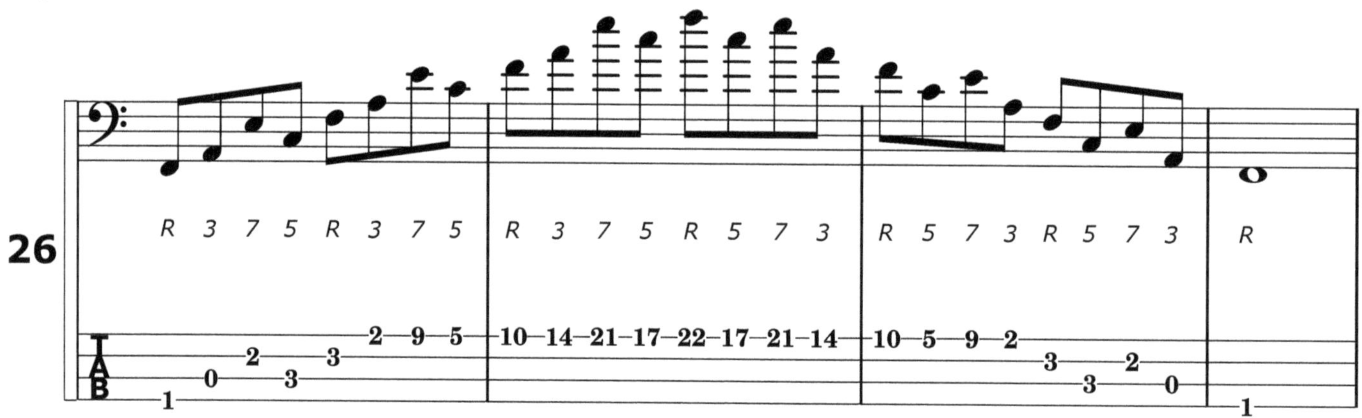

F Major - Root Pattern 3

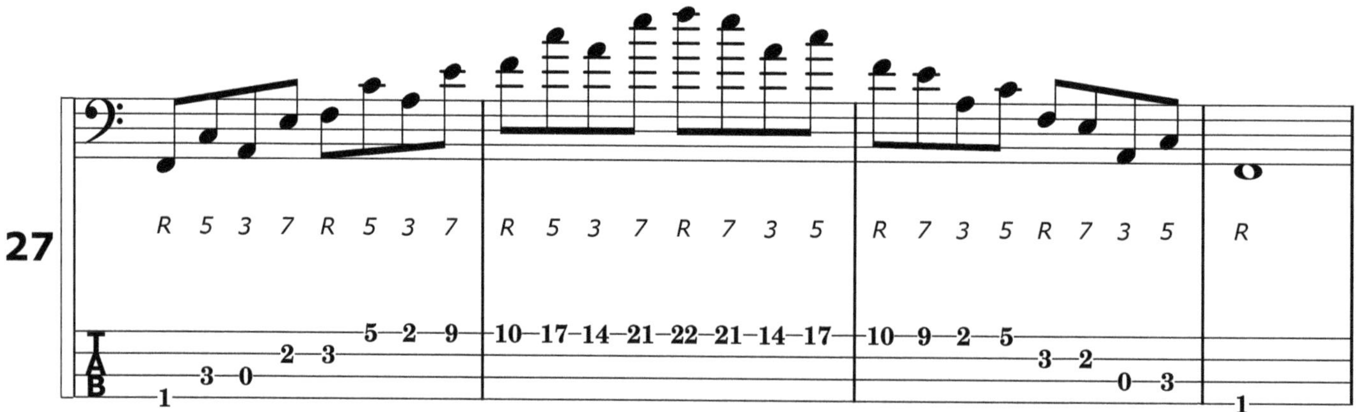

F Major - Root Pattern 4

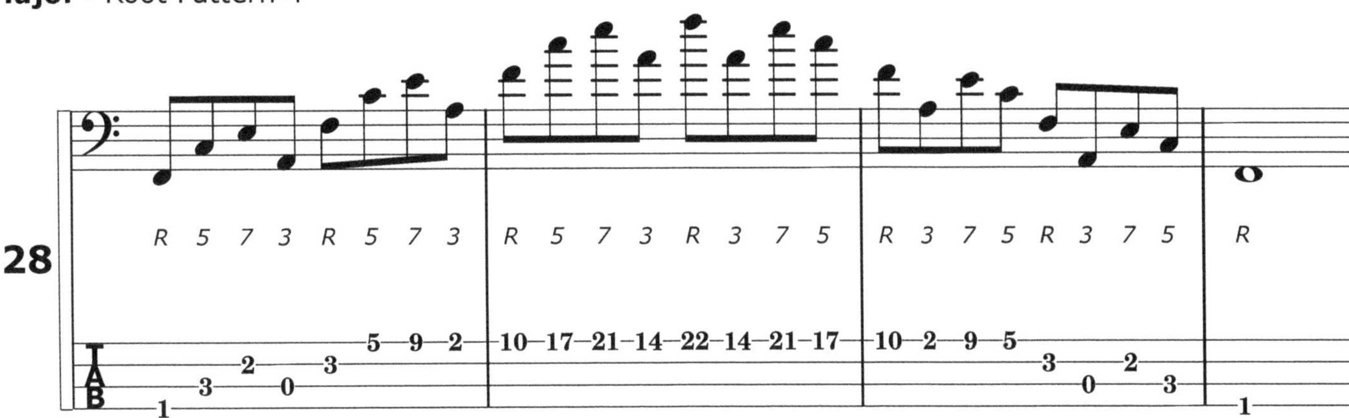

F Major - Root Pattern 5

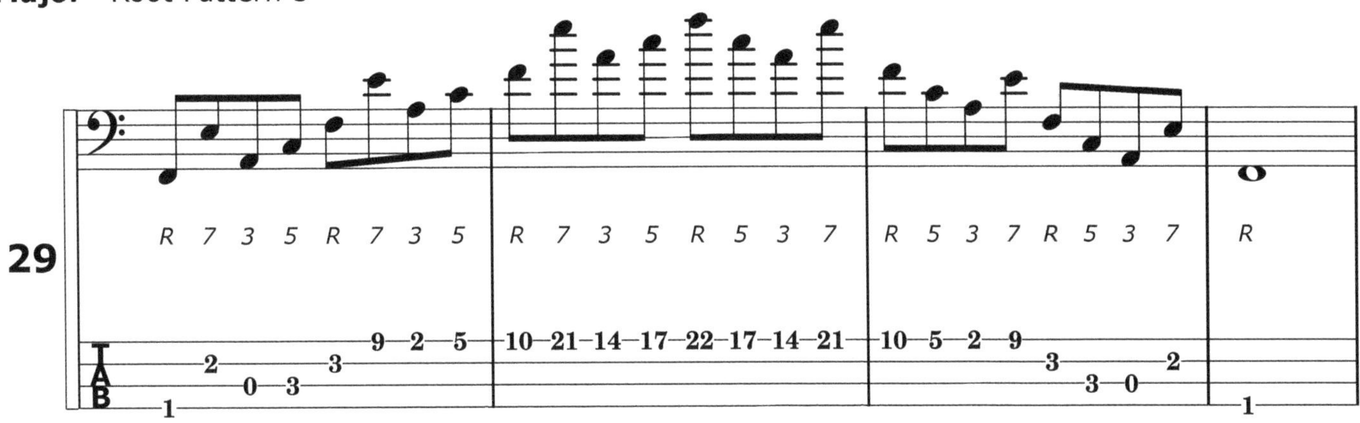

F Major - Root Pattern 6

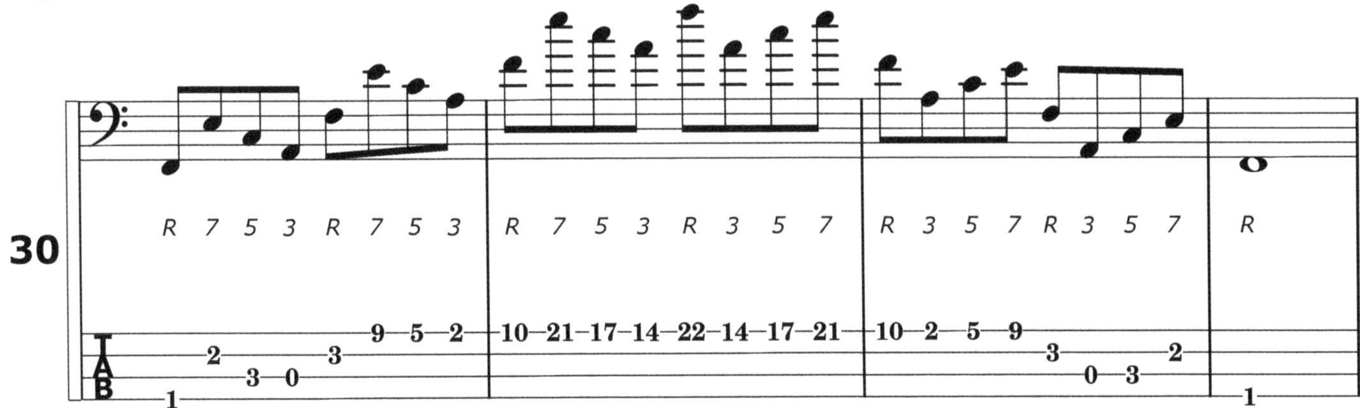

F Major - Third Pattern 1

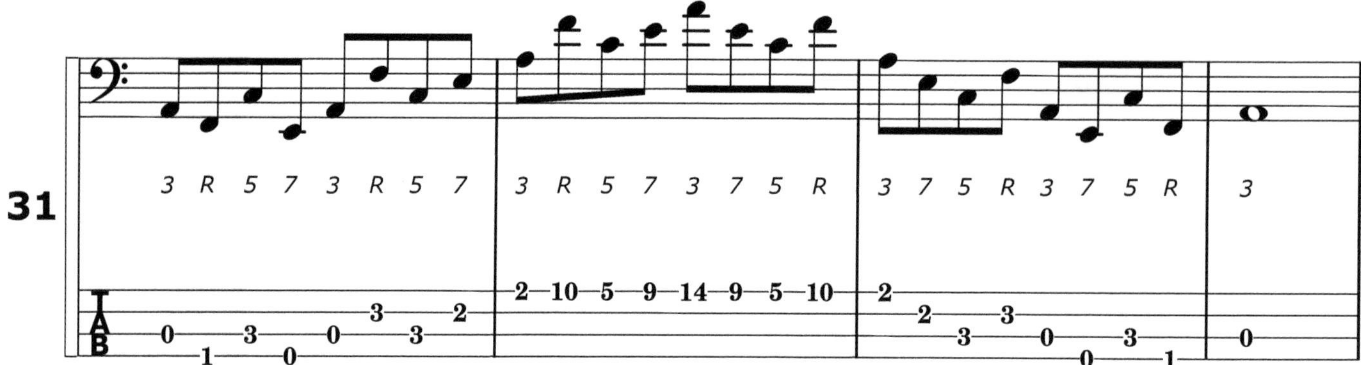

F Major - Third Pattern 2

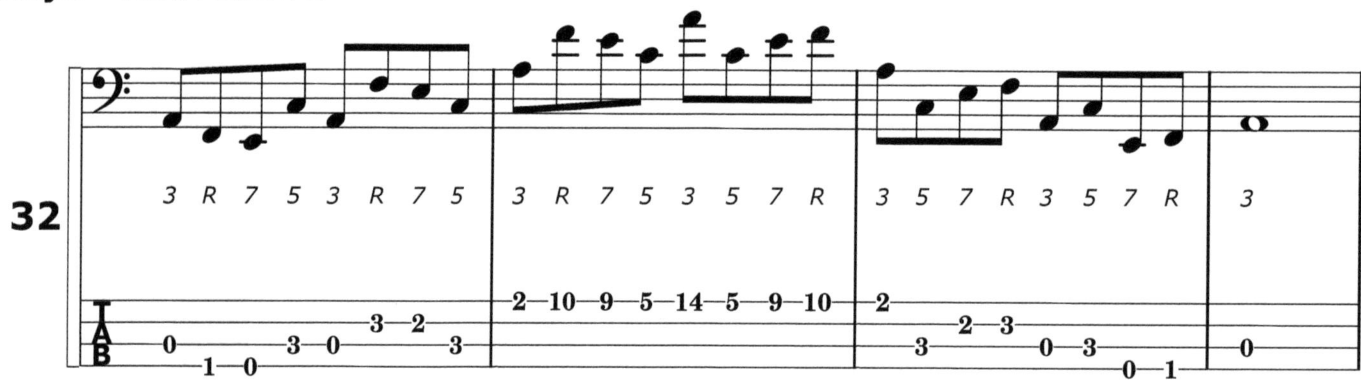

F Major - Third Pattern 3

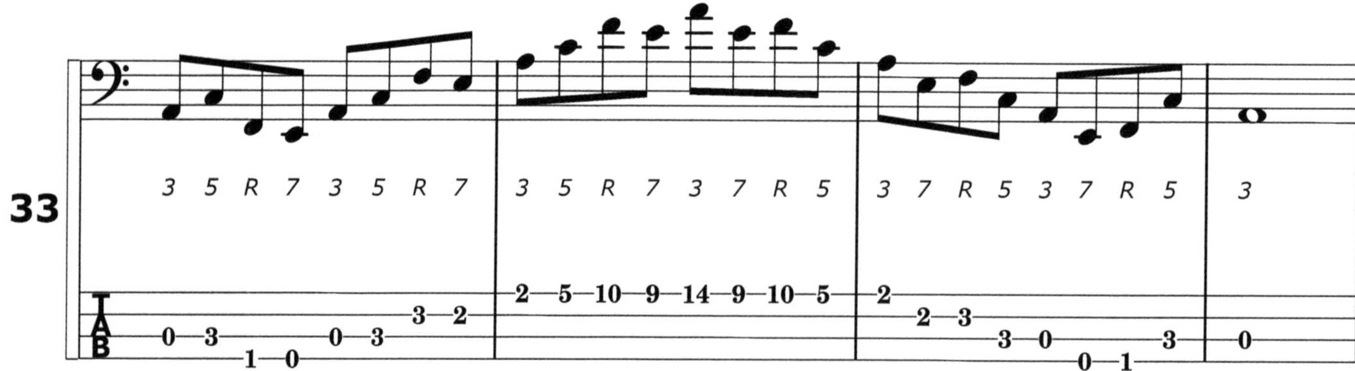

F Major - Third Pattern 4

34 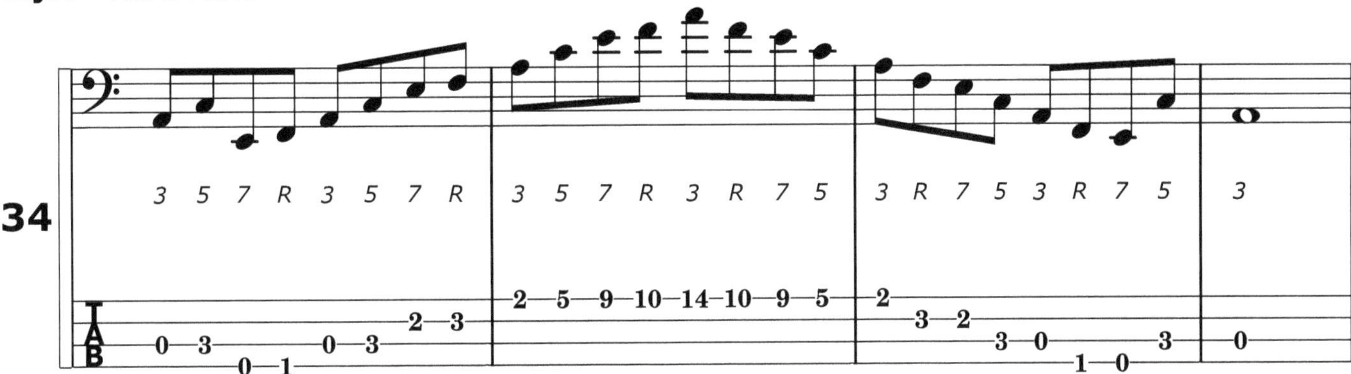

F Major - Third Pattern 5

35 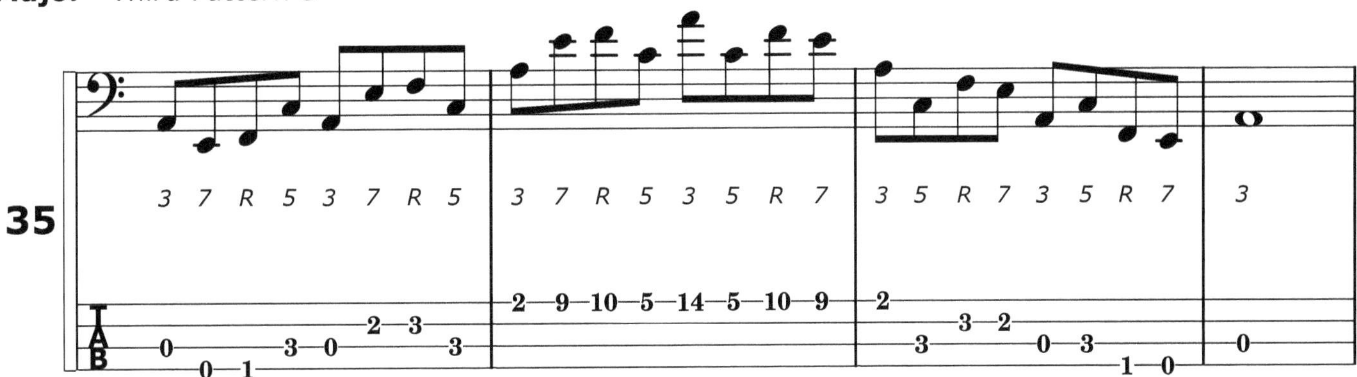

F Major - Third Pattern 6

36 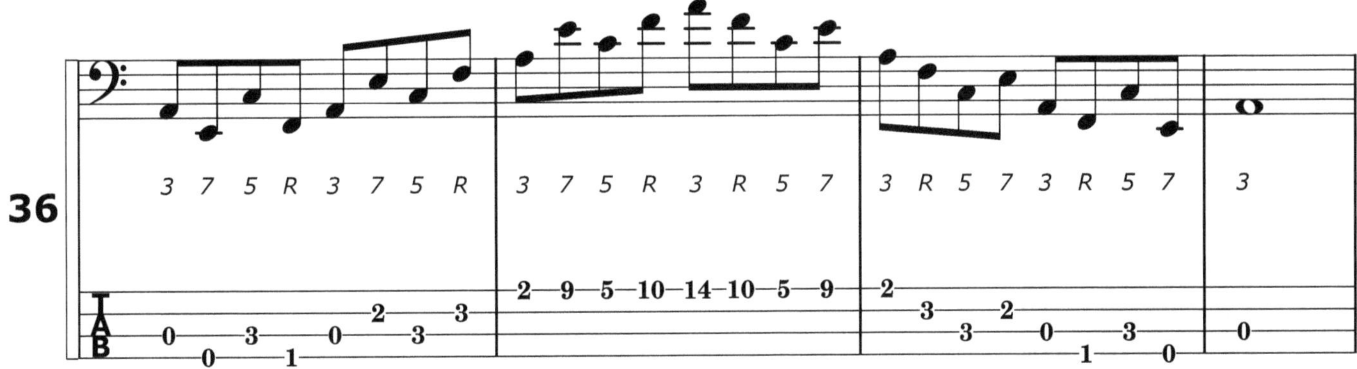

F Major - Fifth Pattern 1

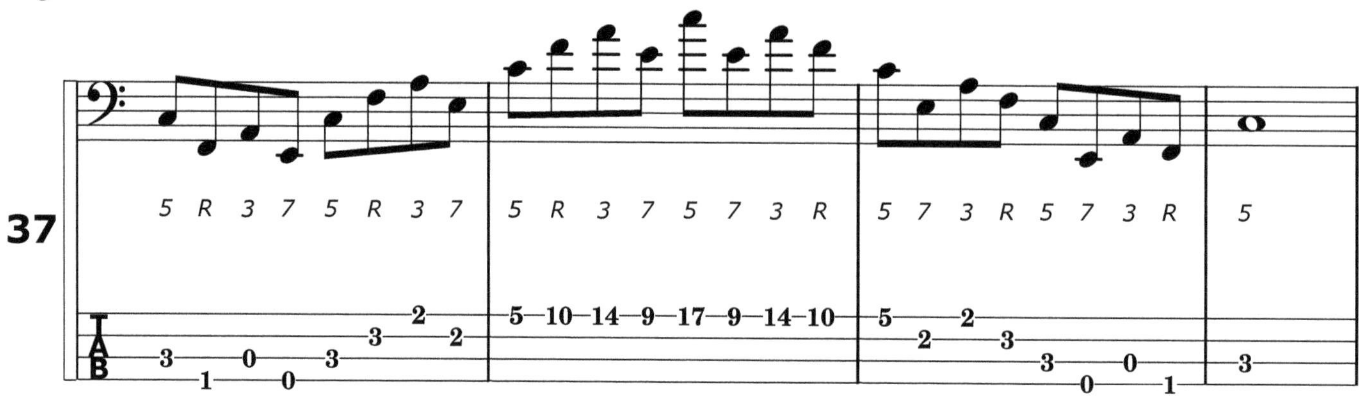

F Major - Fifth Pattern 2

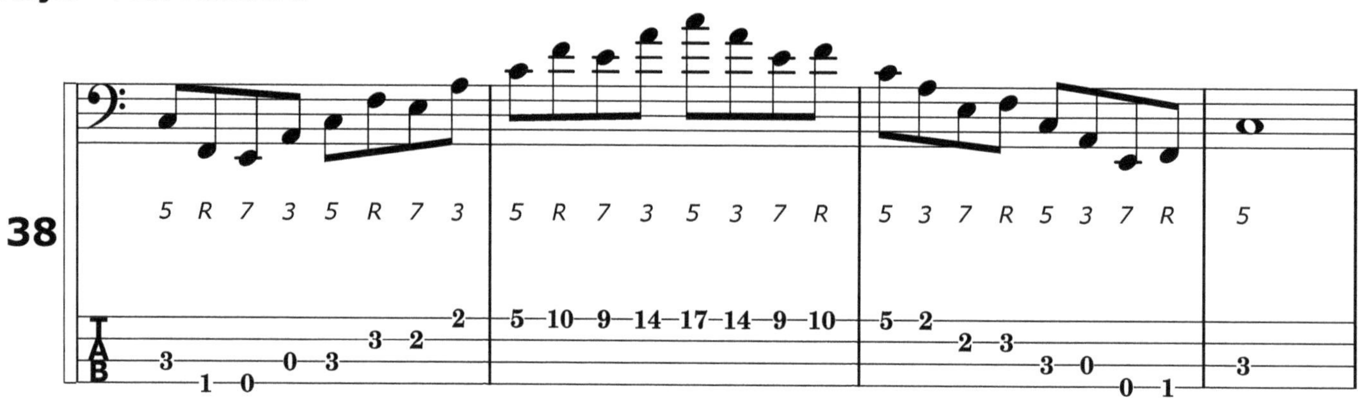

F Major - Fifth Pattern 3

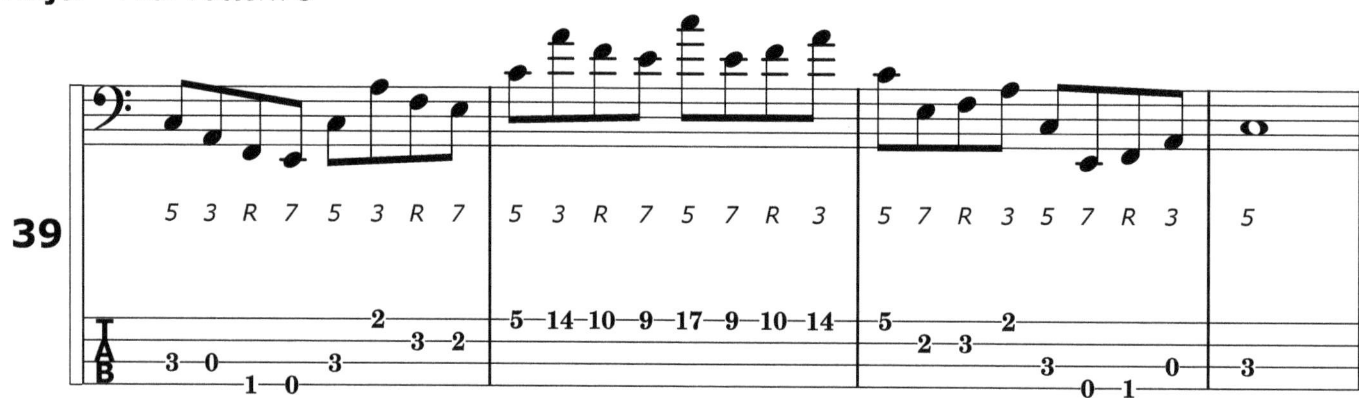

F Major - Fifth Pattern 4

40

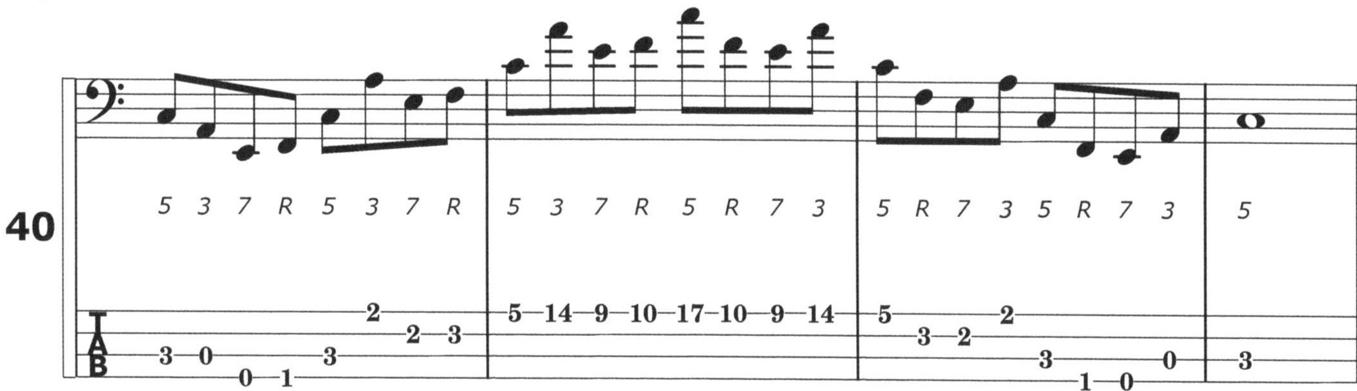

F Major - Fifth Pattern 5

41

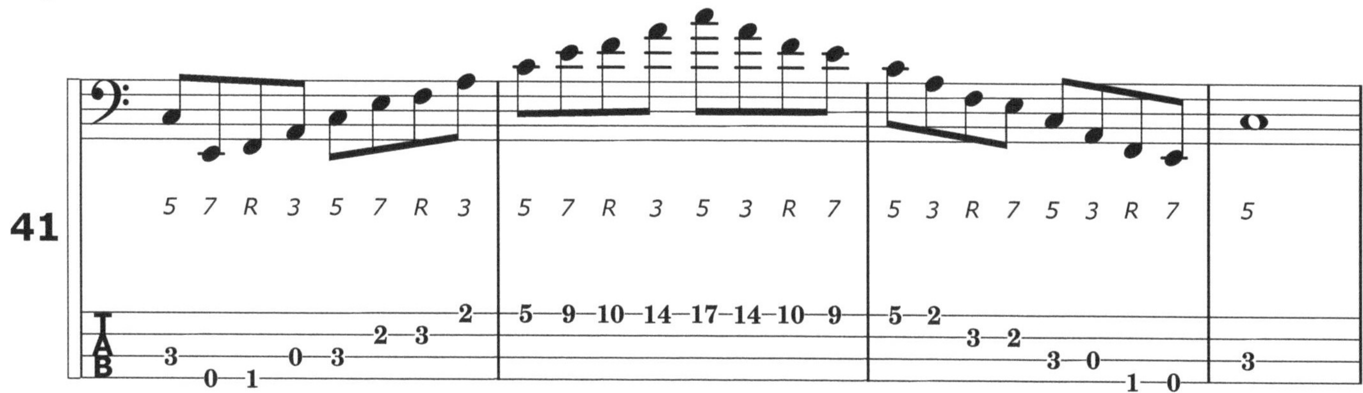

F Major - Fifth Pattern 6

42

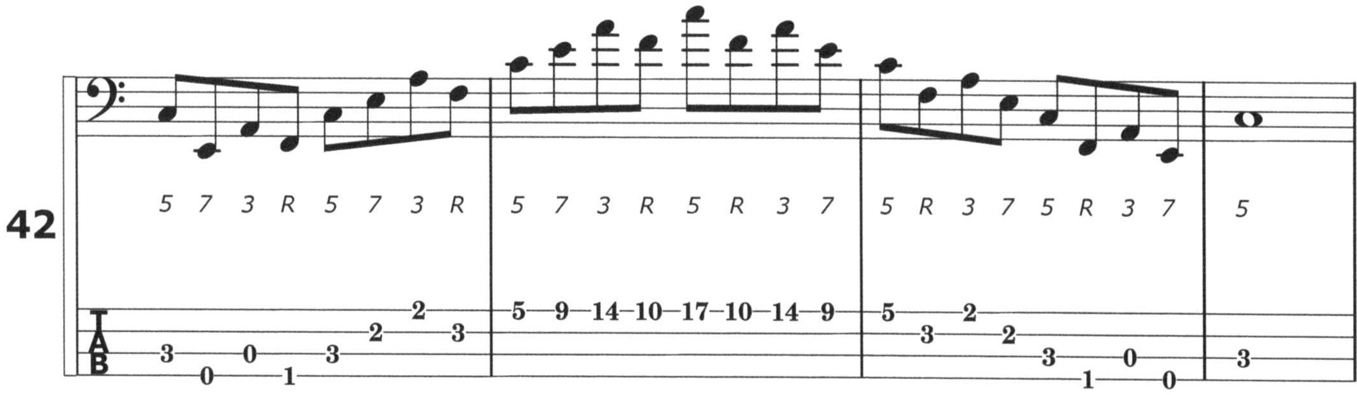

F Major - Seventh Pattern 1

43

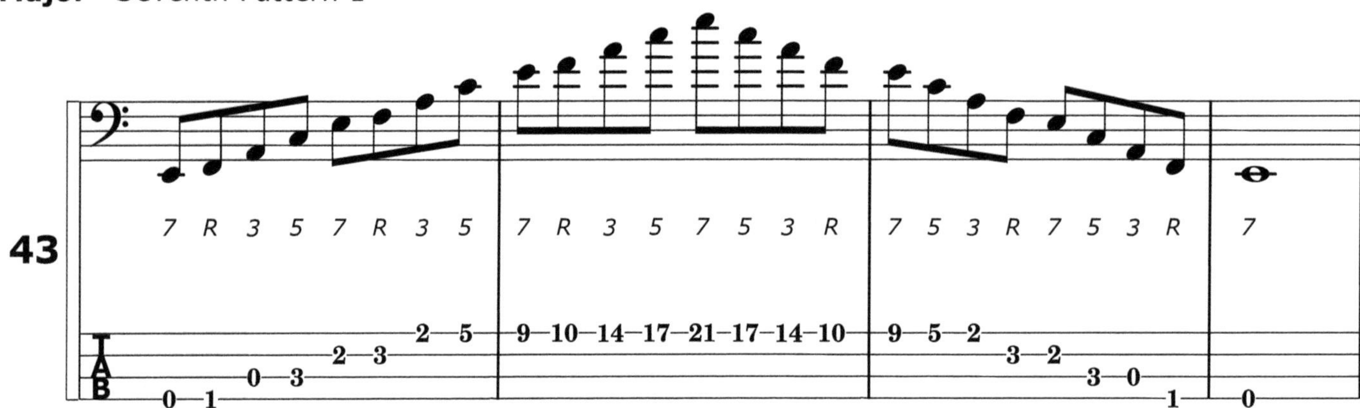

F Major - Seventh Pattern 2

44

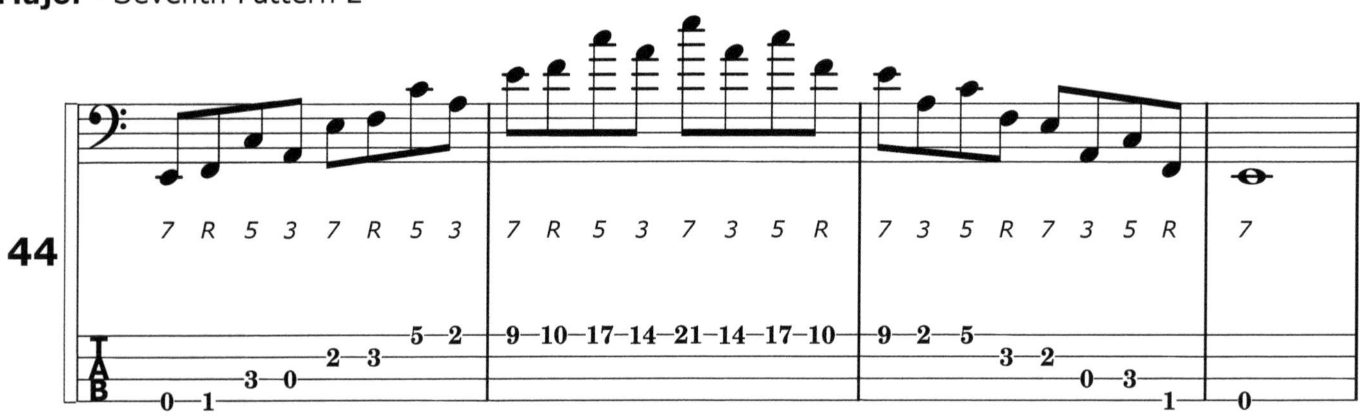

F Major - Seventh Pattern 3

45

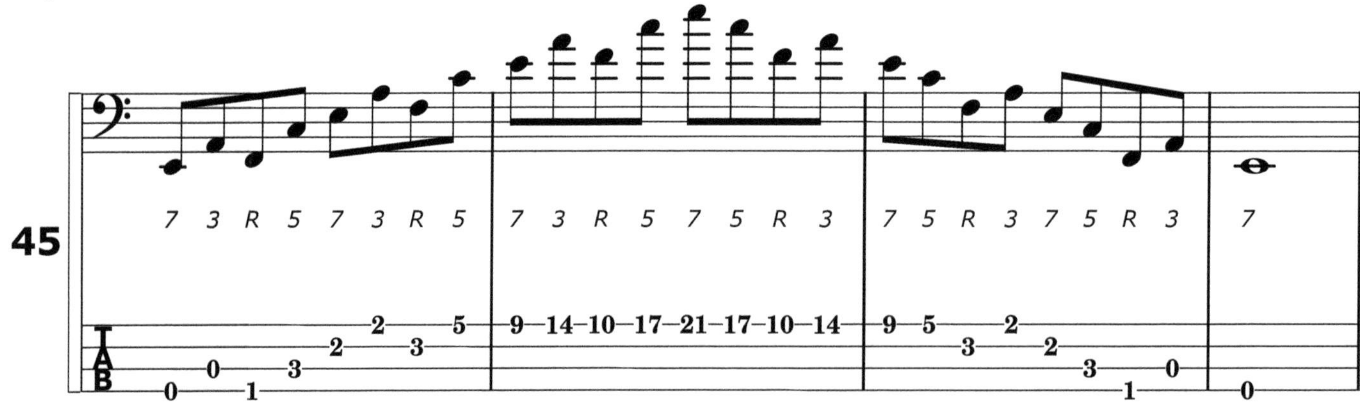

F Major - Seventh Pattern 4

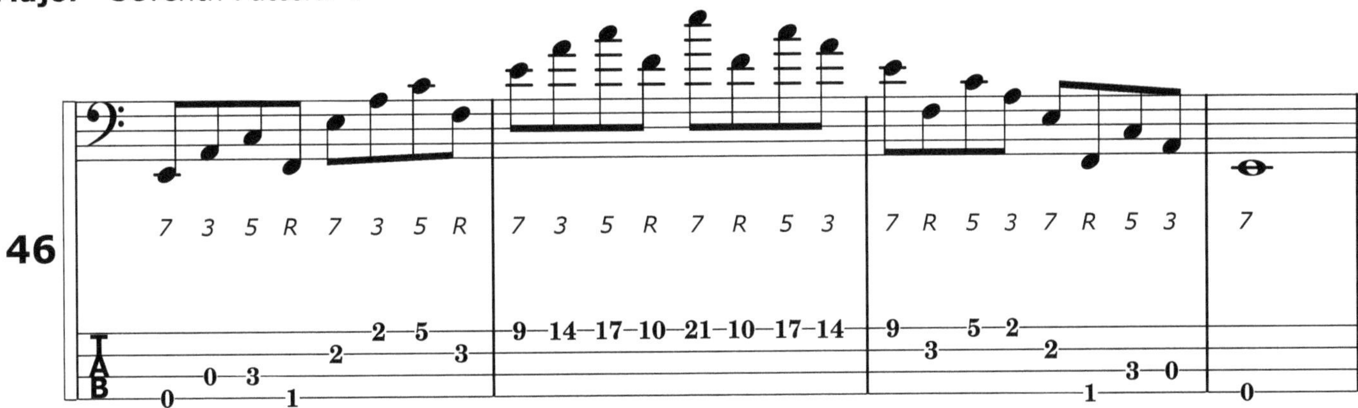

F Major - Seventh Pattern 5

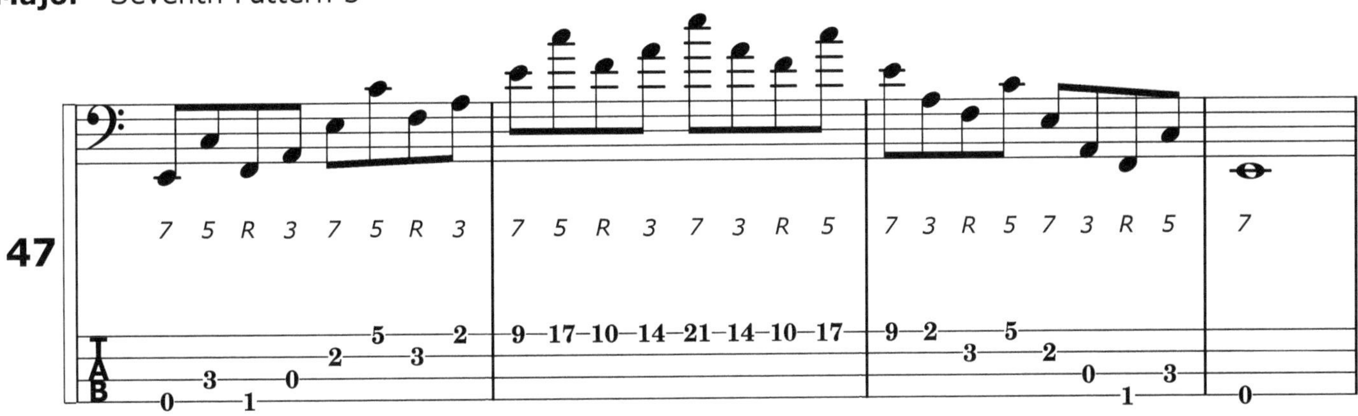

F Major - Seventh Pattern 6

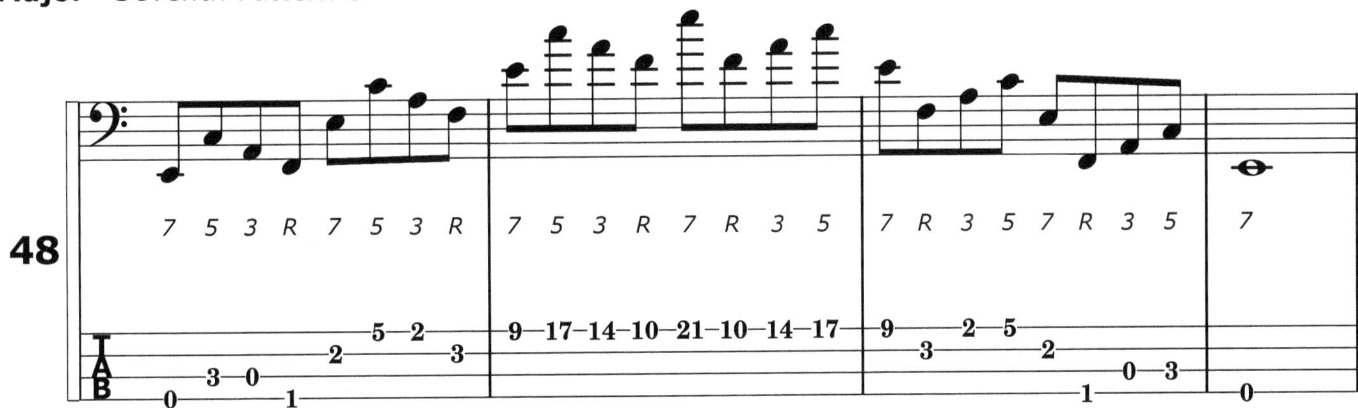

G Major - Root Pattern 1

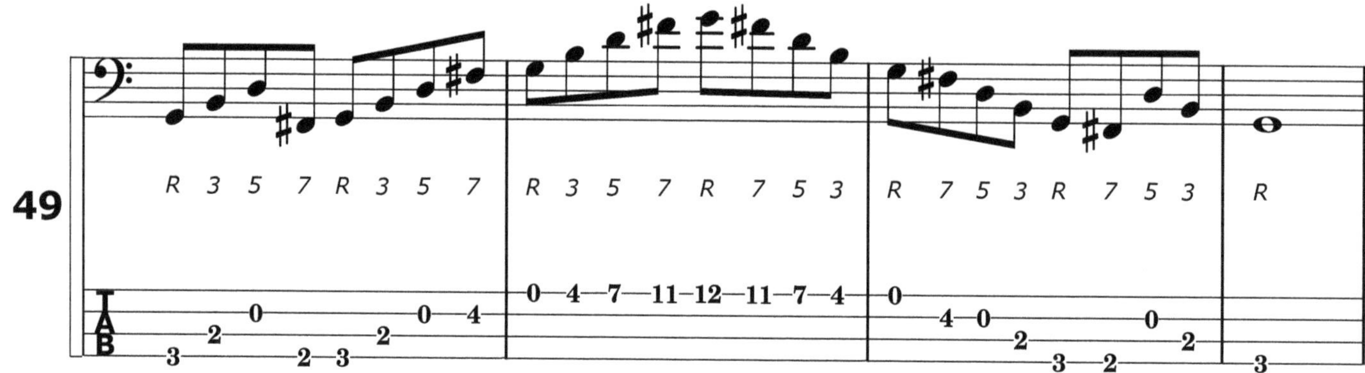

G Major - Root Pattern 2

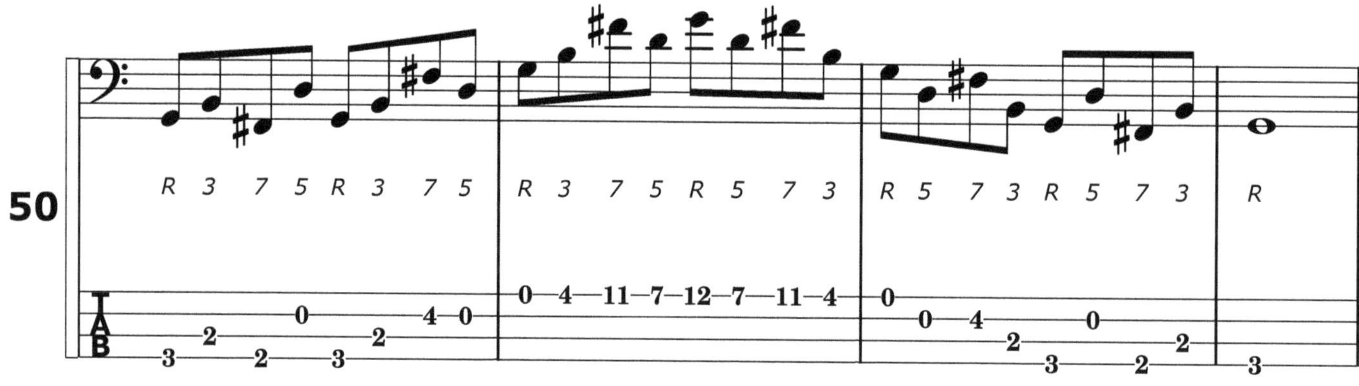

G Major - Root Pattern 3

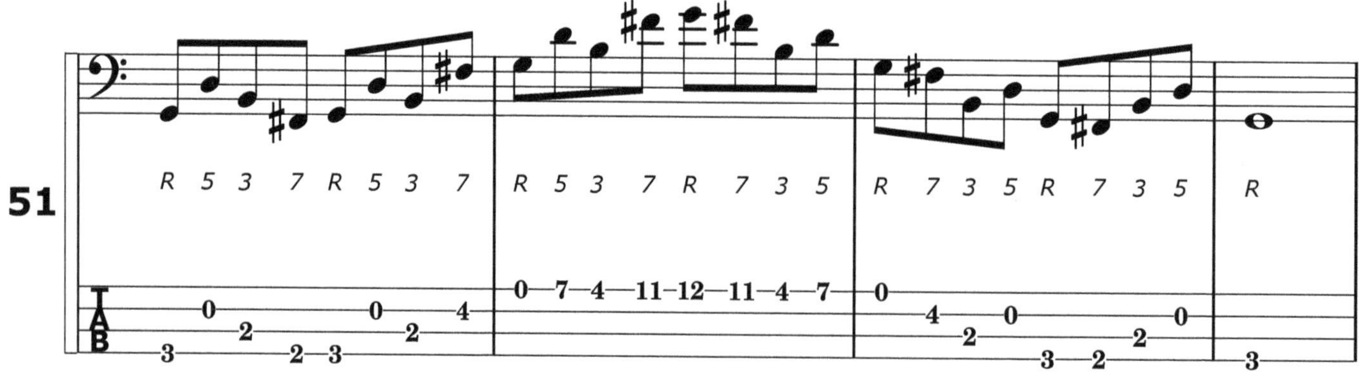

G Major - Root Pattern 4

52

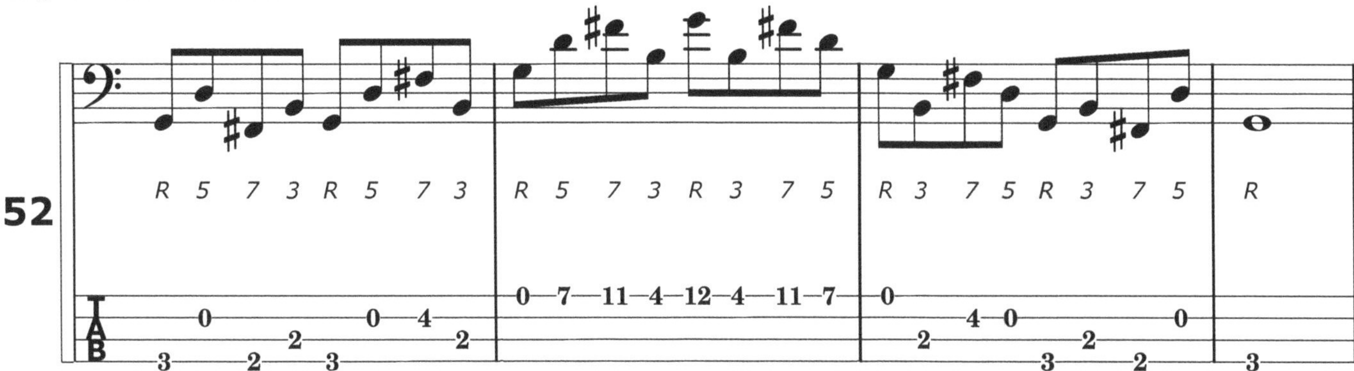

G Major - Root Pattern 5

53

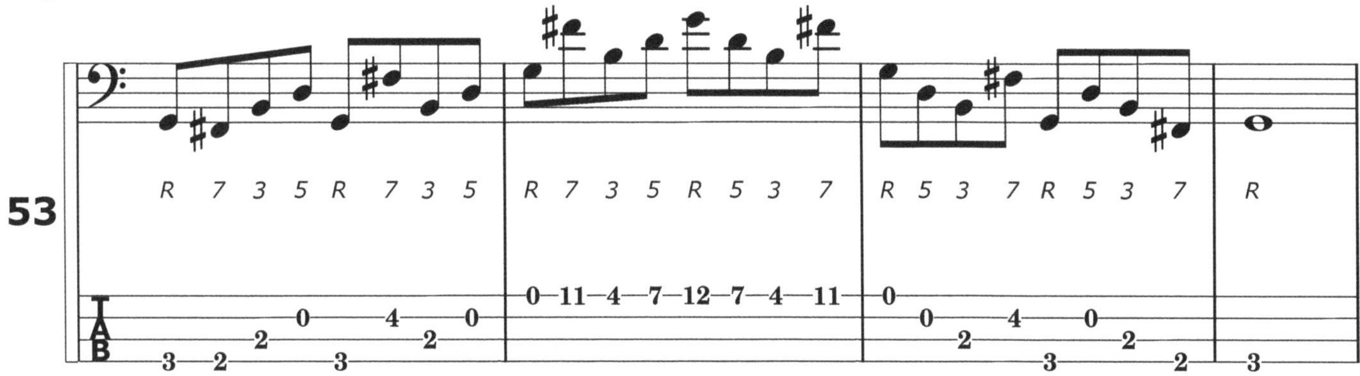

G Major - Root Pattern 6

54

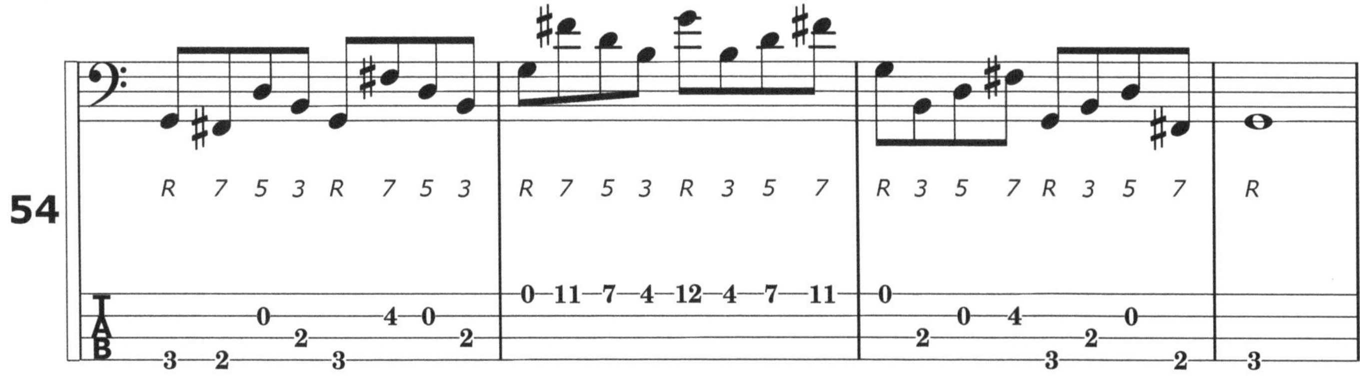

G Major - Third Pattern 1

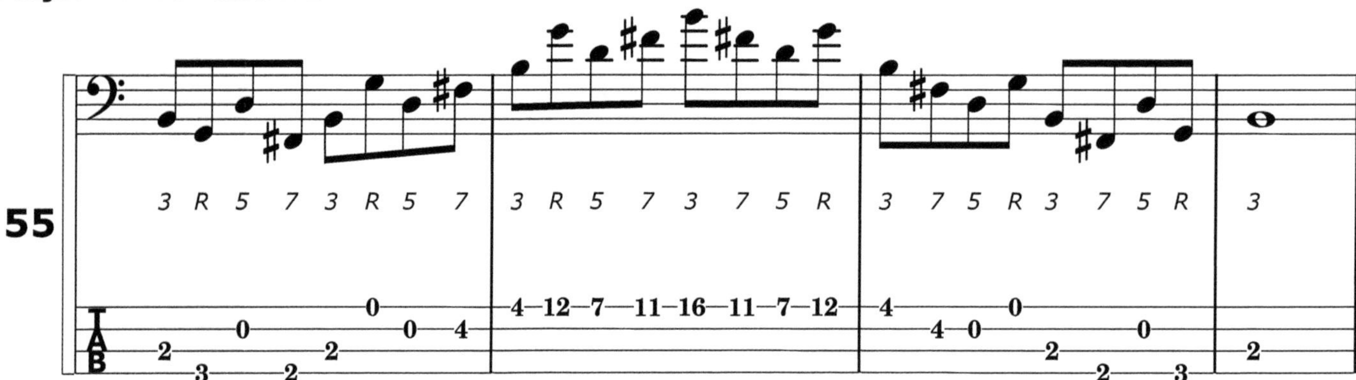

G Major - Third Pattern 2

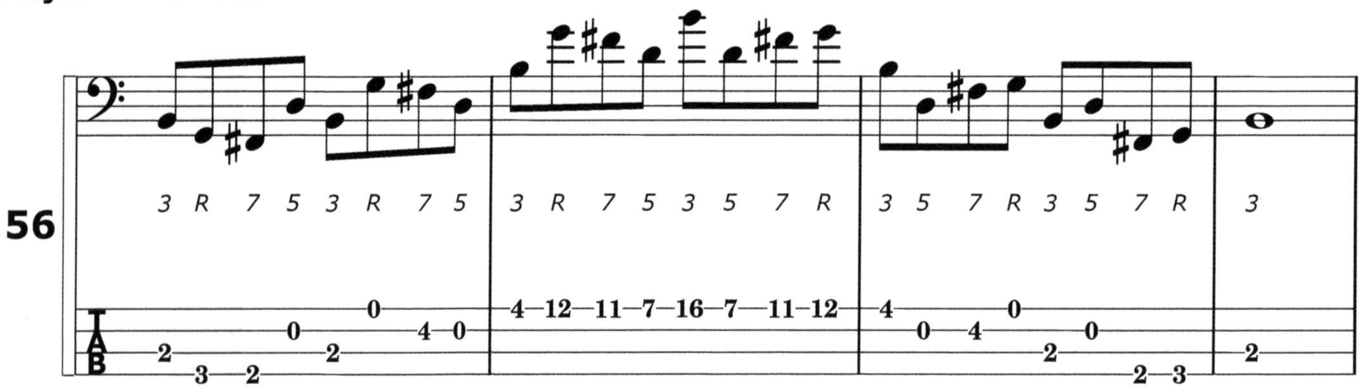

G Major - Third Pattern 3

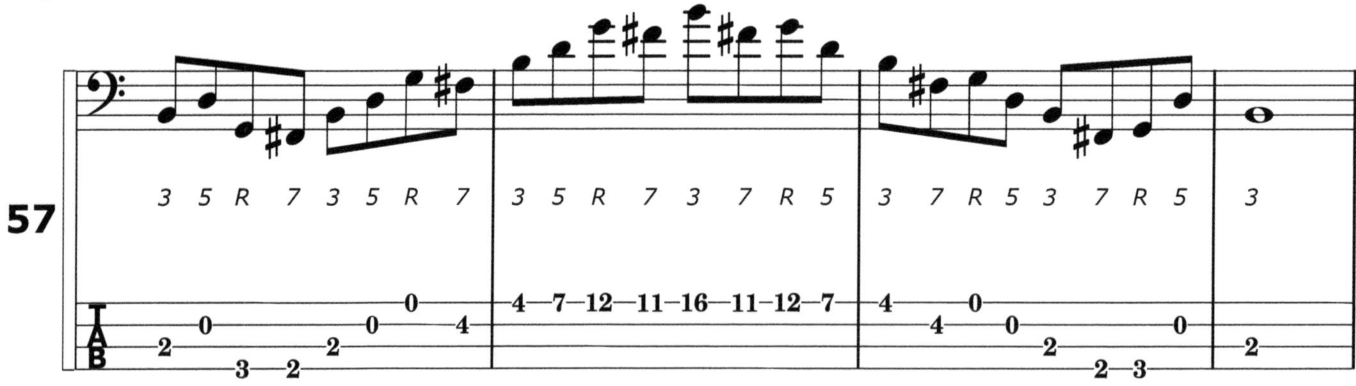

G Major - Third Pattern 4

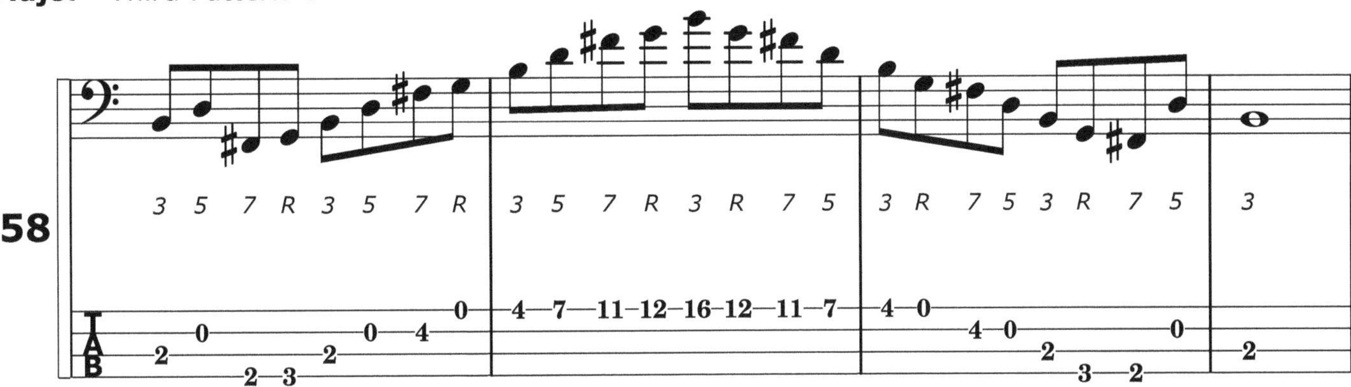

G Major - Third Pattern 5

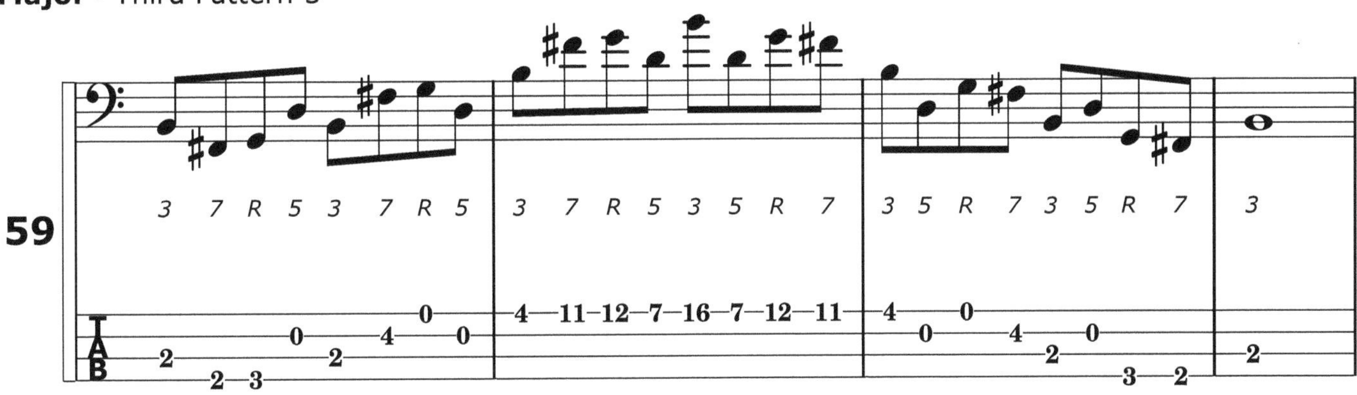

G Major - Third Pattern 6

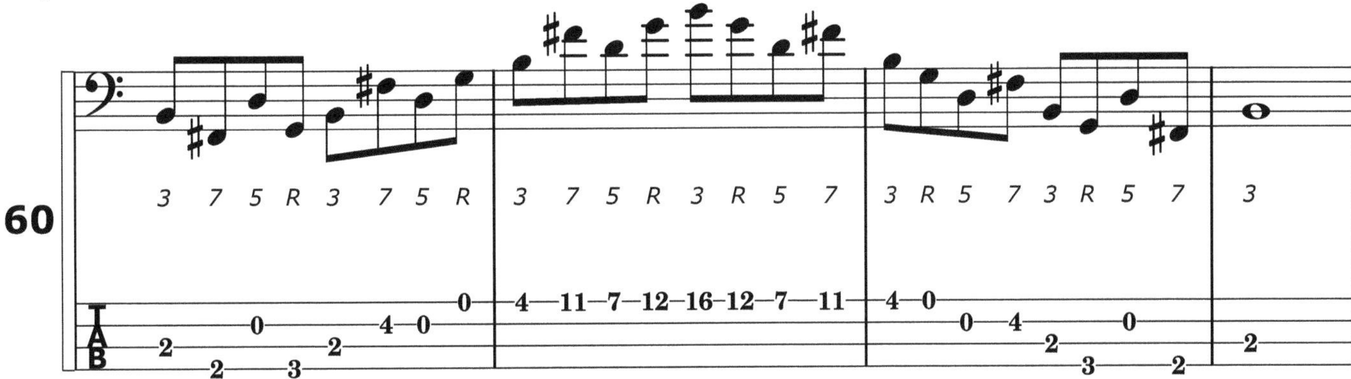

G Major - Fifth Pattern 1

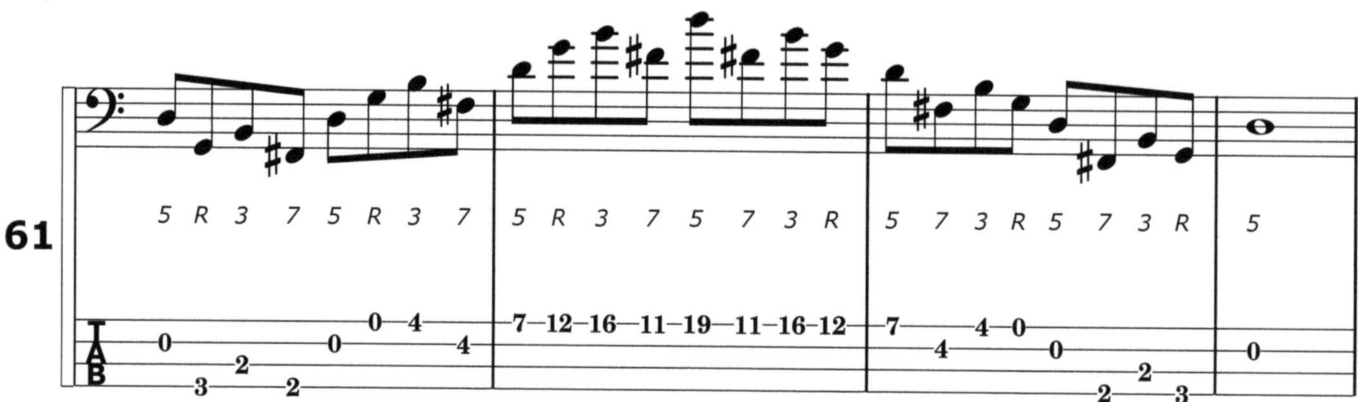

G Major - Fifth Pattern 2

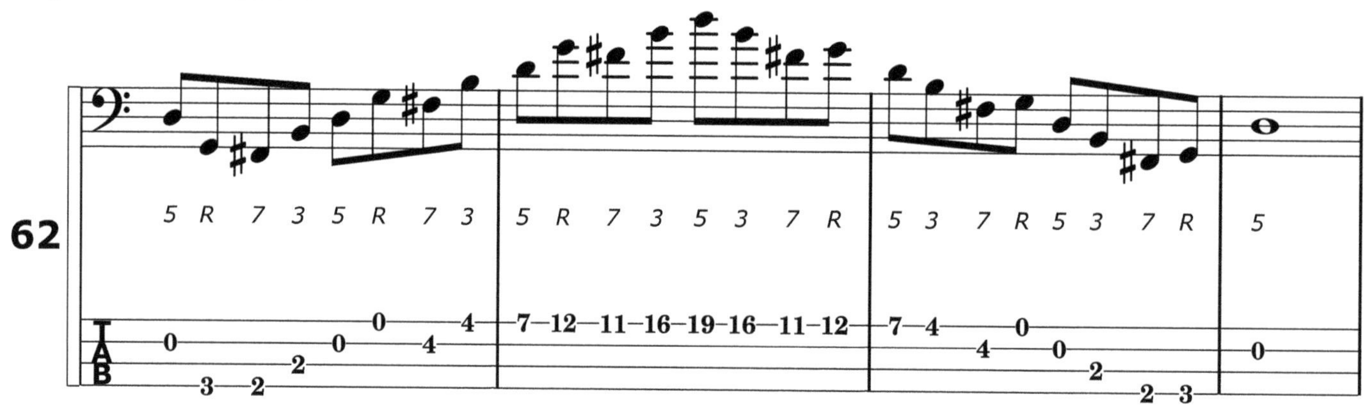

G Major - Fifth Pattern 3

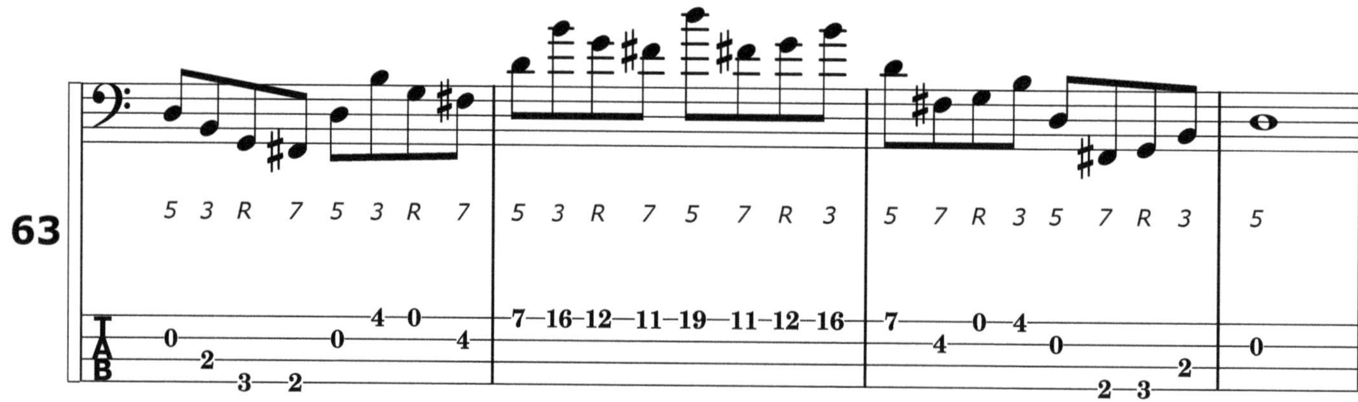

G Major - Fifth Pattern 4

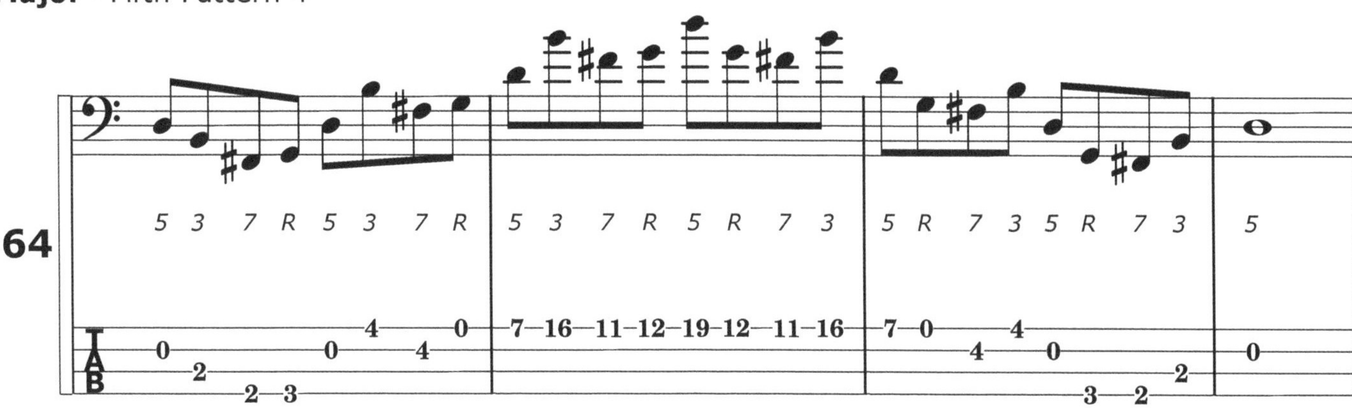

G Major - Fifth Pattern 5

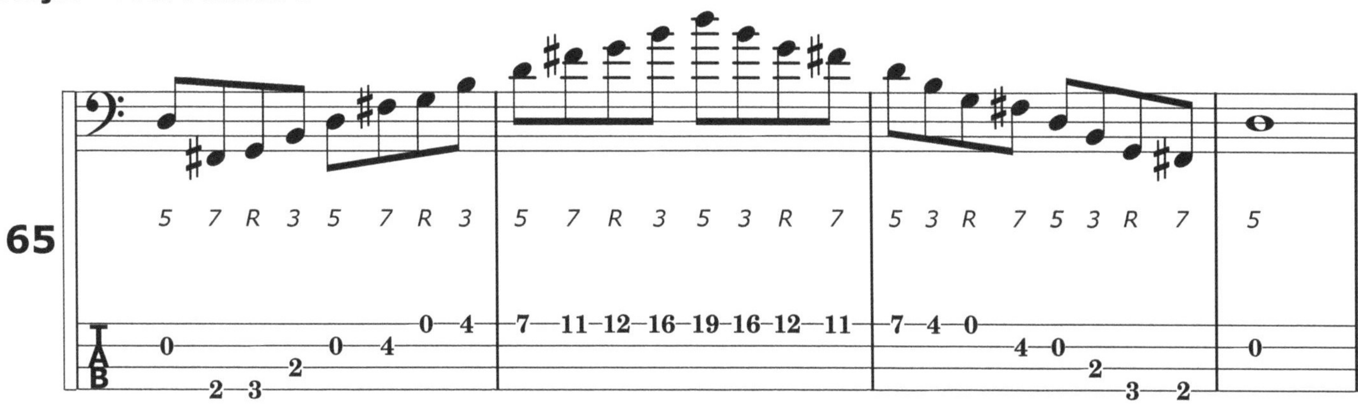

G Major - Fifth Pattern 6

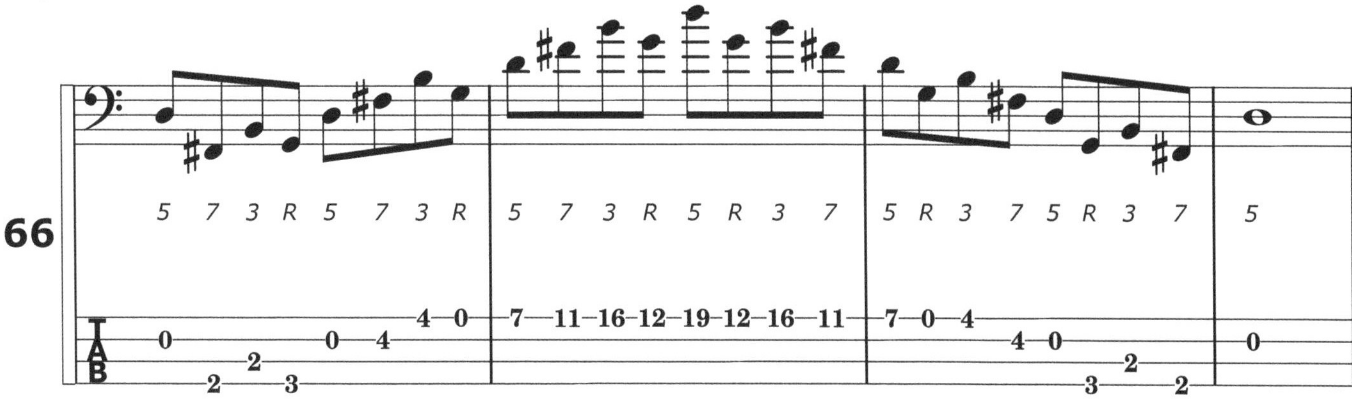

G Major - Seventh Pattern 1

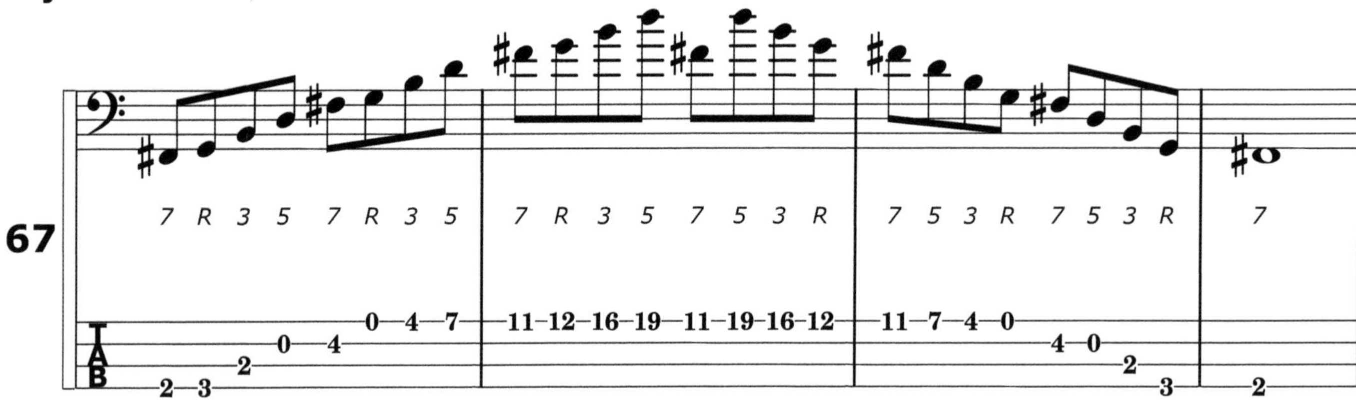

G Major - Seventh Pattern 2

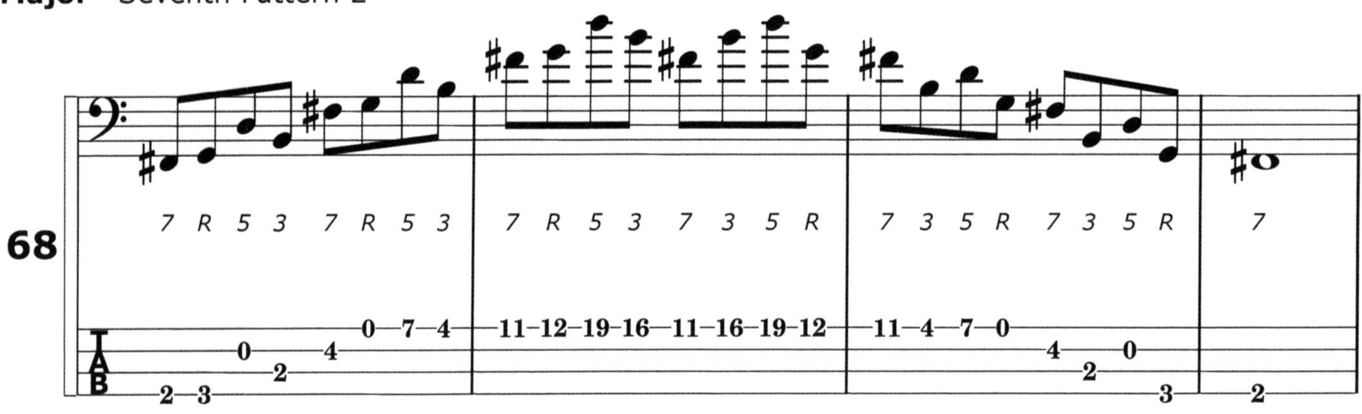

G Major - Seventh Pattern 3

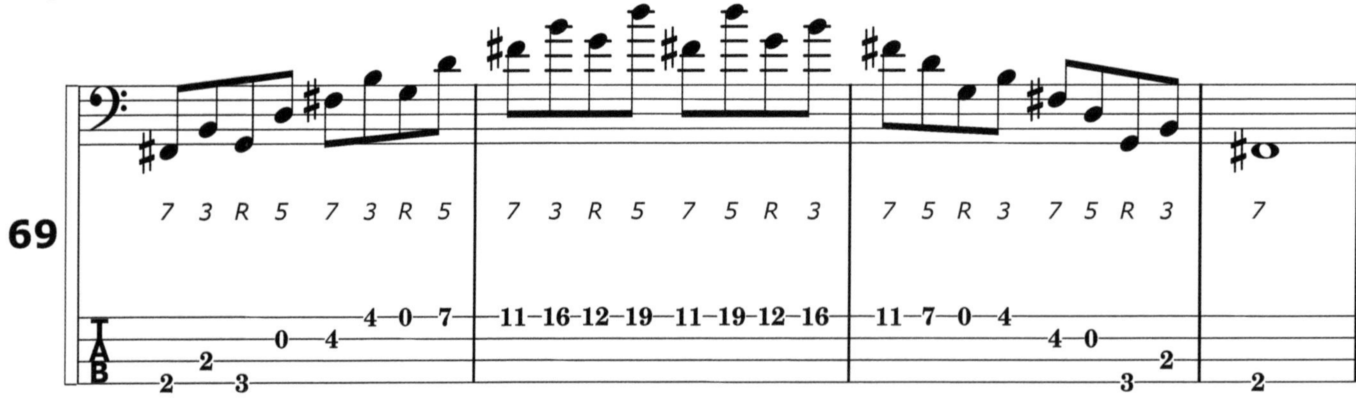

G Major - Seventh Pattern 4

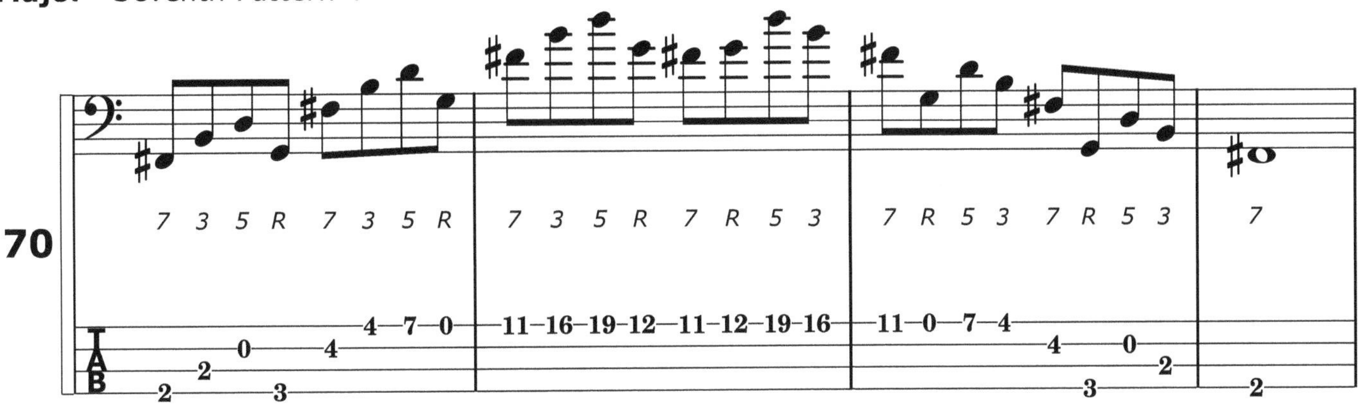

G Major - Seventh Pattern 5

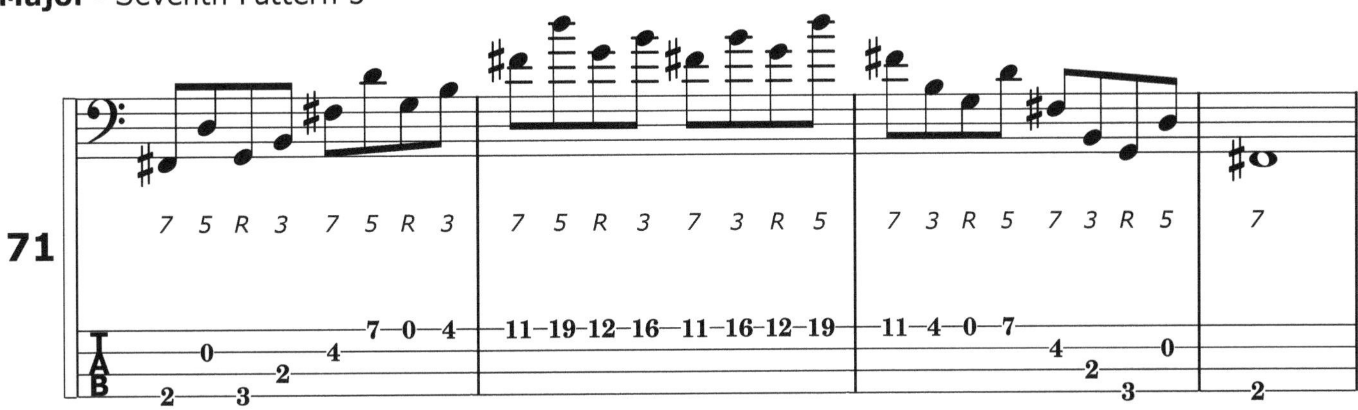

G Major - Seventh Pattern 6

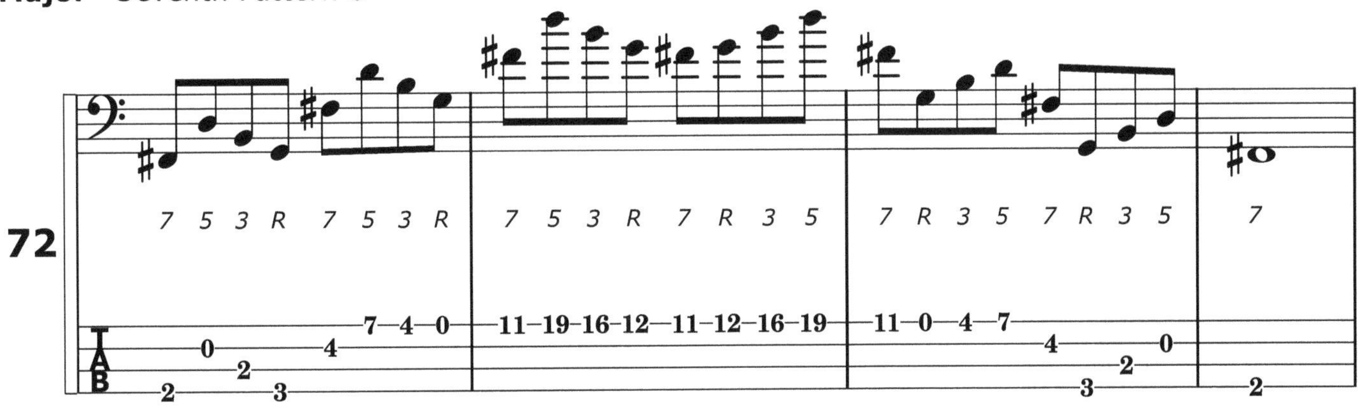

B♭ Major - Root Pattern 1

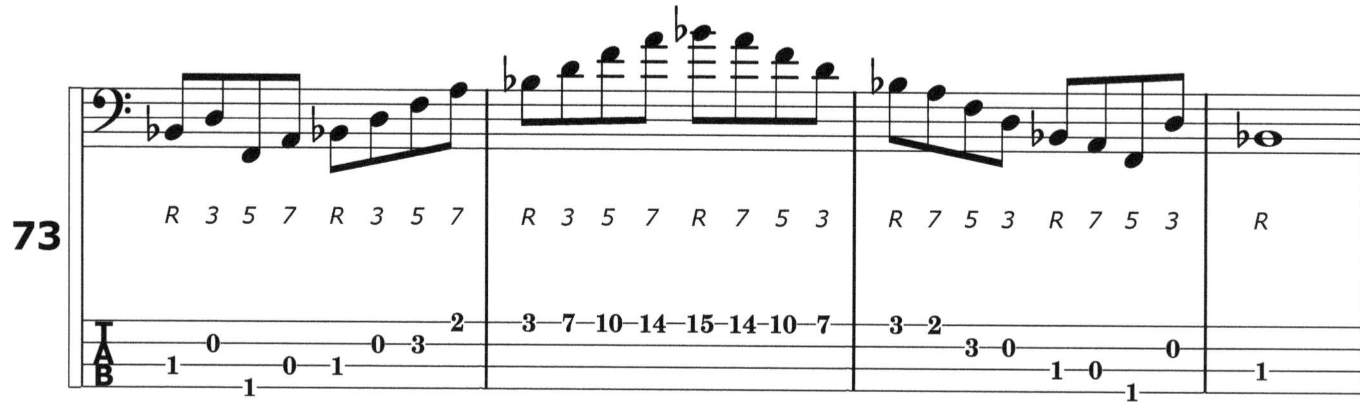

B♭ Major - Root Pattern 2

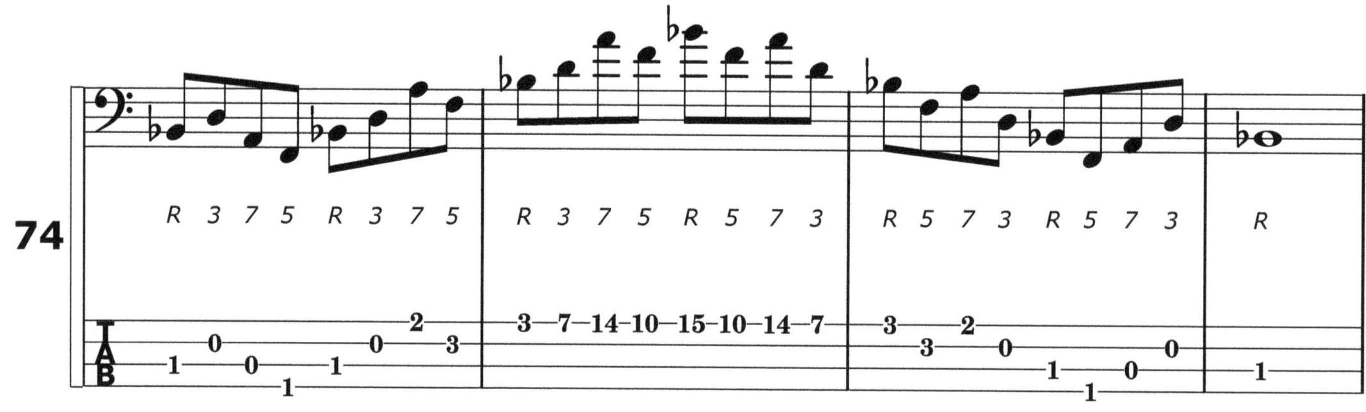

B♭ Major - Root Pattern 3

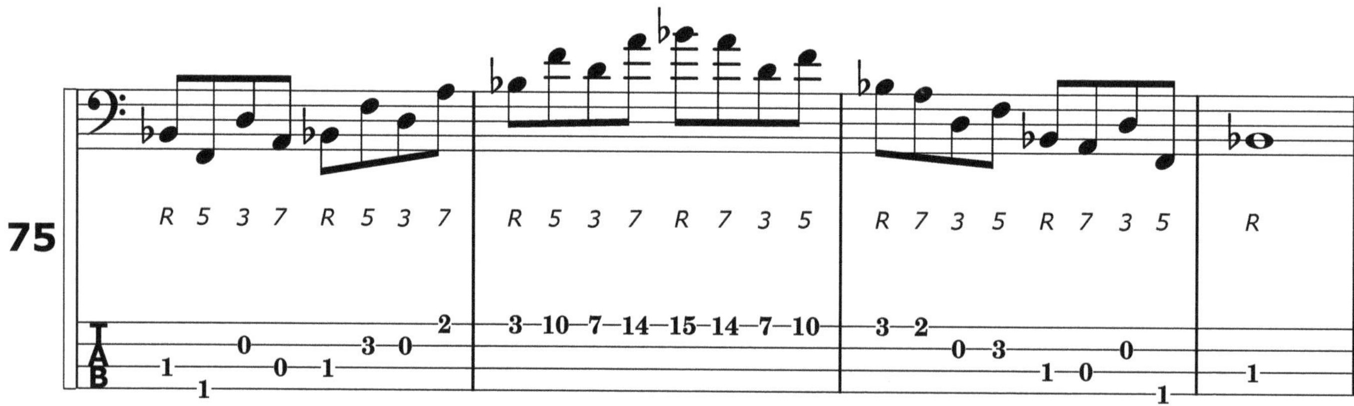

B♭ Major - Root Pattern 4

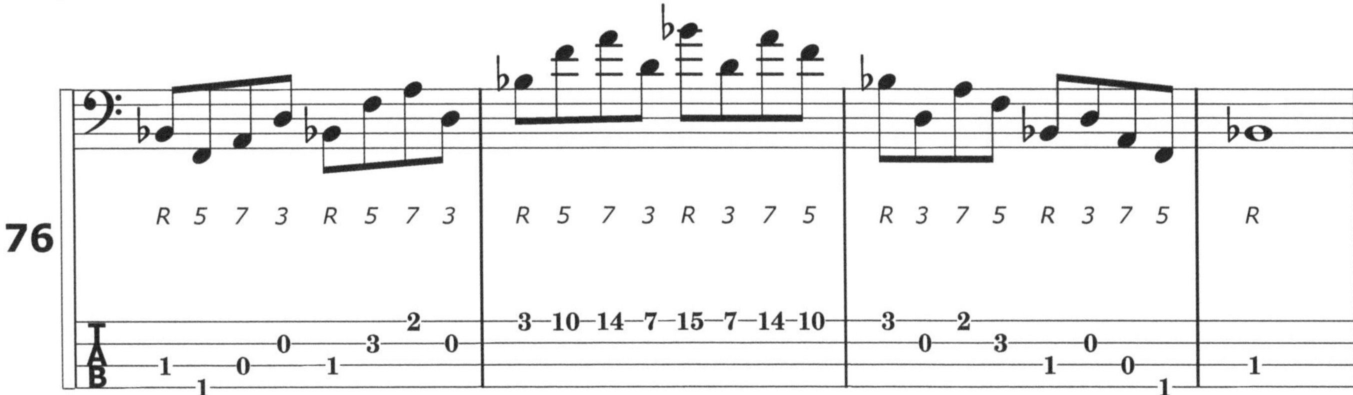

B♭ Major - Root Pattern 5

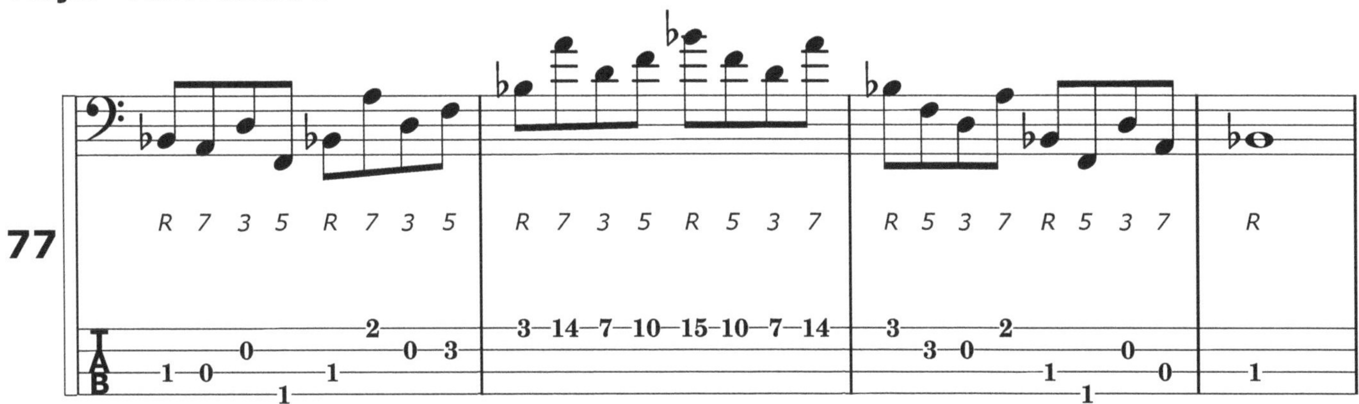

B♭ Major - Root Pattern 6

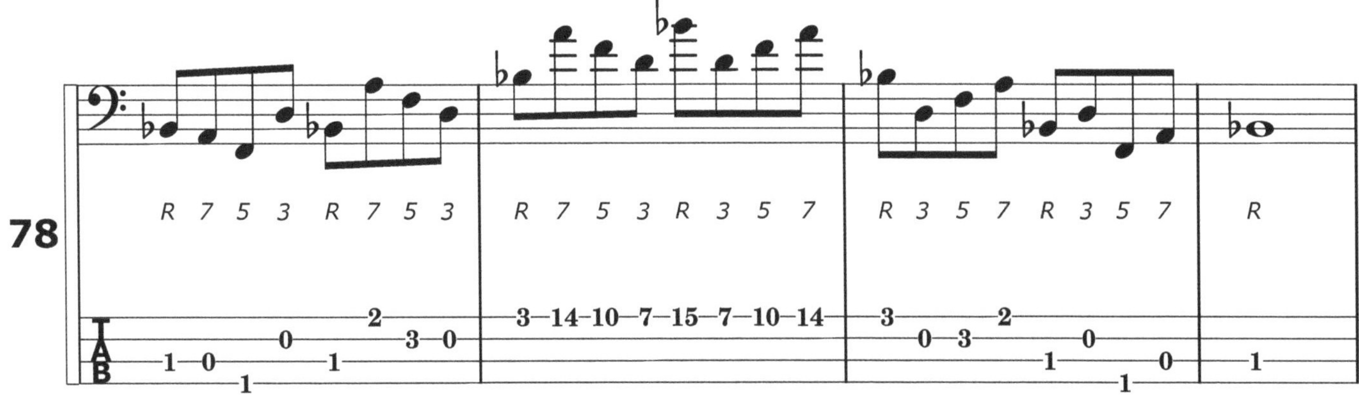

B♭ Major - Third Pattern 1

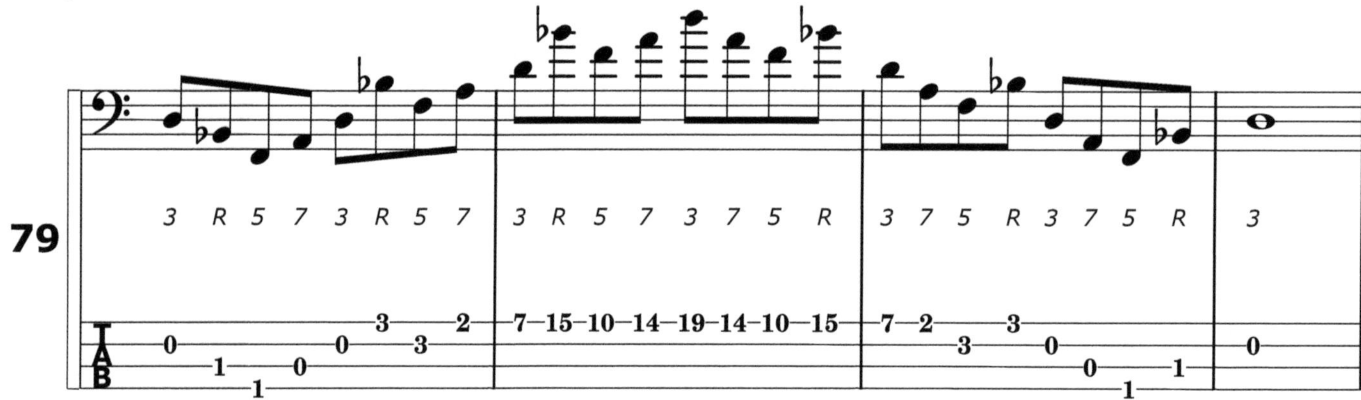

B♭ Major - Third Pattern 2

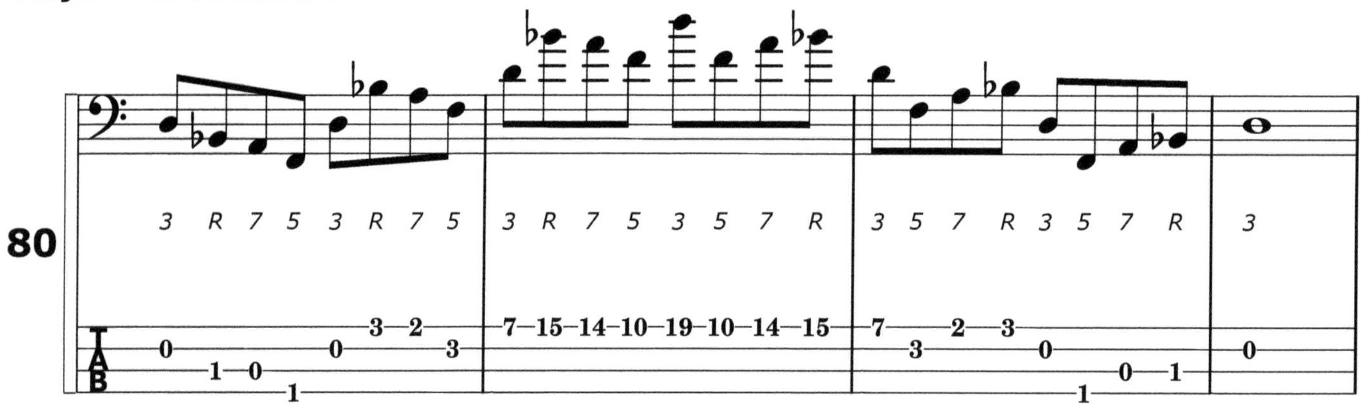

B♭ Major - Third Pattern 3

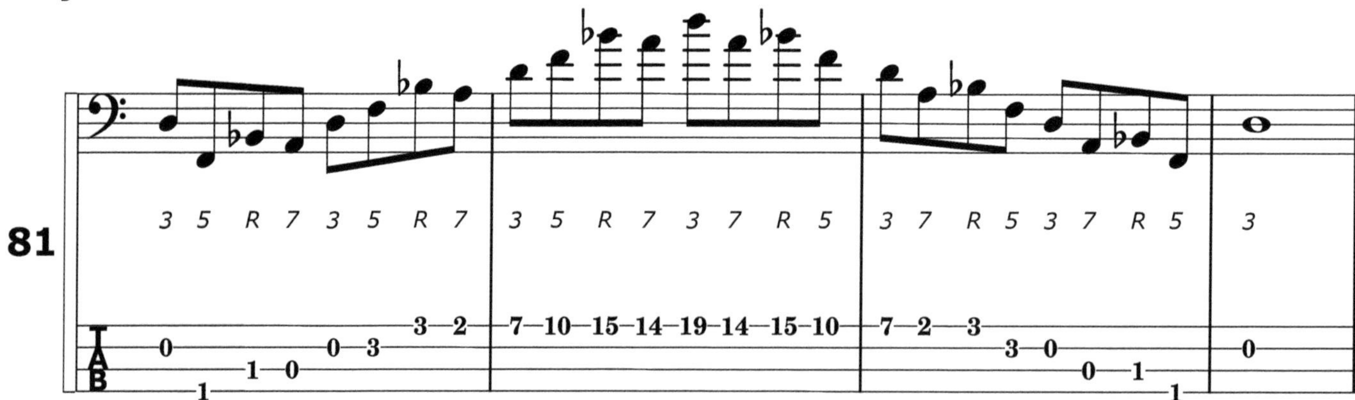

B♭ Major - Third Pattern 4

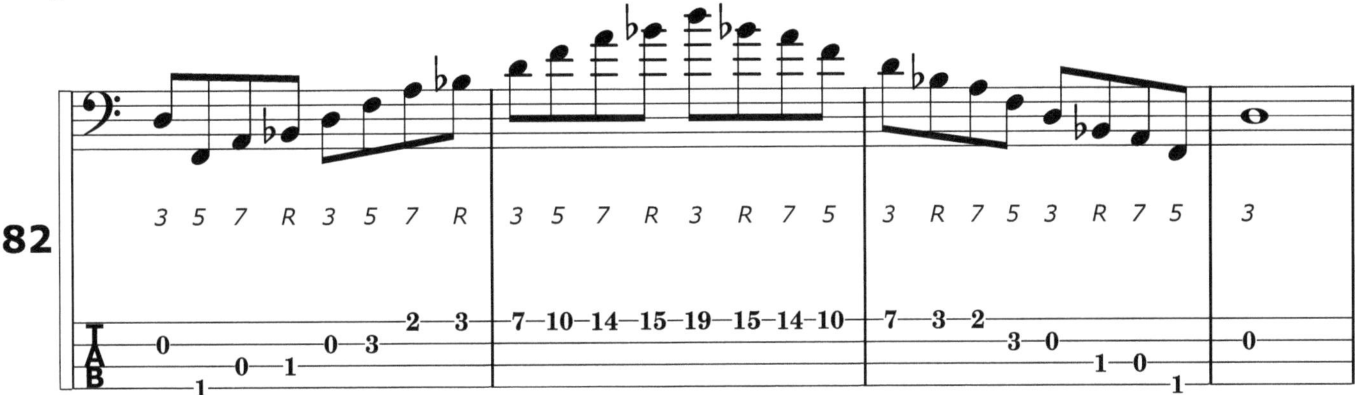

B♭ Major - Third Pattern 5

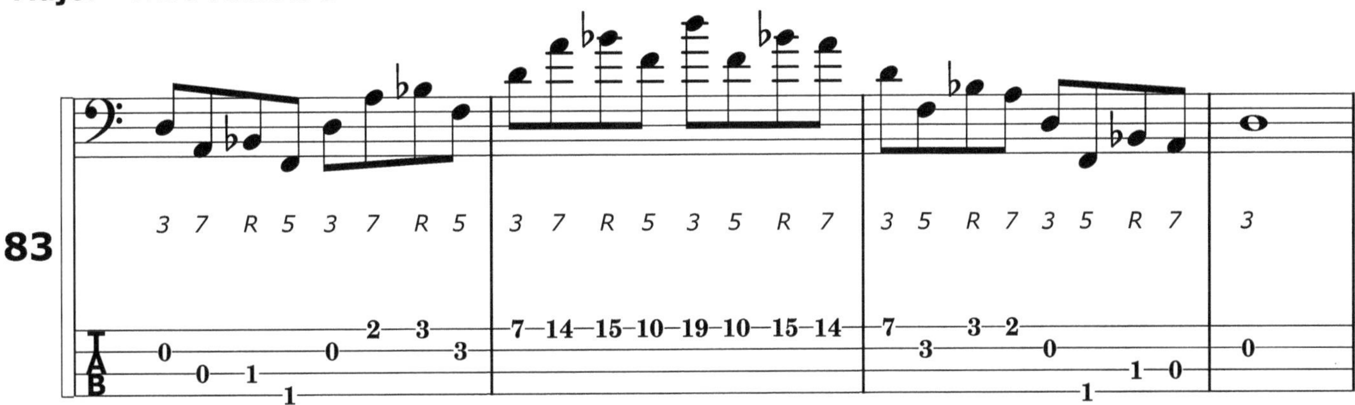

B♭ Major - Third Pattern 6

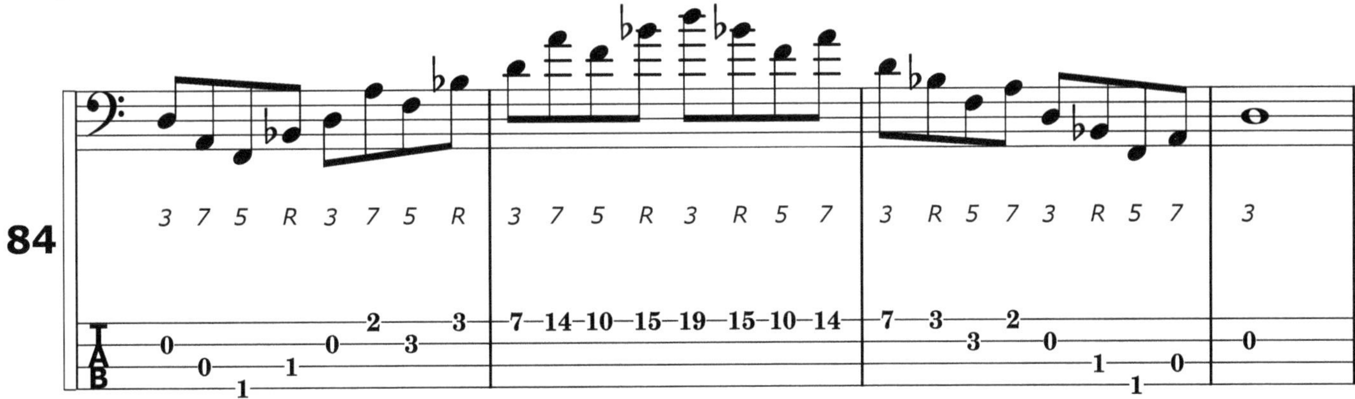

B♭ Major - Fifth Pattern 1

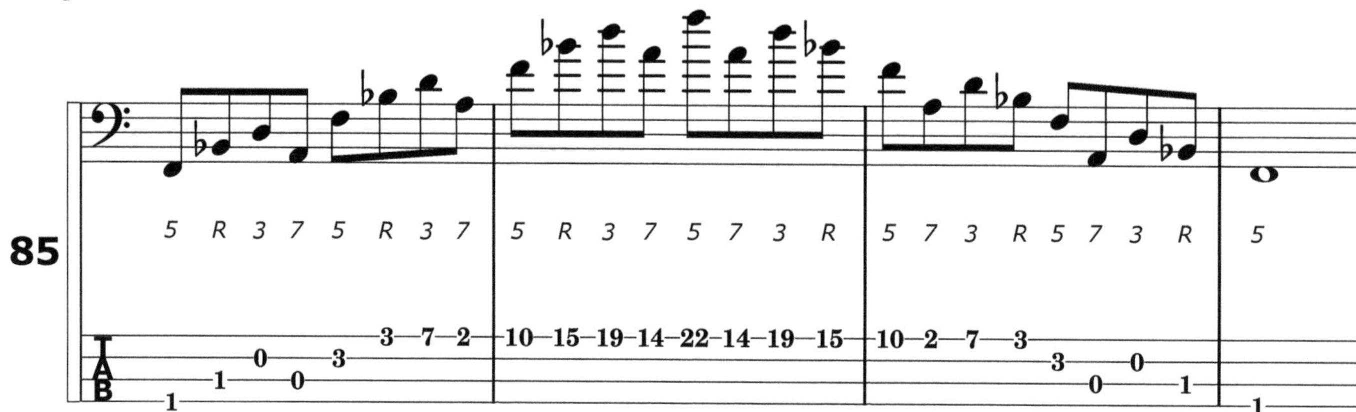

B♭ Major - Fifth Pattern 2

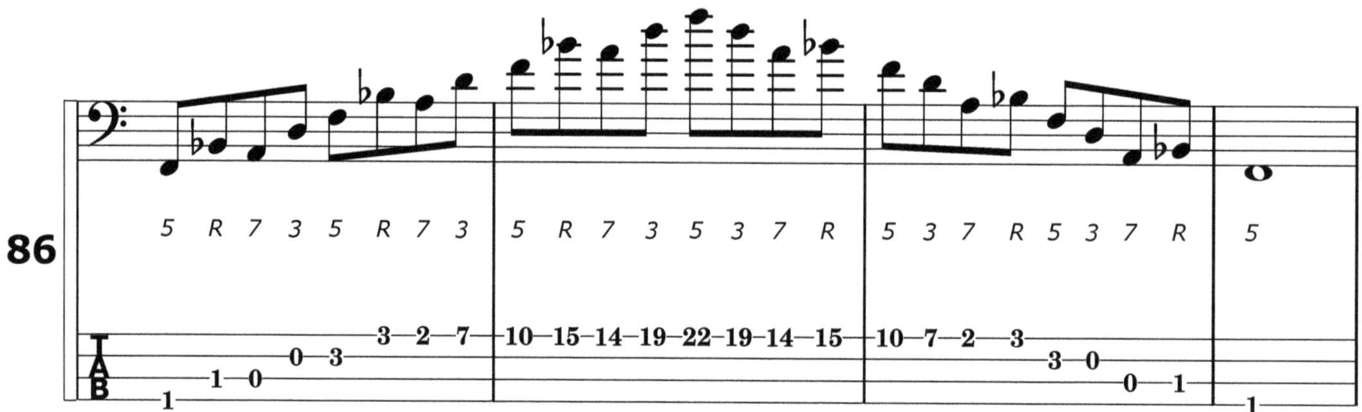

B♭ Major - Fifth Pattern 3

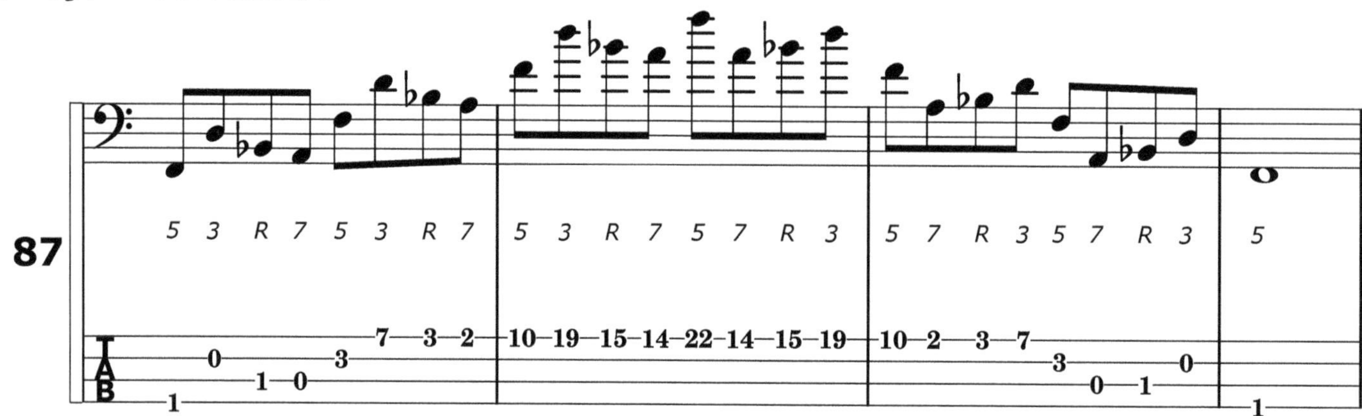

B♭ Major - Fifth Pattern 4

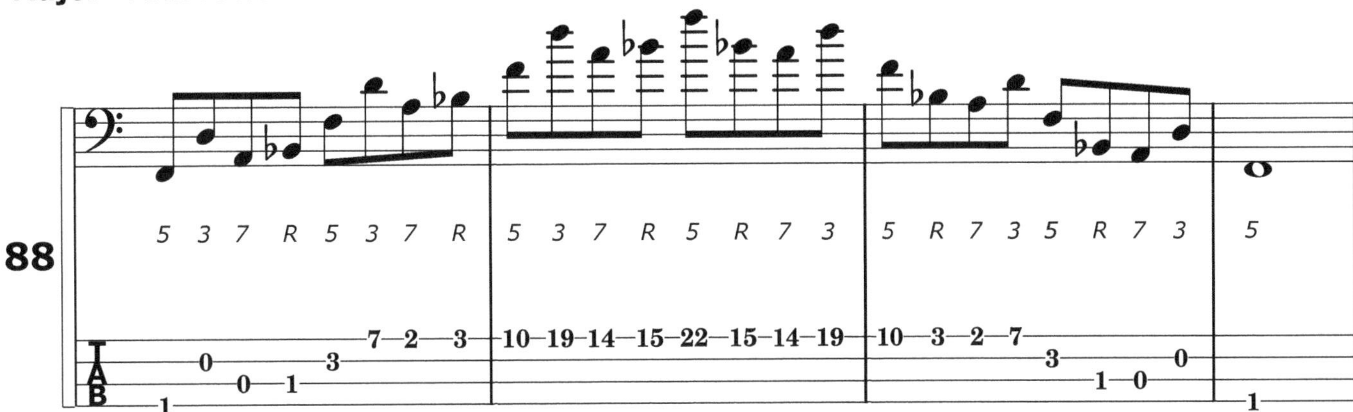

B♭ Major - Fifth Pattern 5

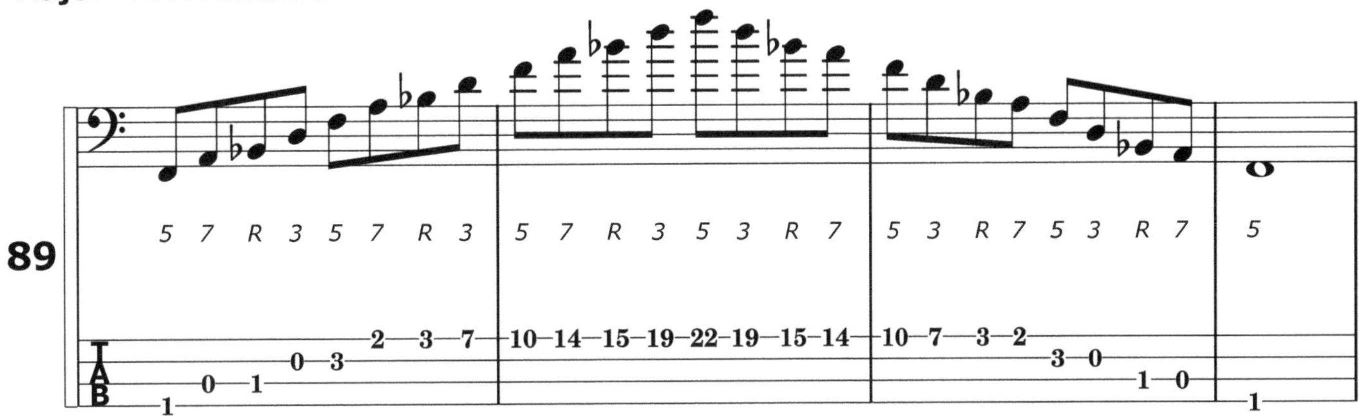

B♭ Major - Fifth Pattern 6

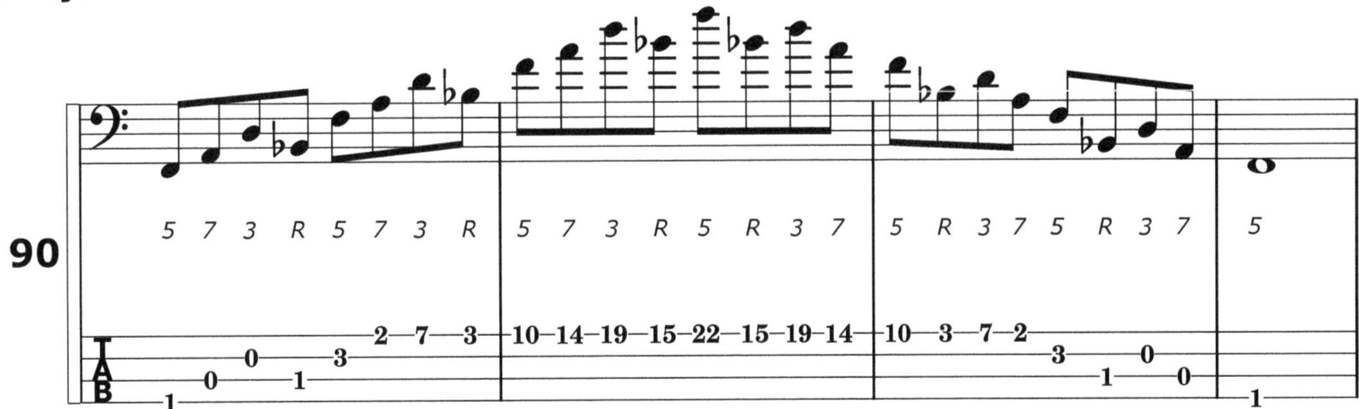

B♭ Major - Seventh Pattern 1

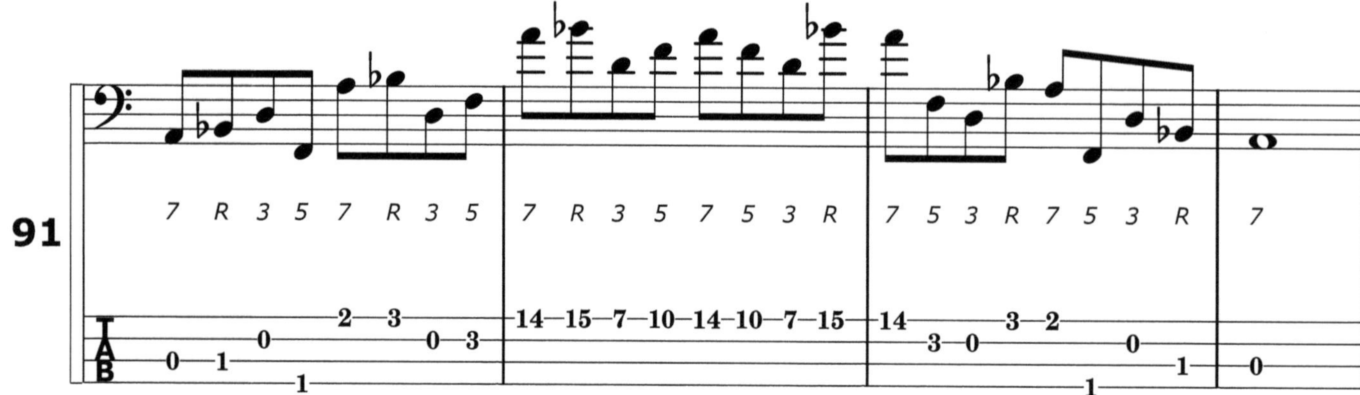

B♭ Major - Seventh Pattern 2

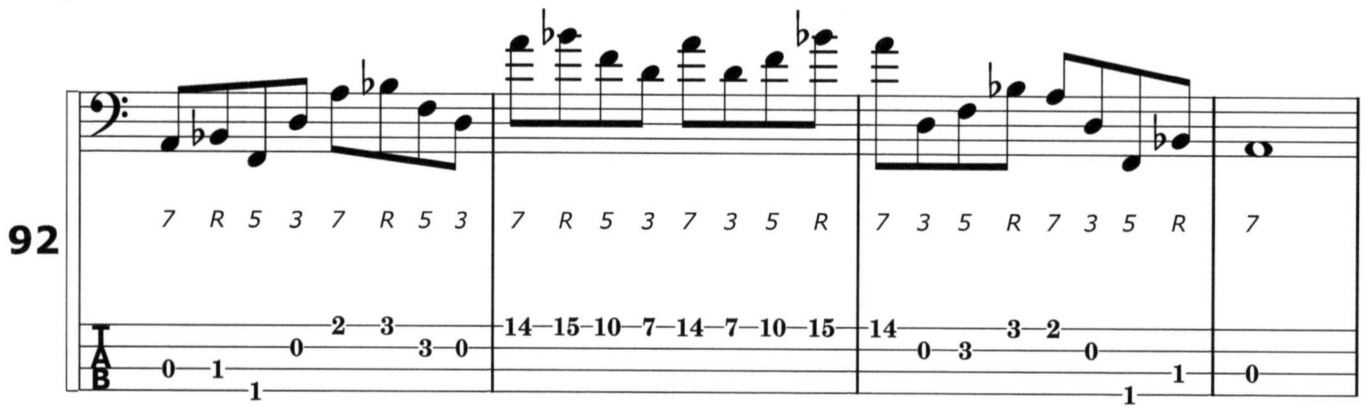

B♭ Major - Seventh Pattern 3

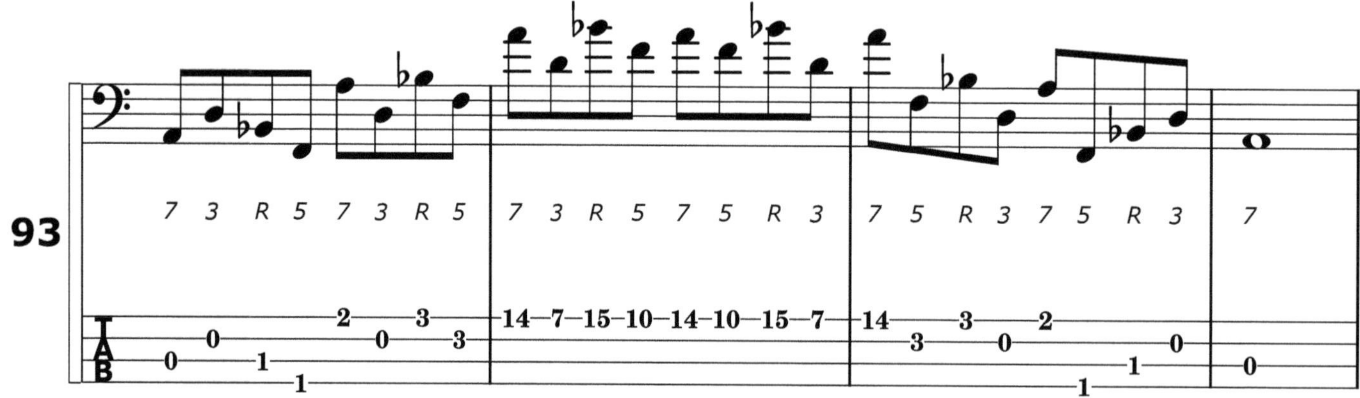

B♭ Major - Seventh Pattern 4

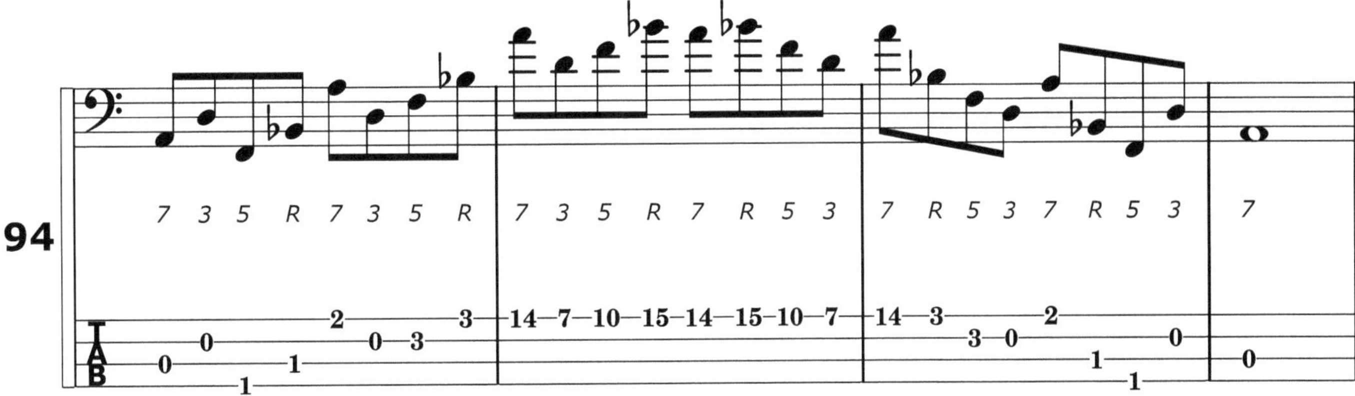

B♭ Major - Seventh Pattern 5

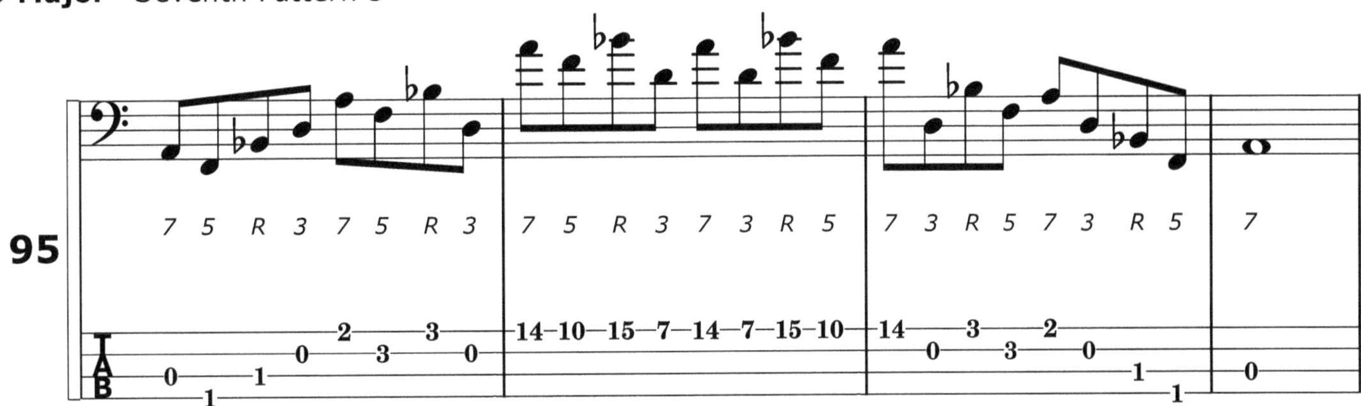

B♭ Major - Seventh Pattern 6

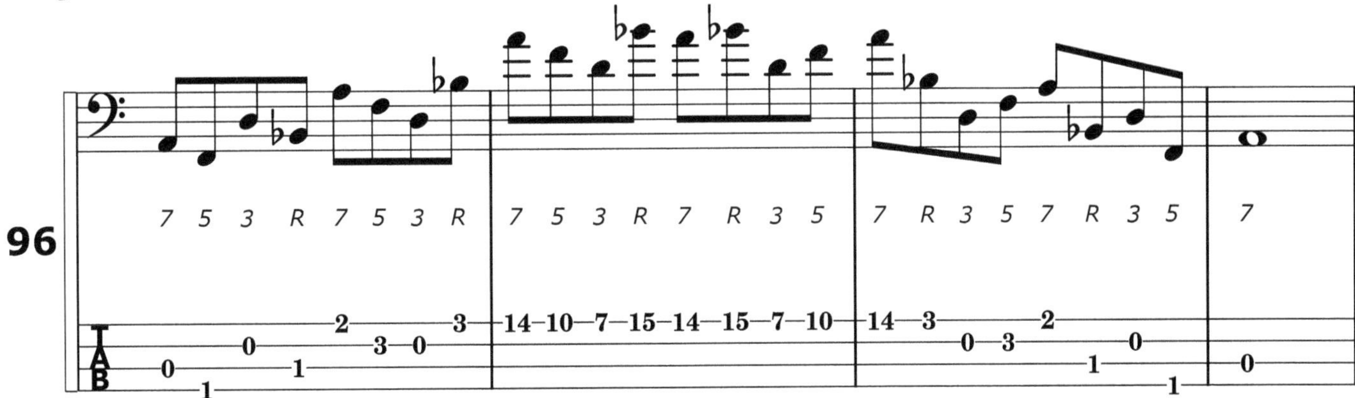

D Major - Root Pattern 1

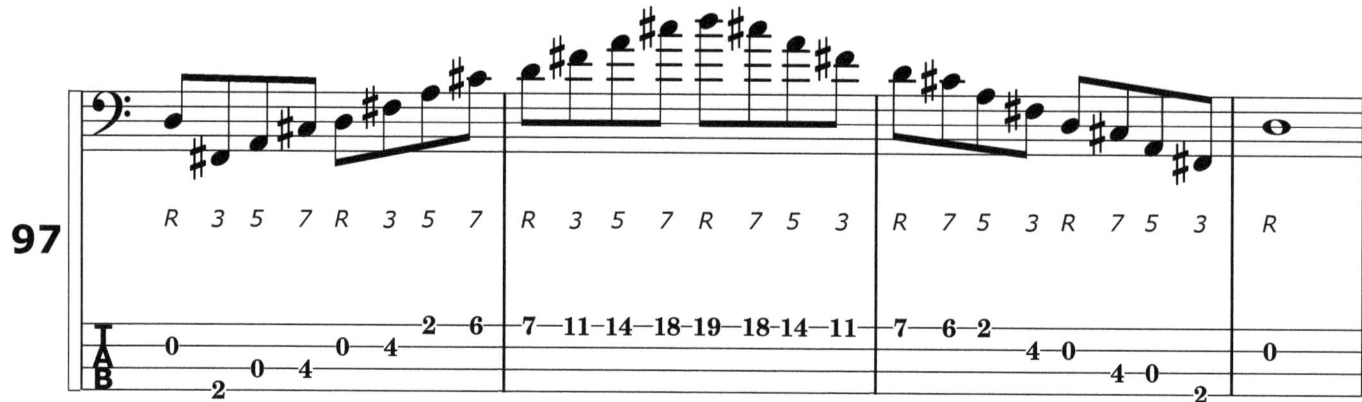

D Major - Root Pattern 2

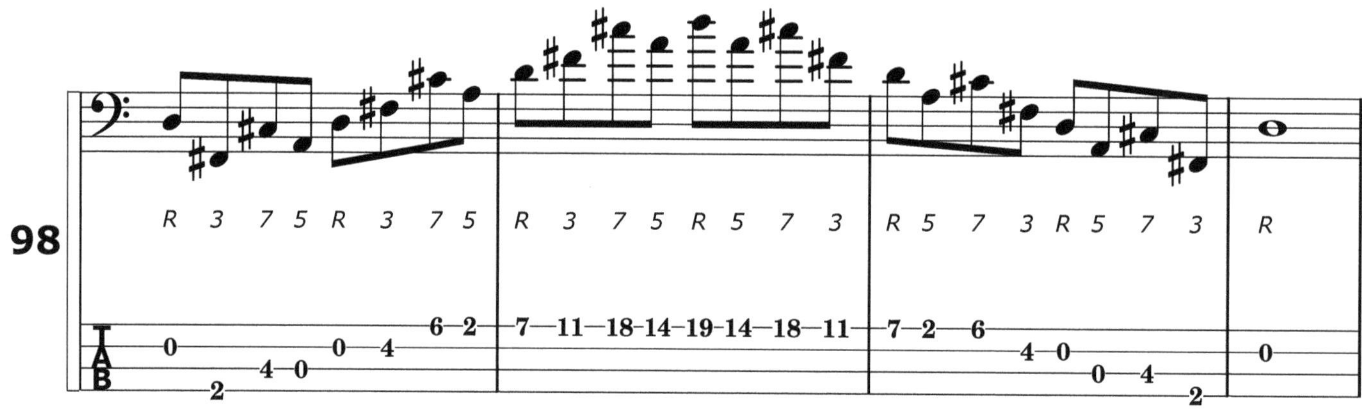

D Major - Root Pattern 3

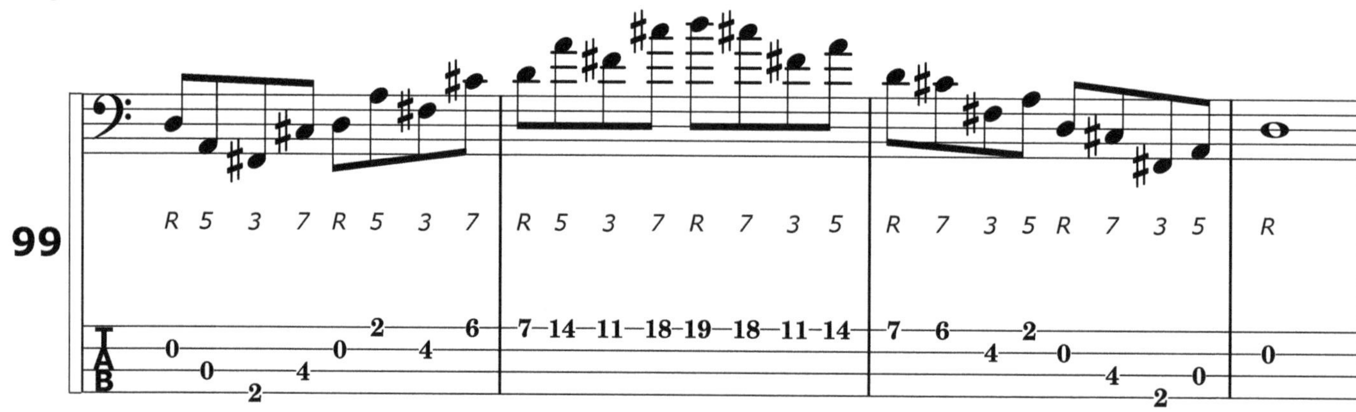

D Major - Root Pattern 4

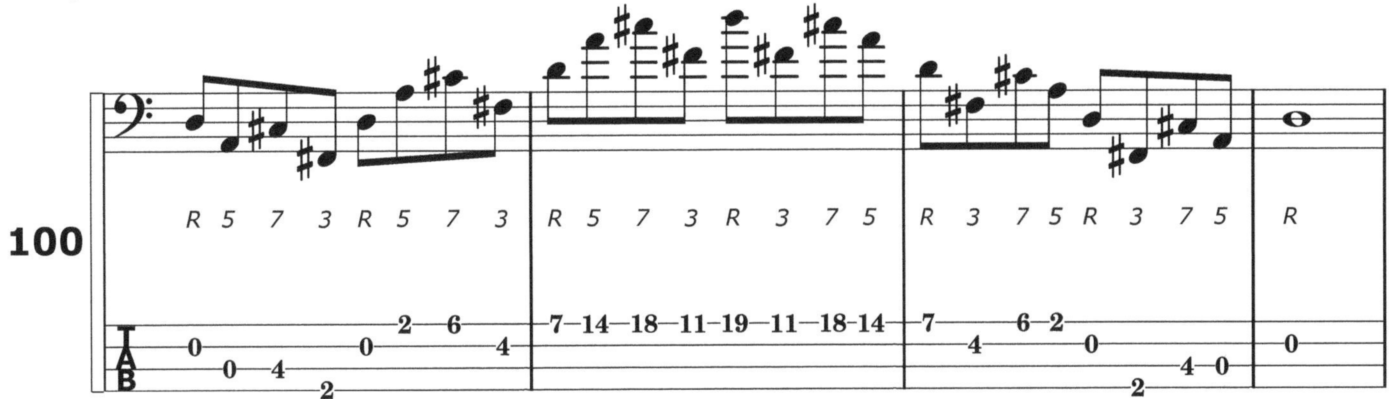

D Major - Root Pattern 5

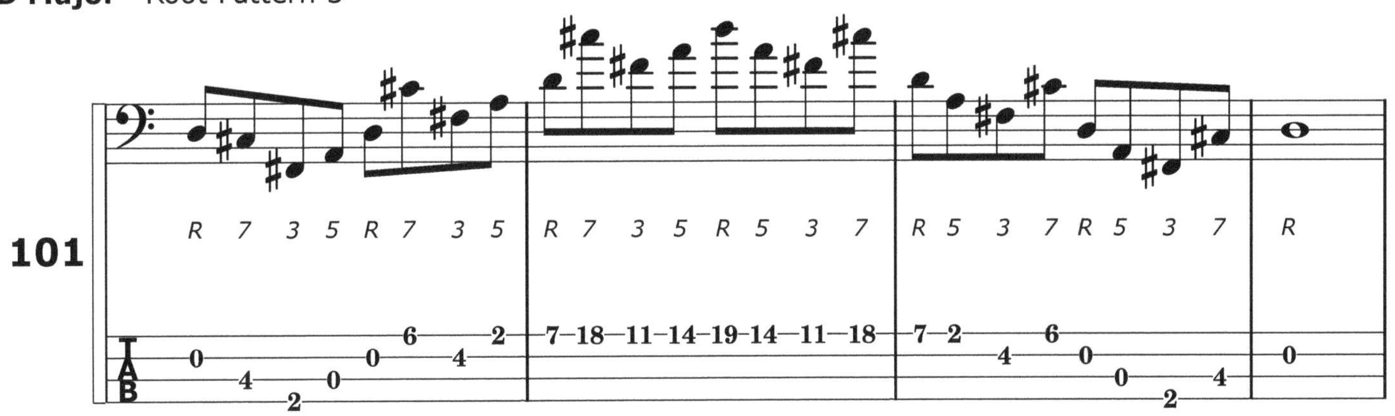

D Major - Root Pattern 6

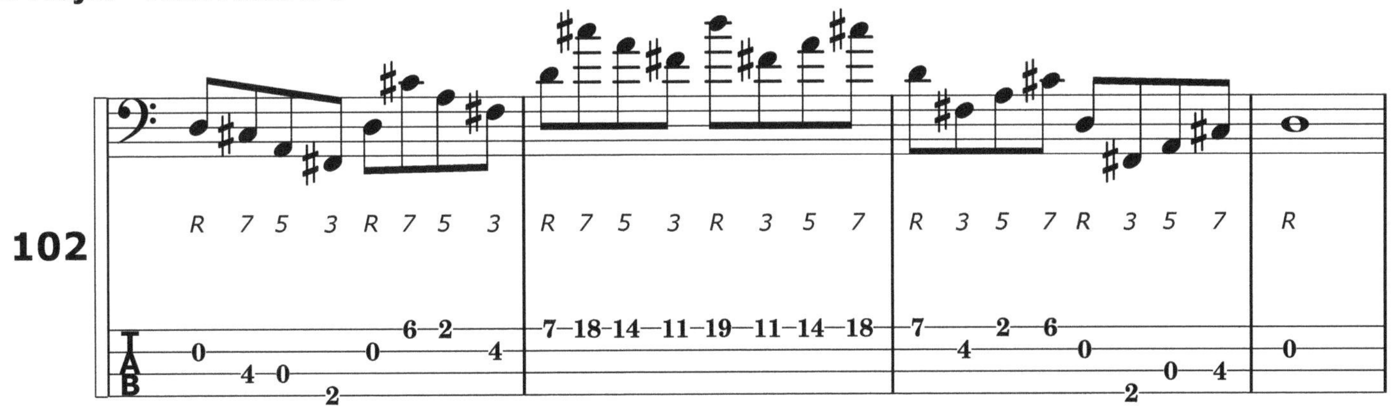

D Major - Third Pattern 1

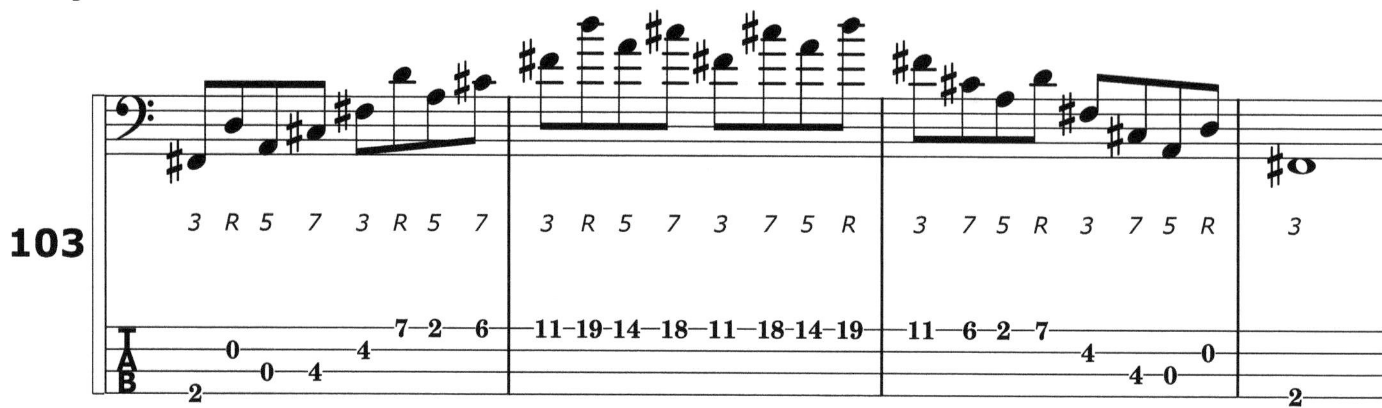

D Major - Third Pattern 2

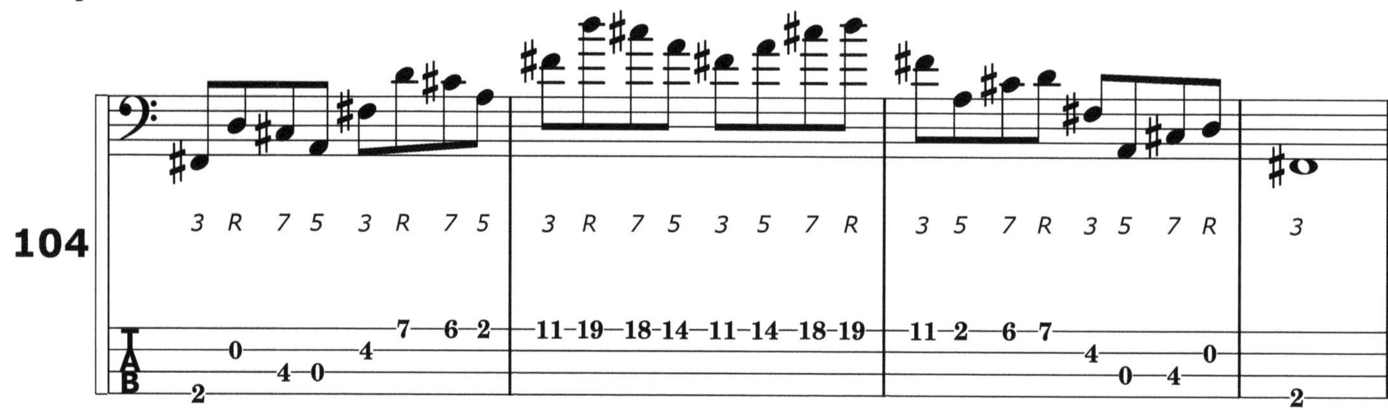

D Major - Third Pattern 3

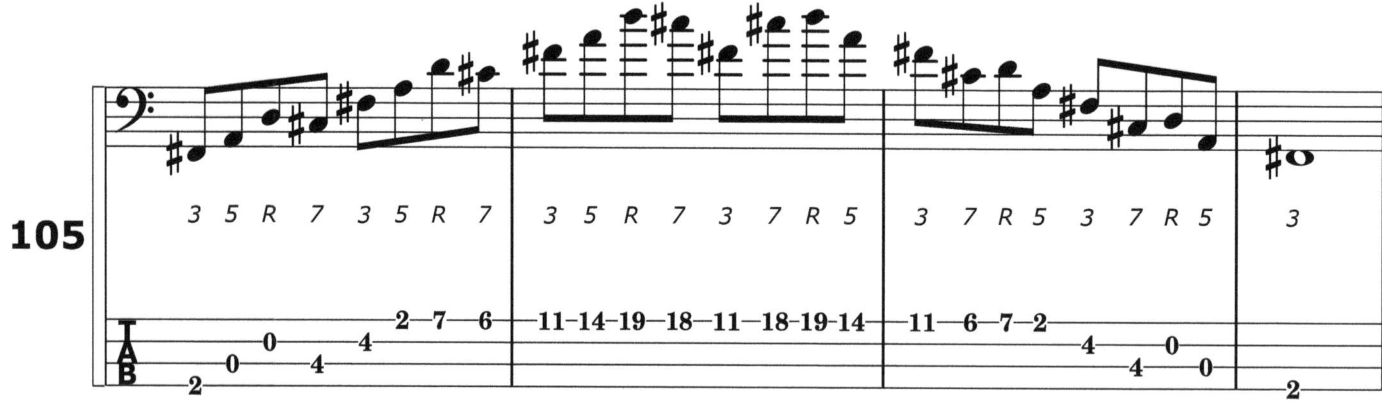

D Major - Third Pattern 4

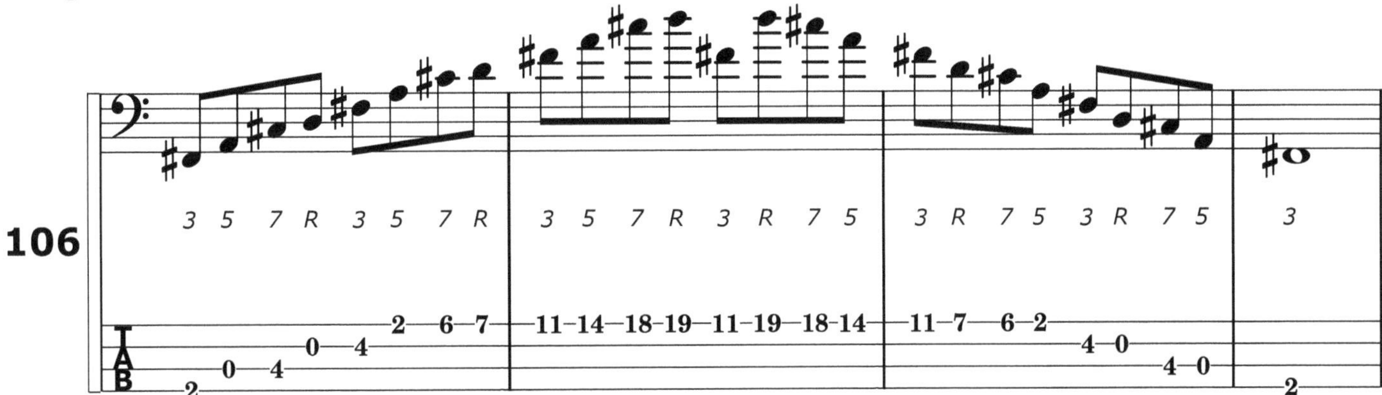

D Major - Third Pattern 5

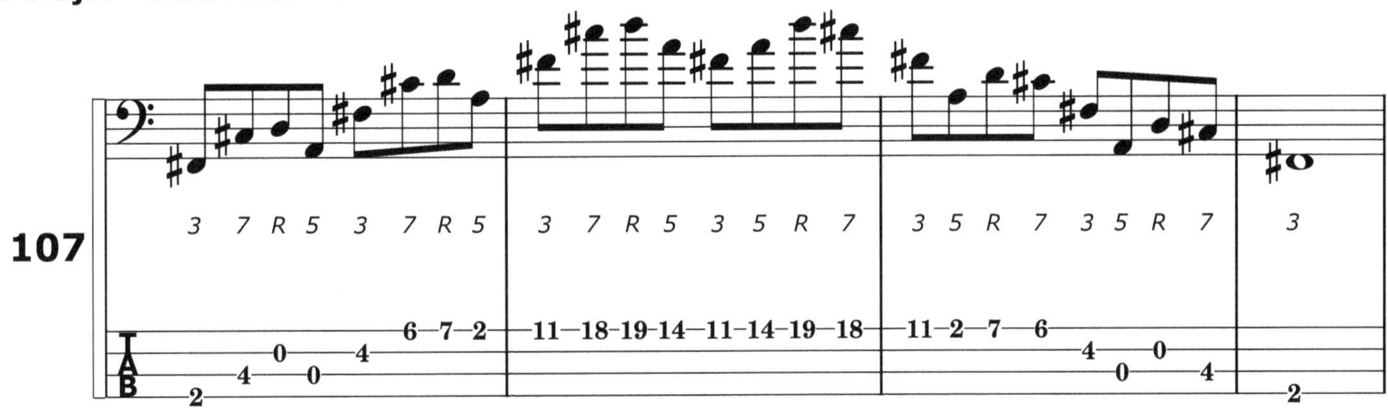

D Major - Third Pattern 6

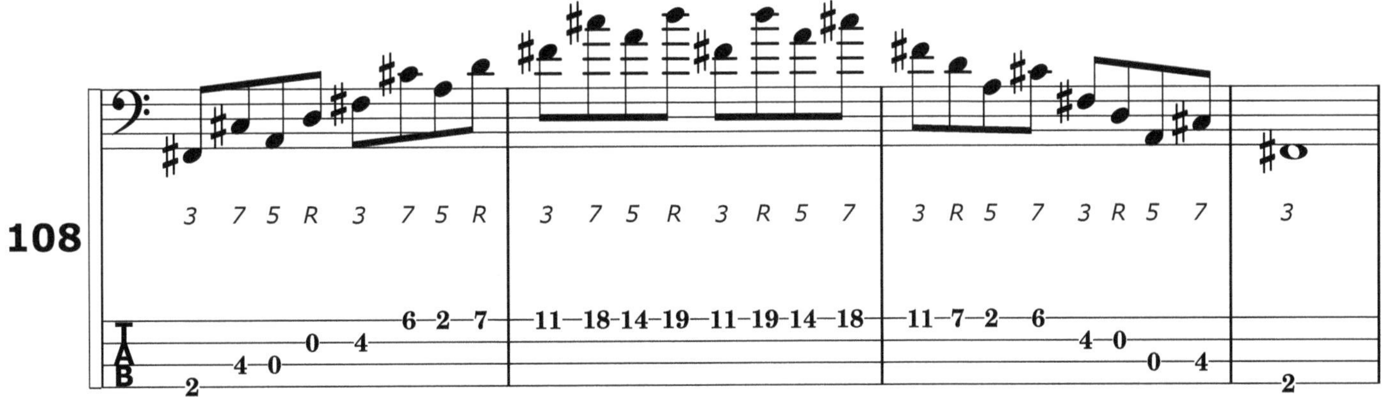

D Major - Fifth Pattern 1

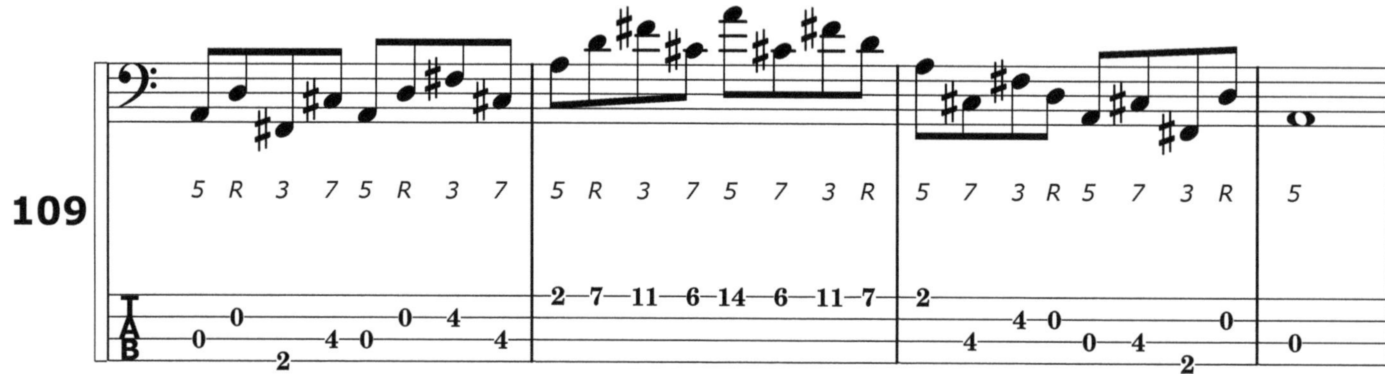

D Major - Fifth Pattern 2

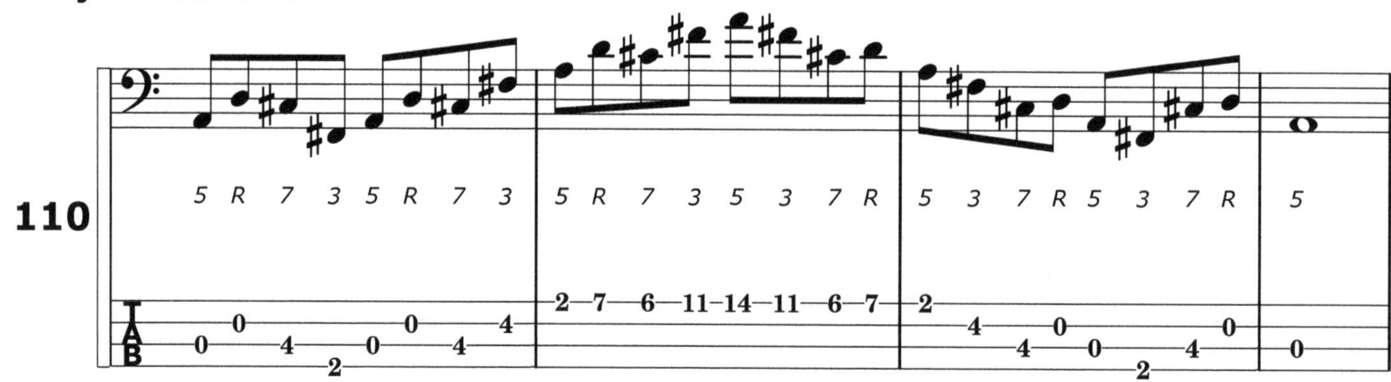

D Major - Fifth Pattern 3

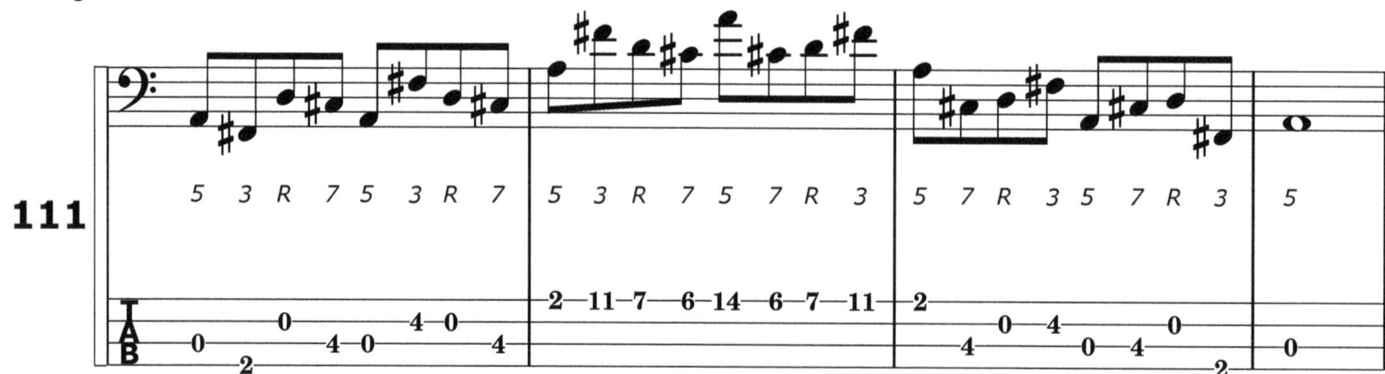

D Major - Fifth Pattern 4

112

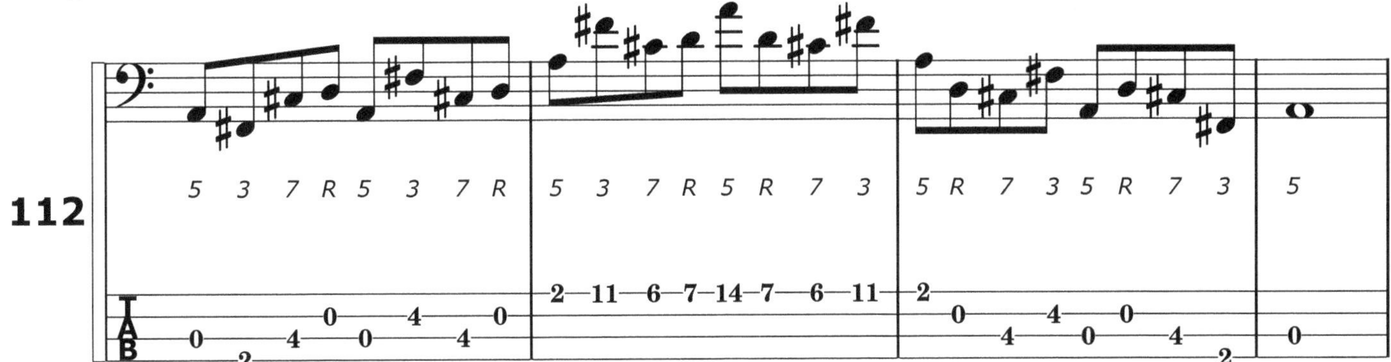

D Major - Fifth Pattern 5

113

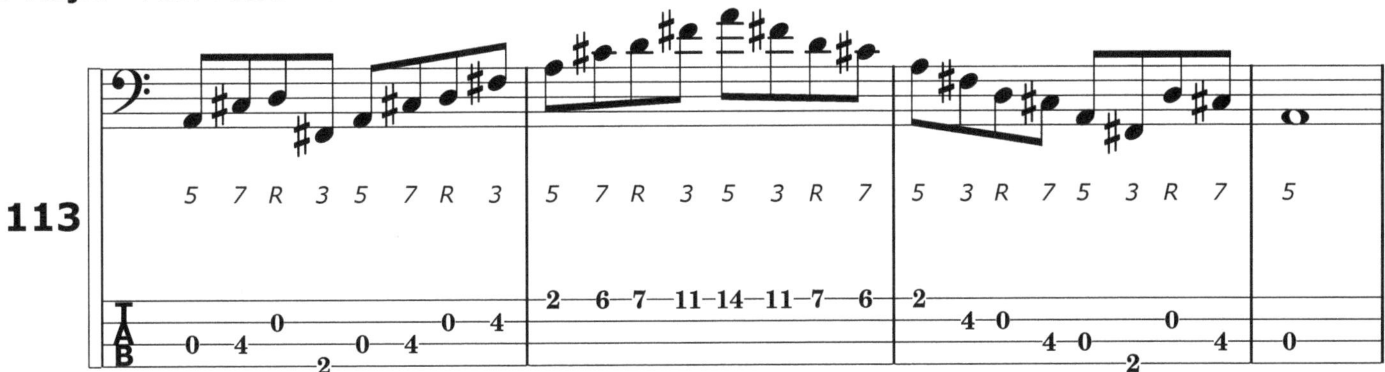

D Major - Fifth Pattern 6

114

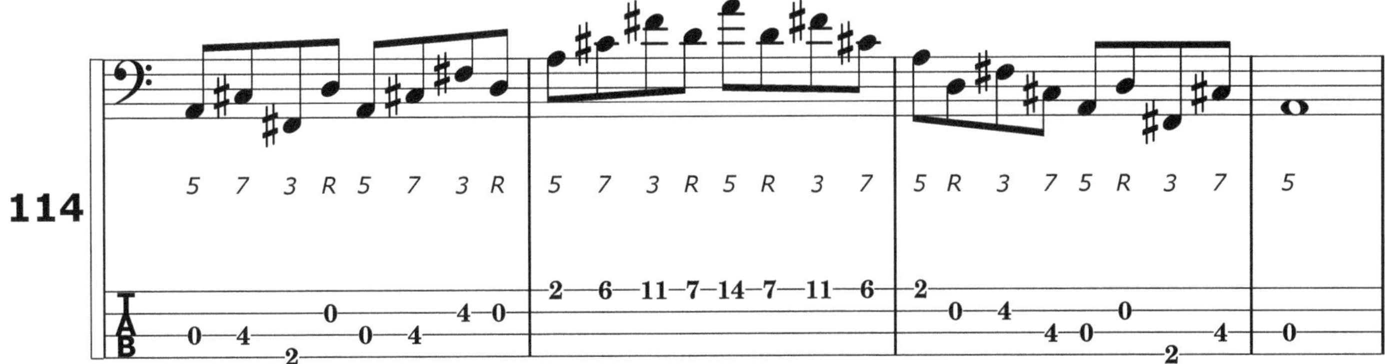

D Major - Seventh Pattern 1

115

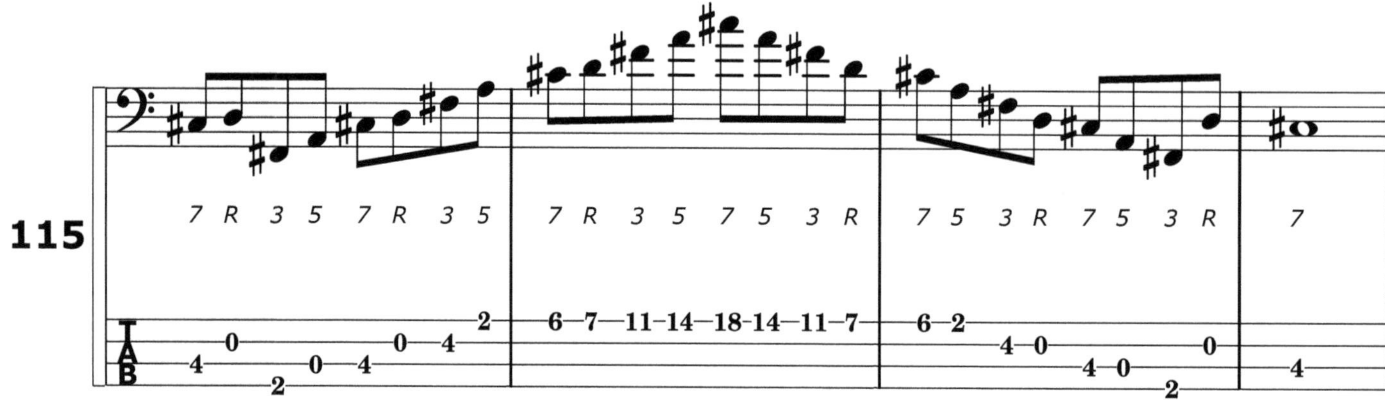

D Major - Seventh Pattern 2

116

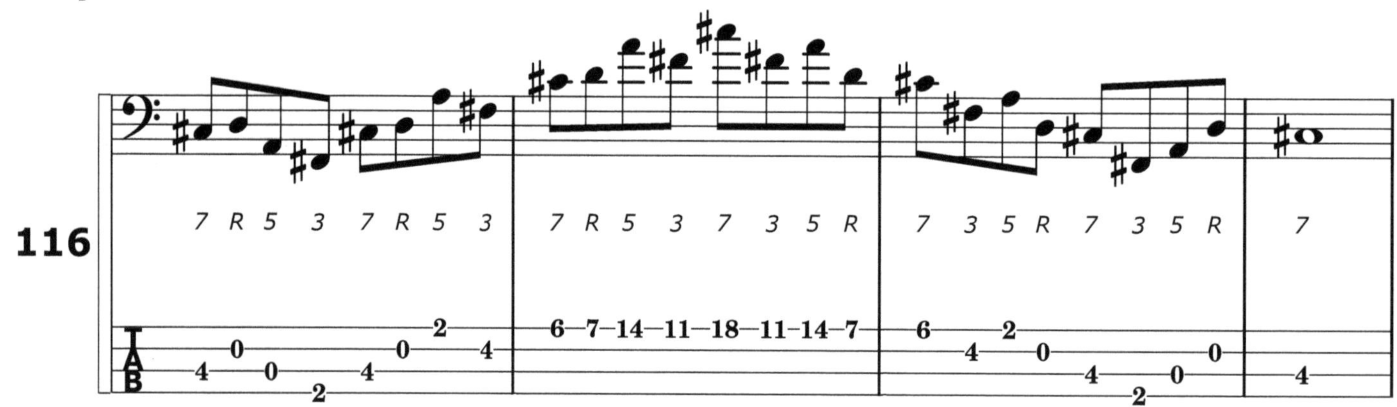

D Major - Seventh Pattern 3

117

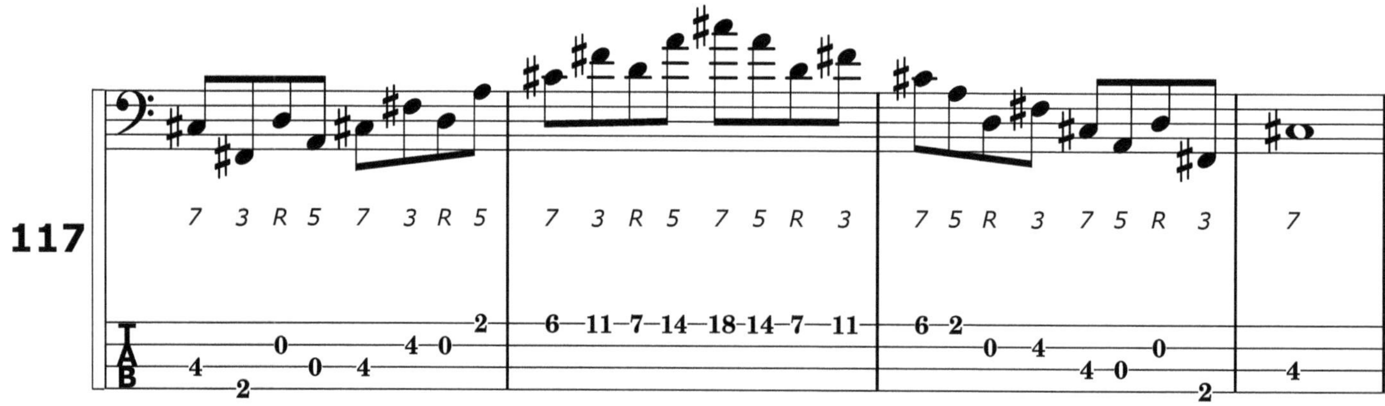

D Major - Seventh Pattern 4

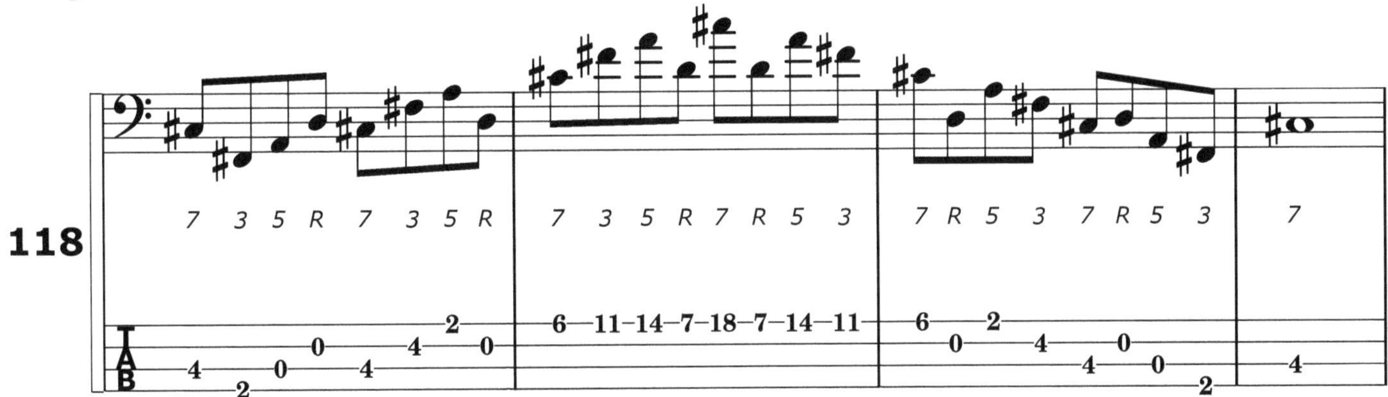

D Major - Seventh Pattern 5

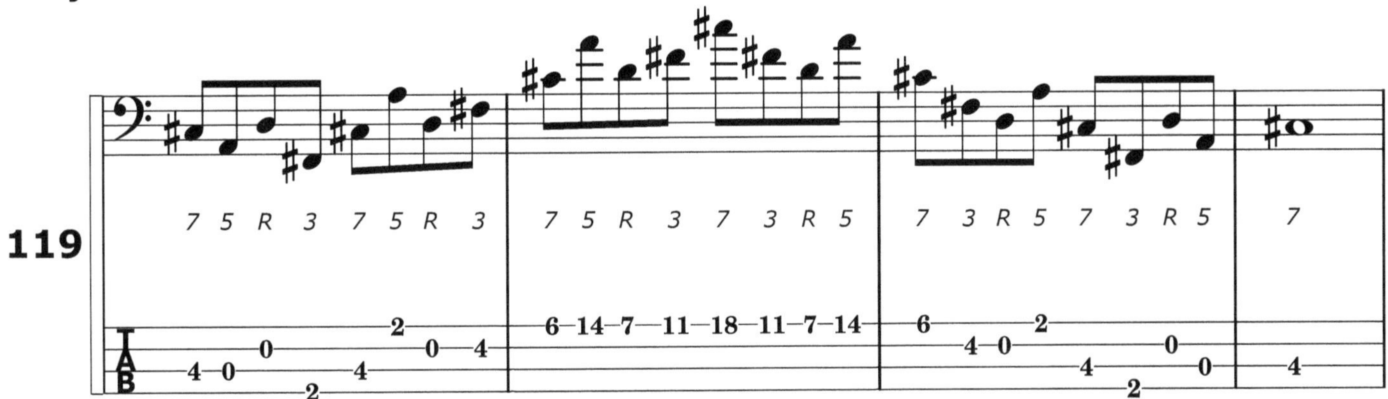

D Major - Seventh Pattern 6

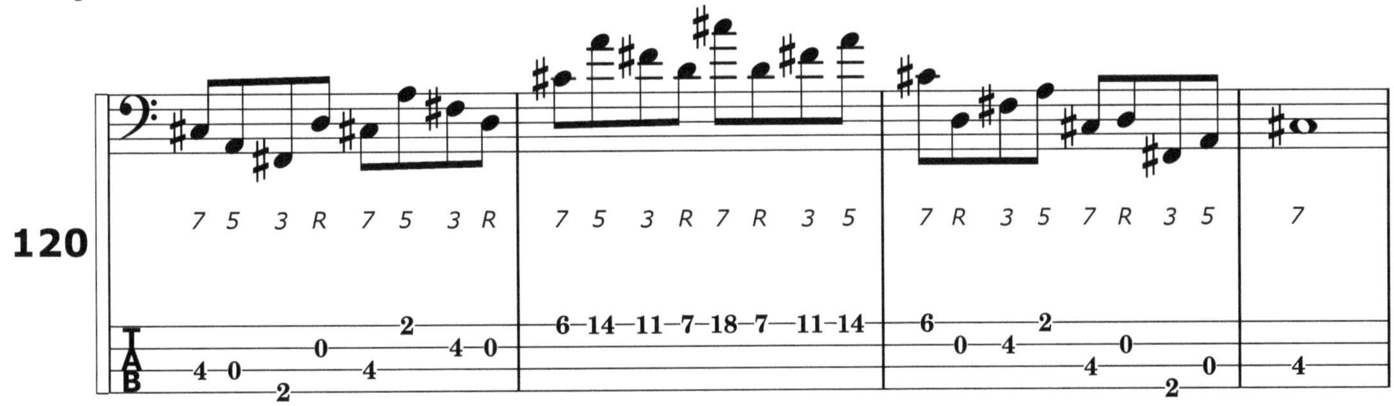

E♭ Major - Root Pattern 1

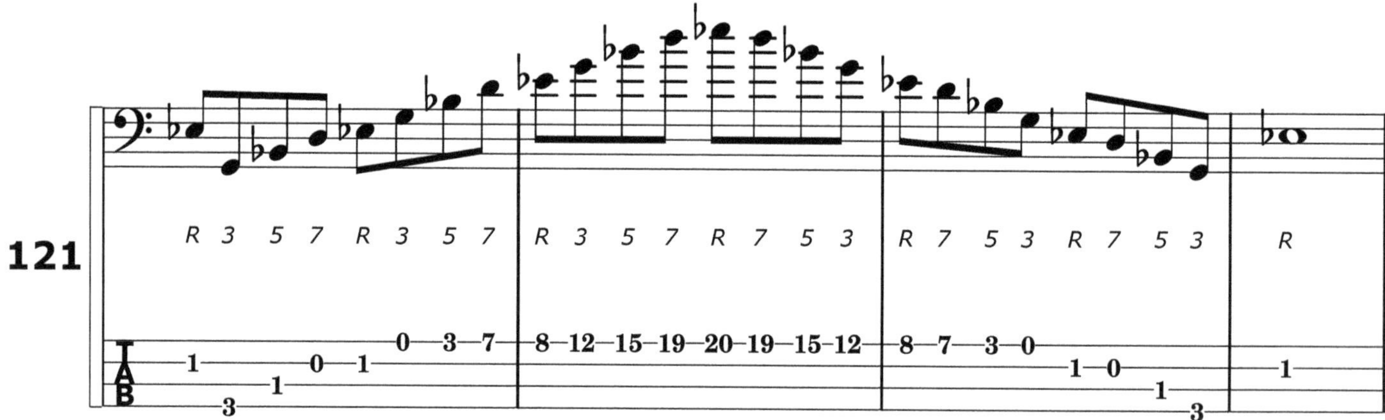

E♭ Major - Root Pattern 2

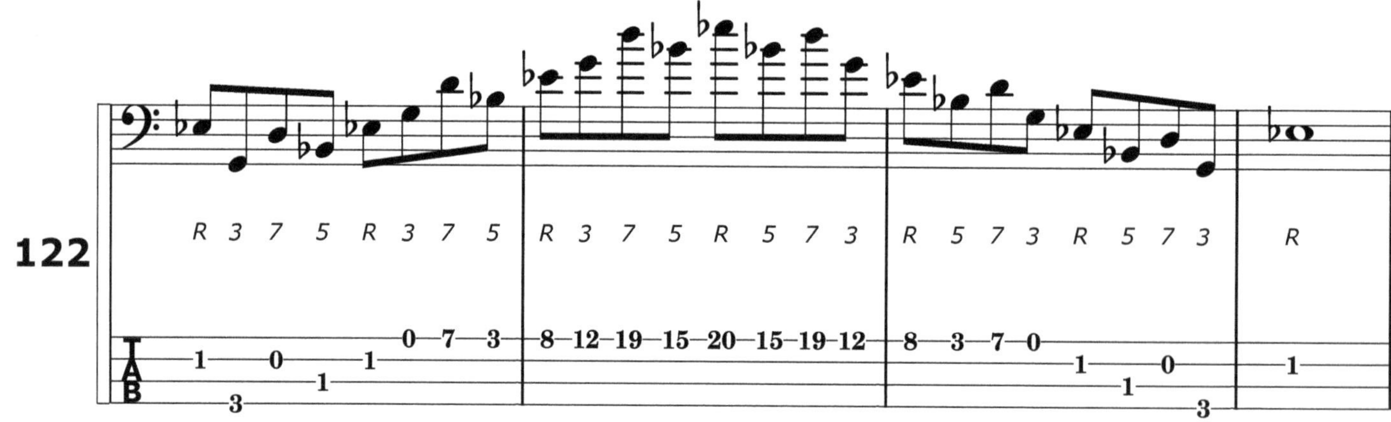

E♭ Major - Root Pattern 3

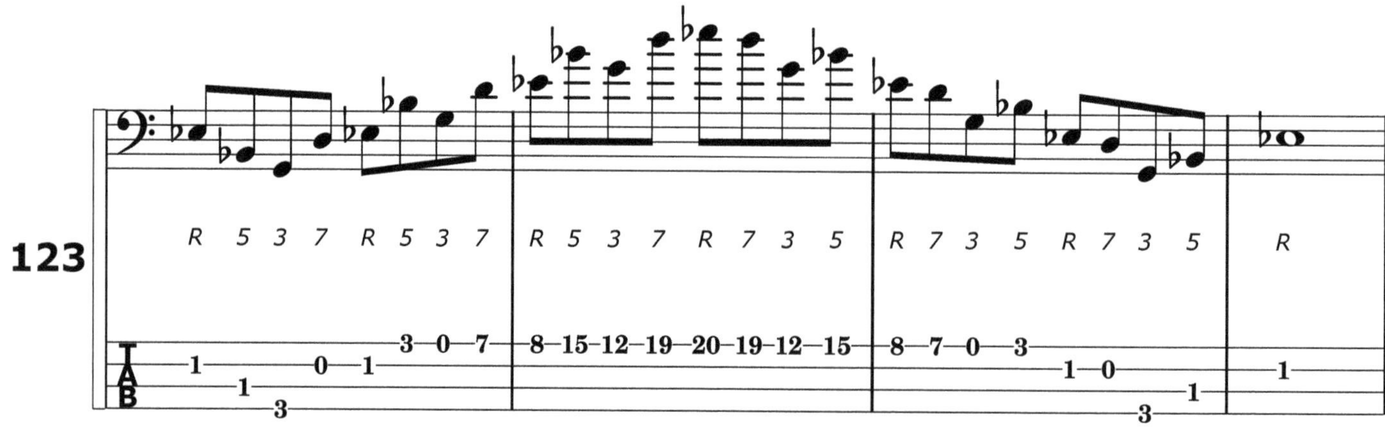

E♭ Major - Root Pattern 4

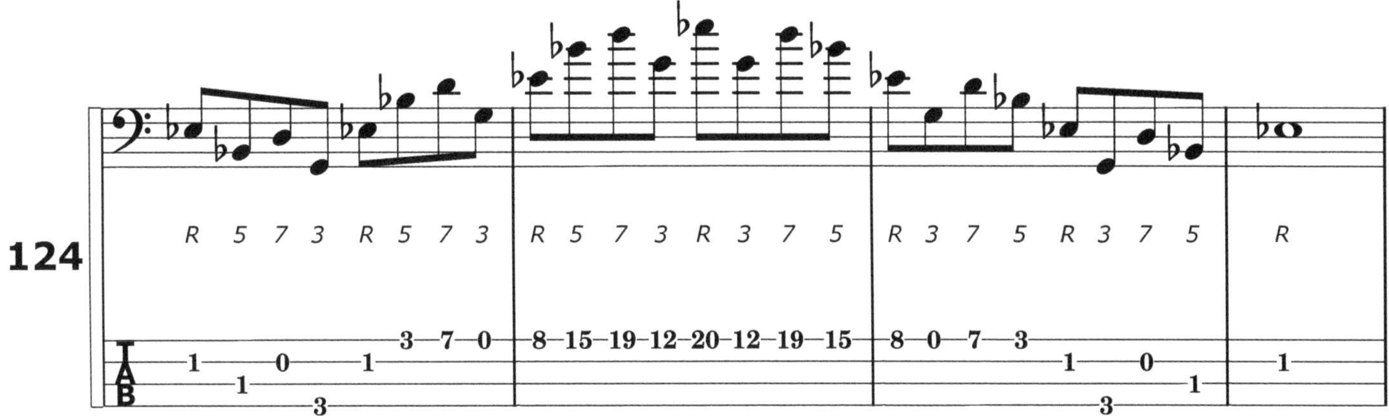

E♭ Major - Root Pattern 5

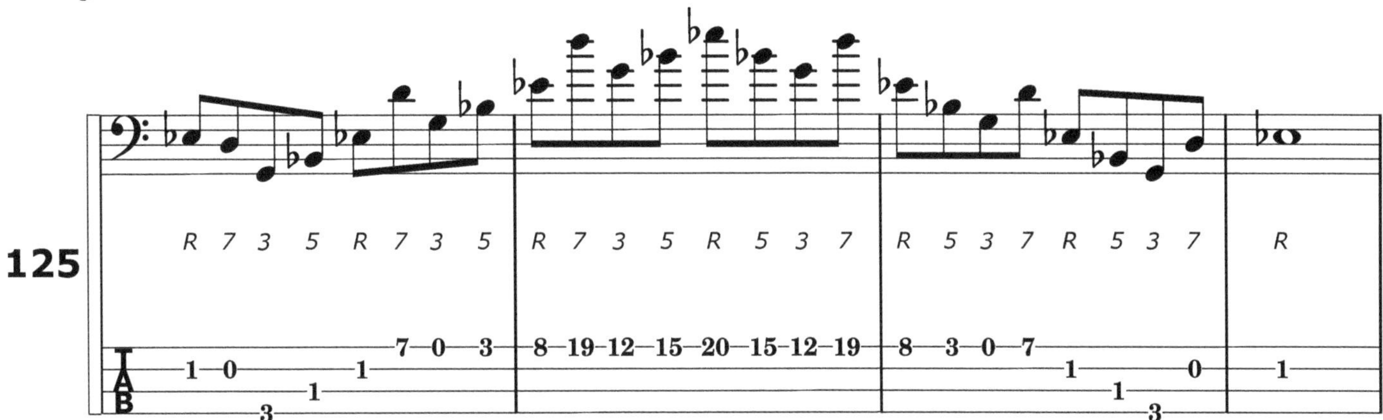

E♭ Major - Root Pattern 6

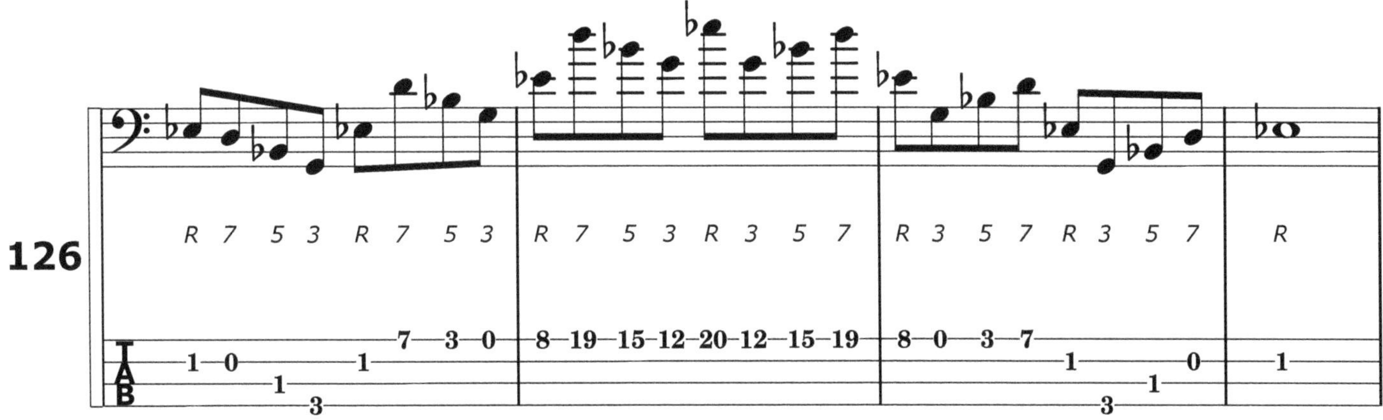

E♭ Major - Third Pattern 1

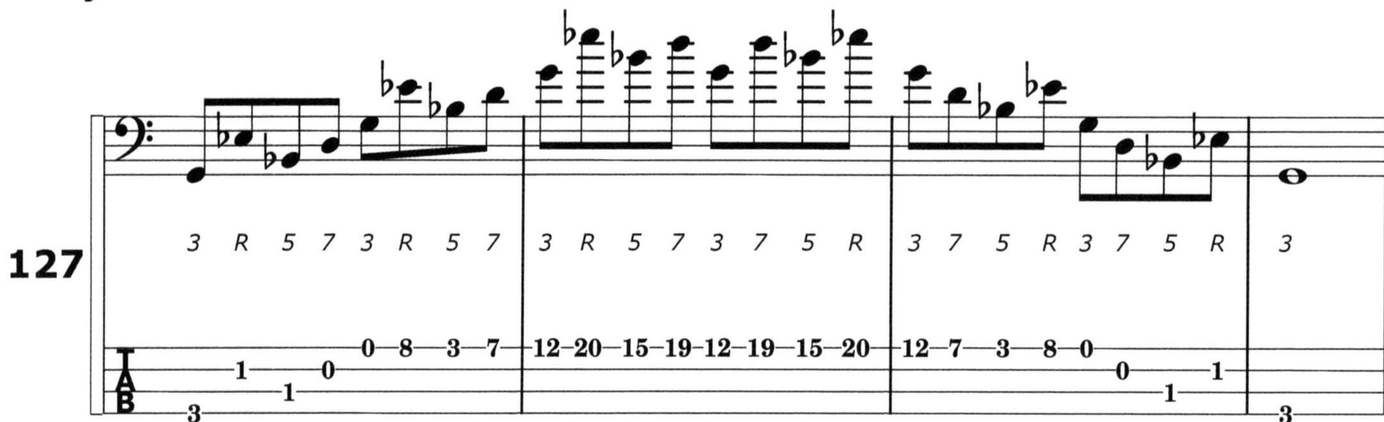

E♭ Major - Third Pattern 2

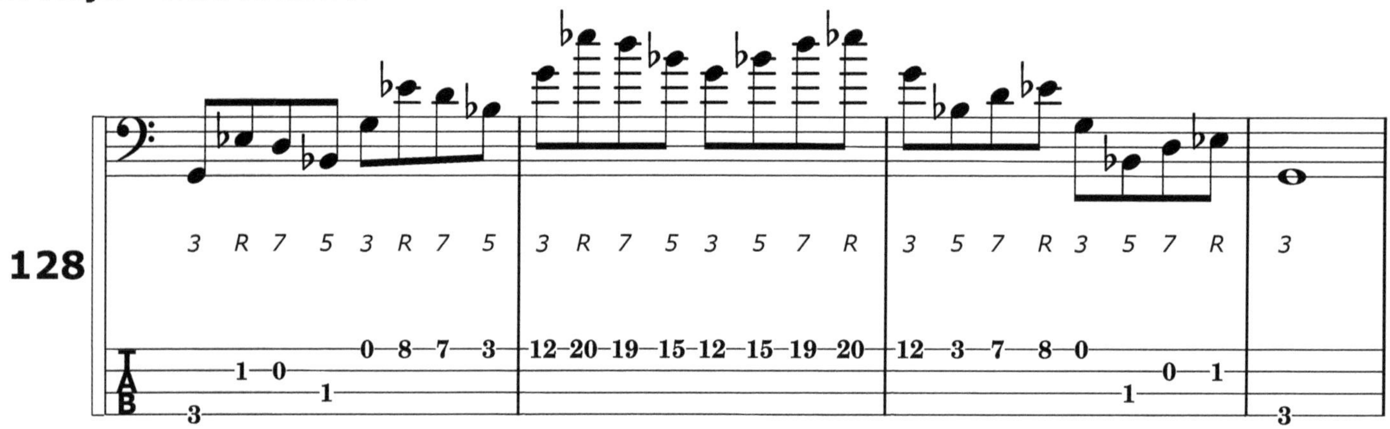

E♭ Major - Third Pattern 3

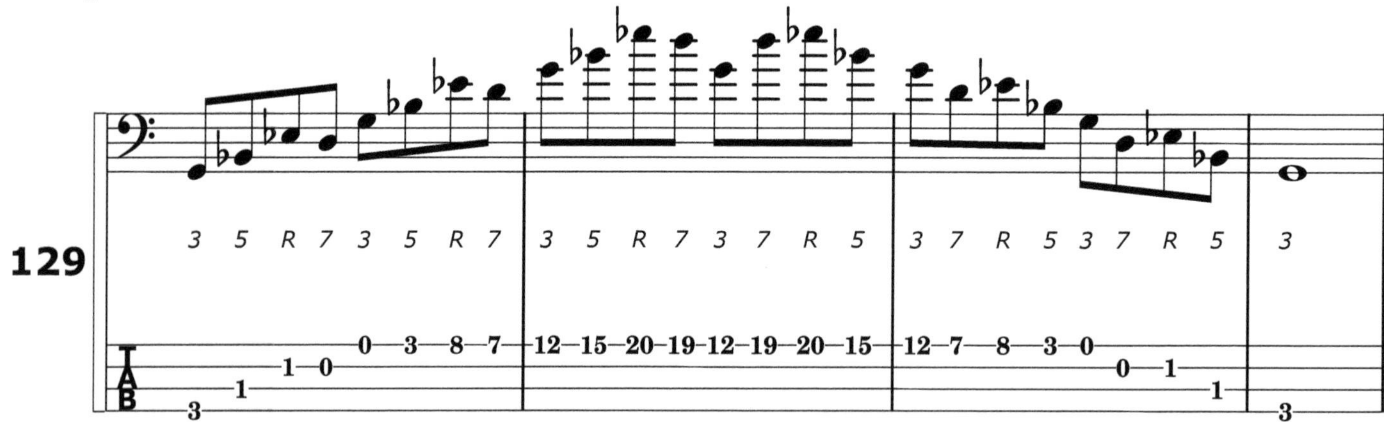

E♭ Major - Third Pattern 4

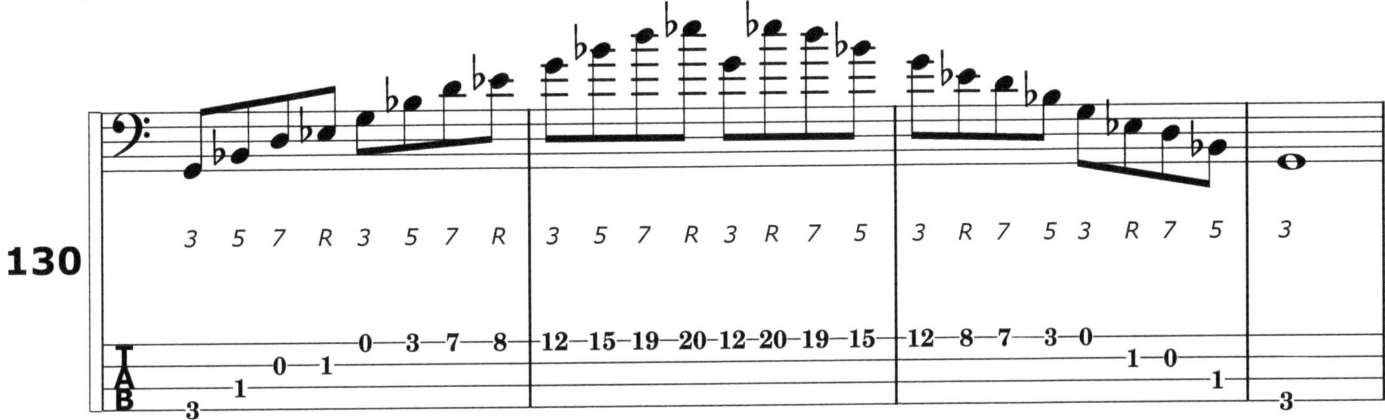

E♭ Major - Third Pattern 5

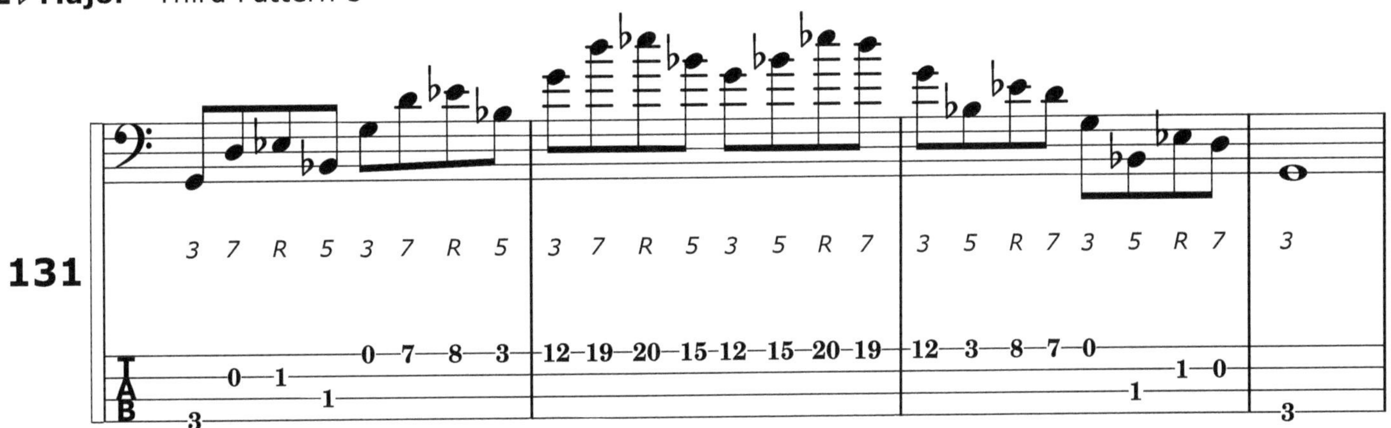

E♭ Major - Third Pattern 6

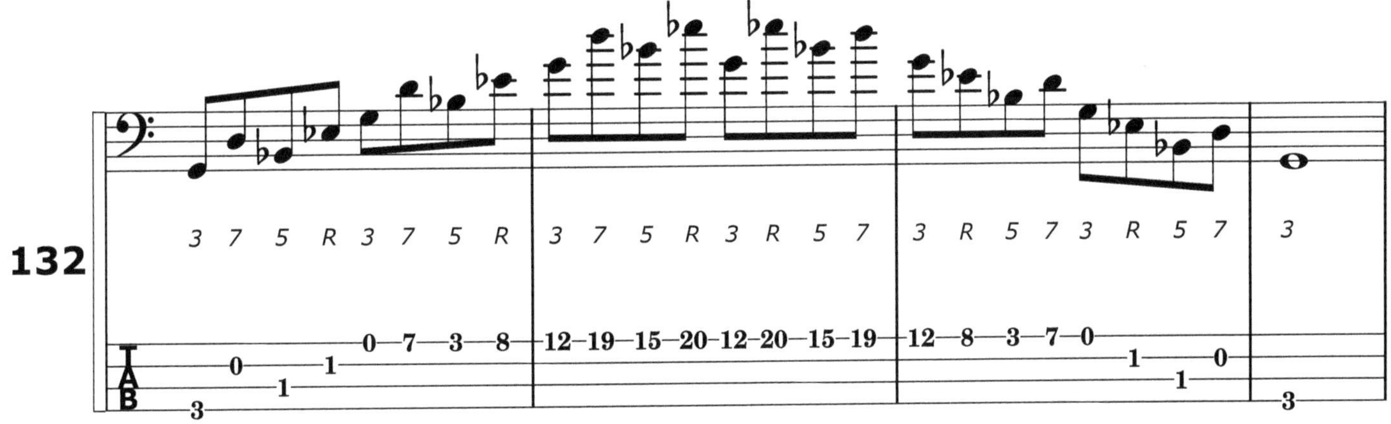

E♭ Major - Fifth Pattern 1

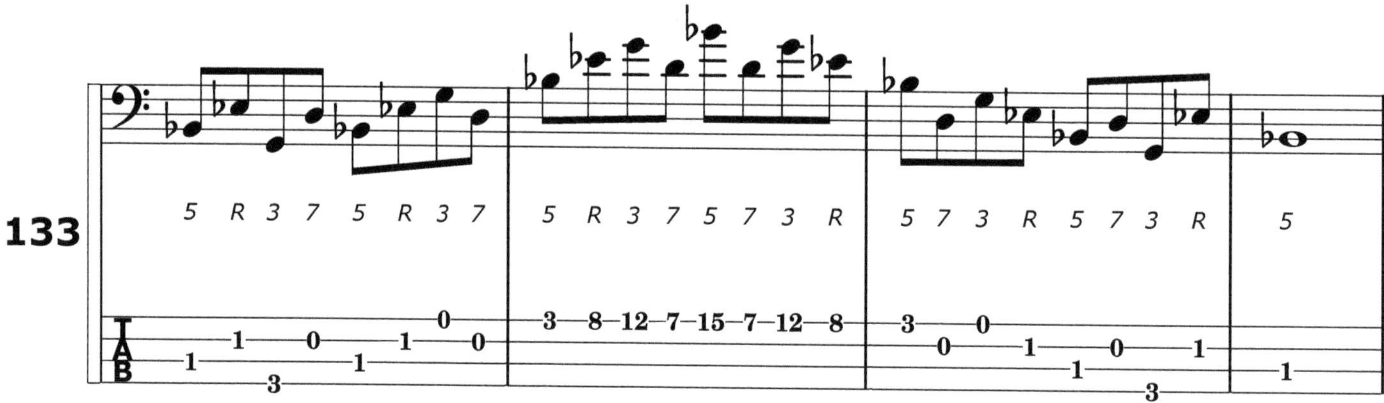

E♭ Major - Fifth Pattern 2

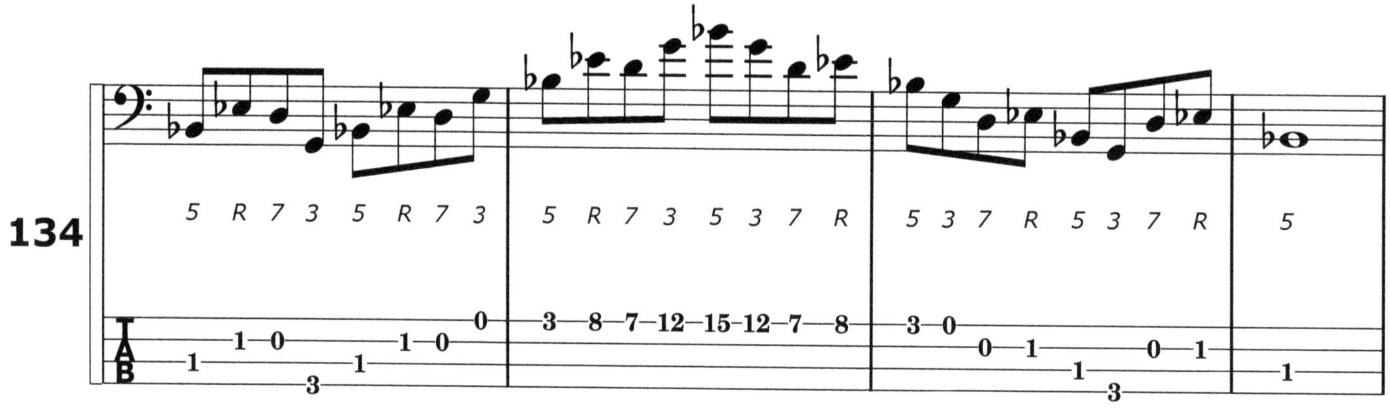

E♭ Major - Fifth Pattern 3

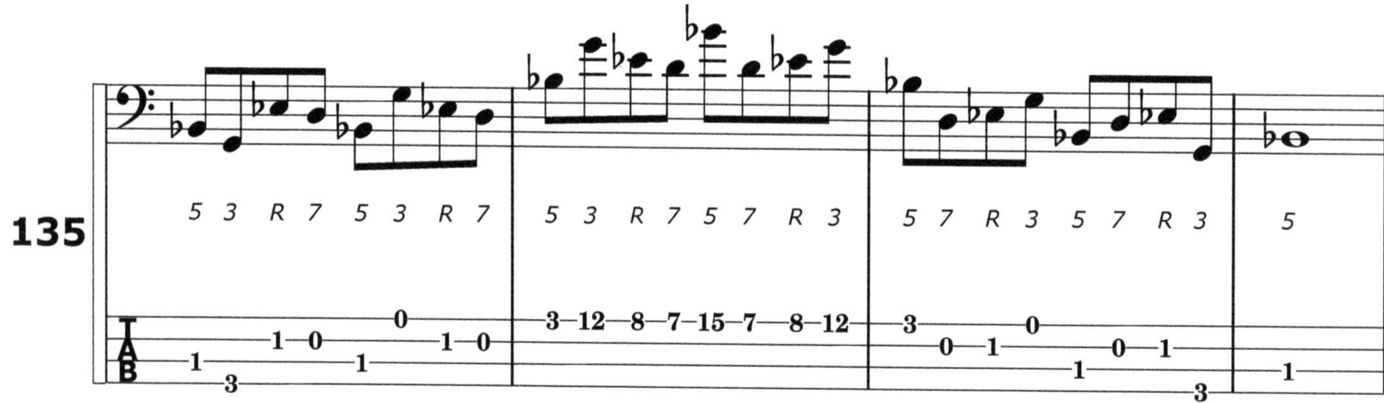

E♭ Major - Fifth Pattern 4

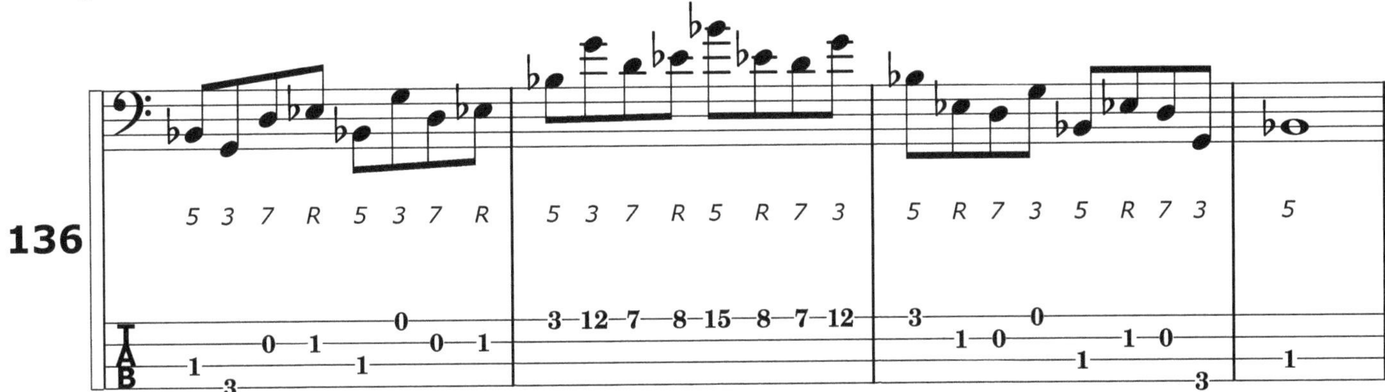

E♭ Major - Fifth Pattern 5

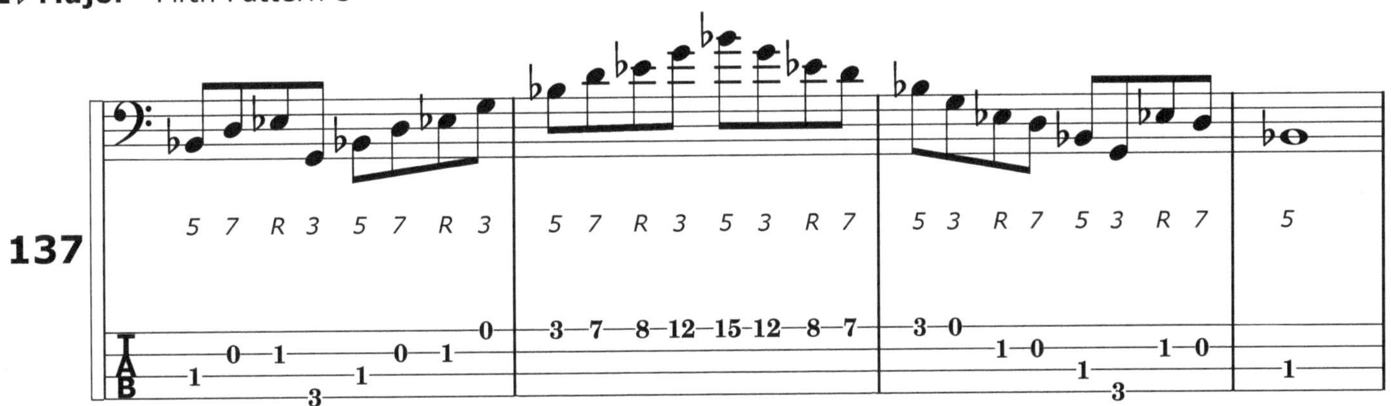

E♭ Major - Fifth Pattern 6

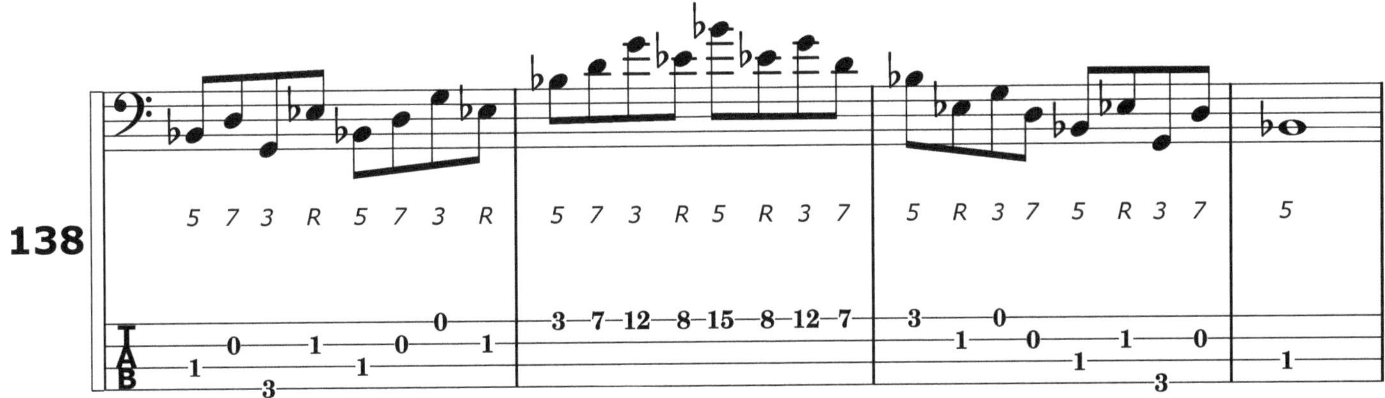

E♭ Major - Seventh Pattern 1

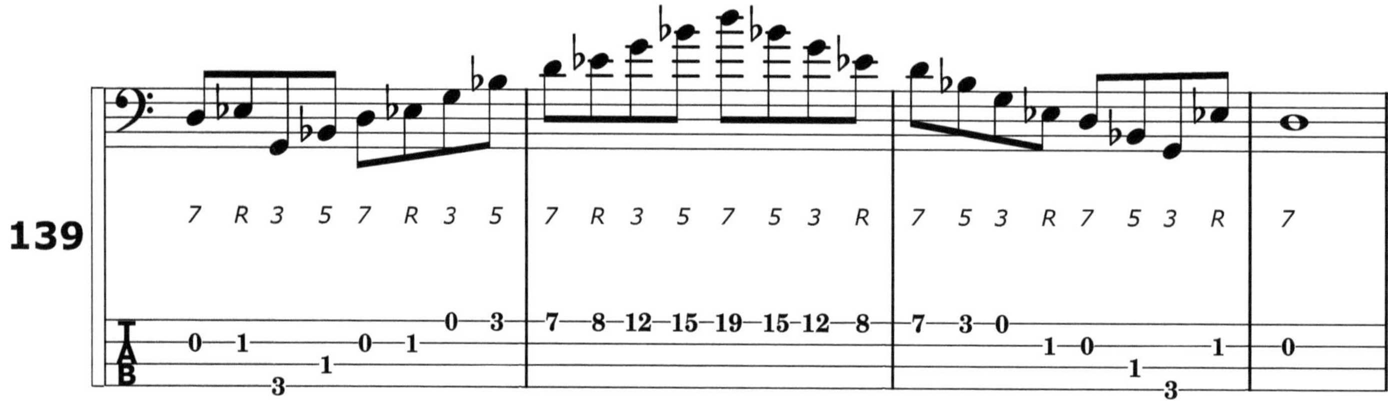

E♭ Major - Seventh Pattern 2

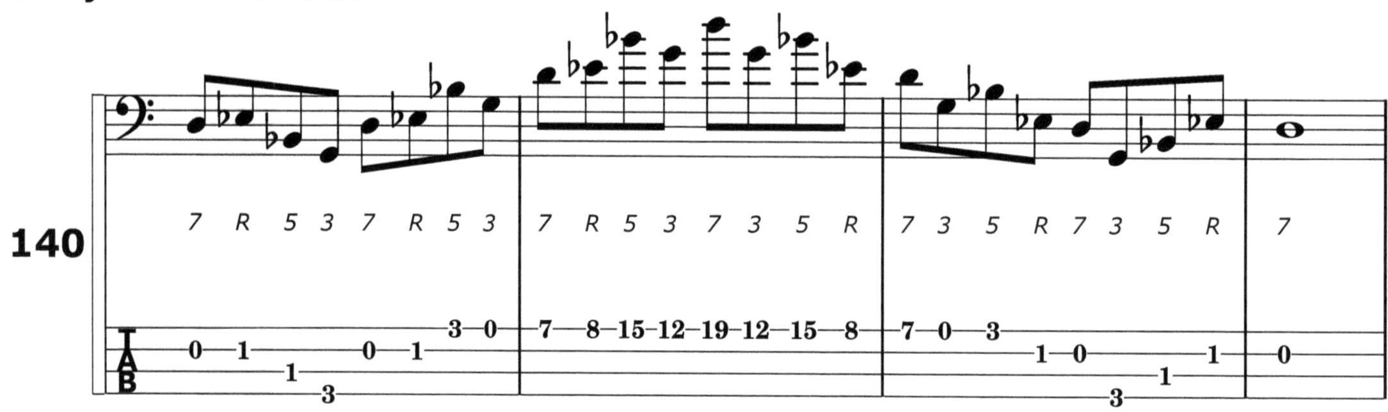

E♭ Major - Seventh Pattern 3

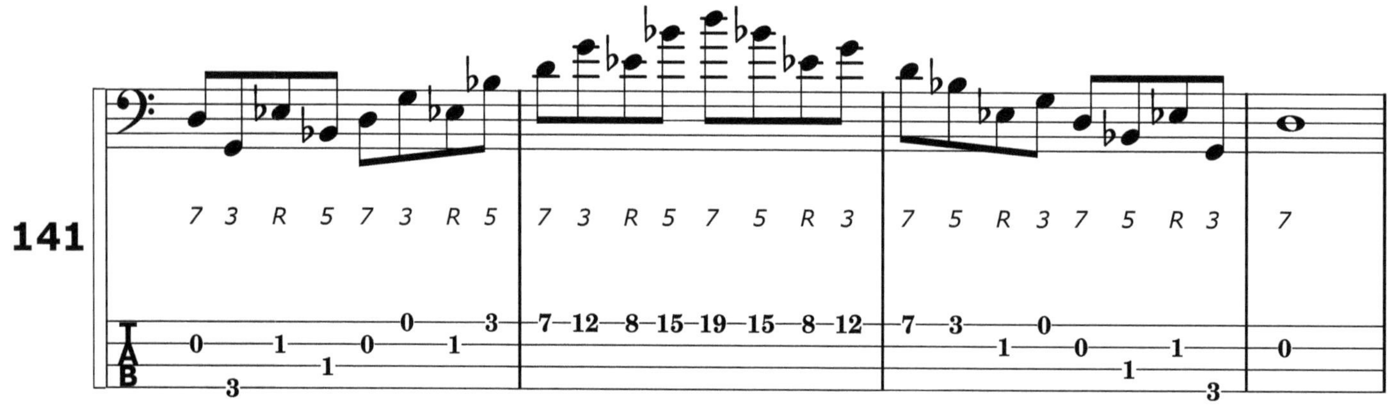

E♭ Major - Seventh Pattern 4

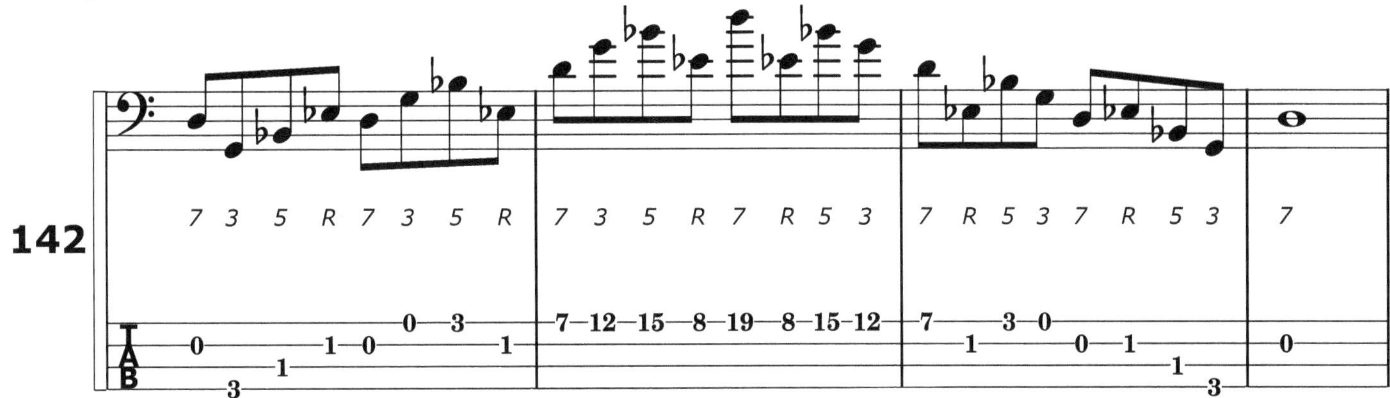

E♭ Major - Seventh Pattern 5

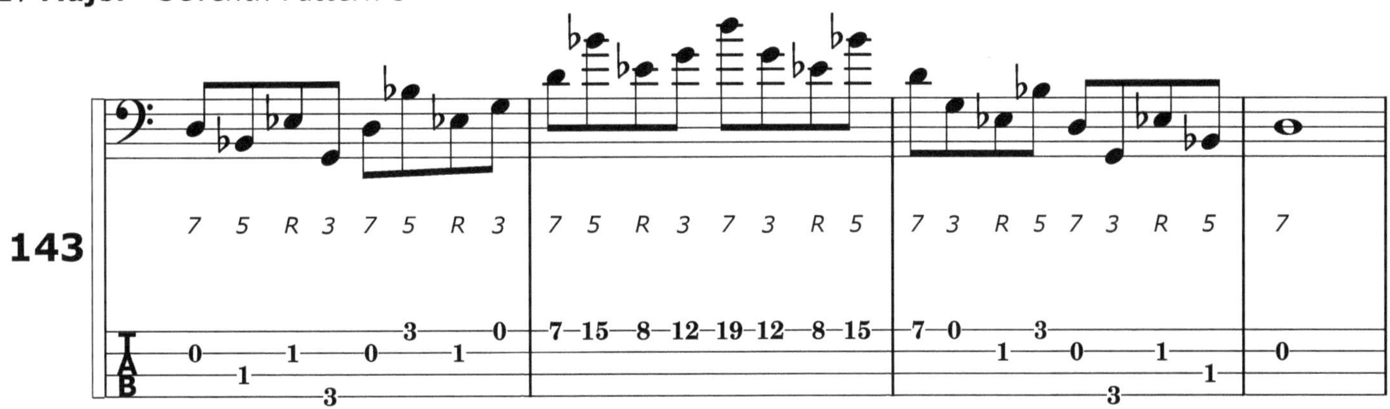

E♭ Major - Seventh Pattern 6

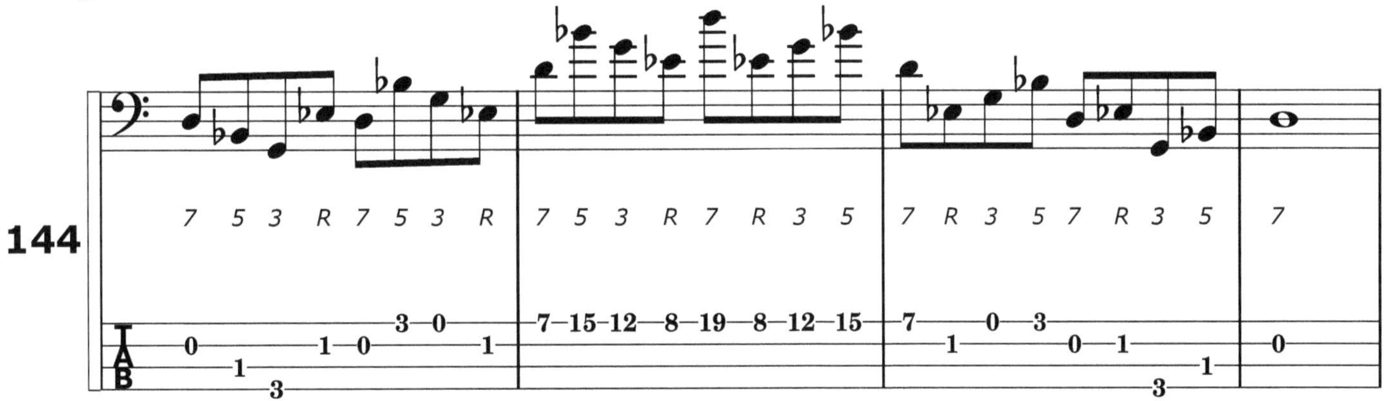

A Major - Root Pattern 1

145

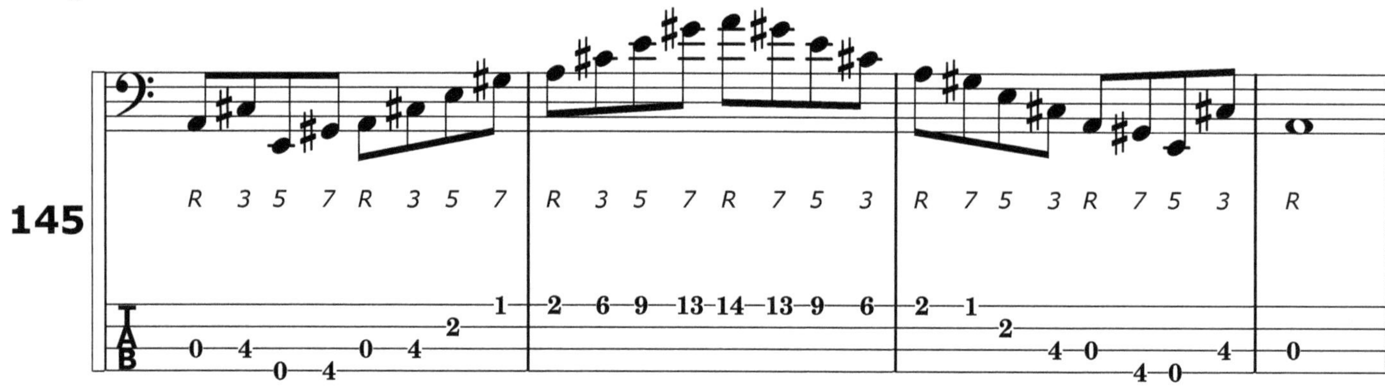

A Major - Root Pattern 2

146

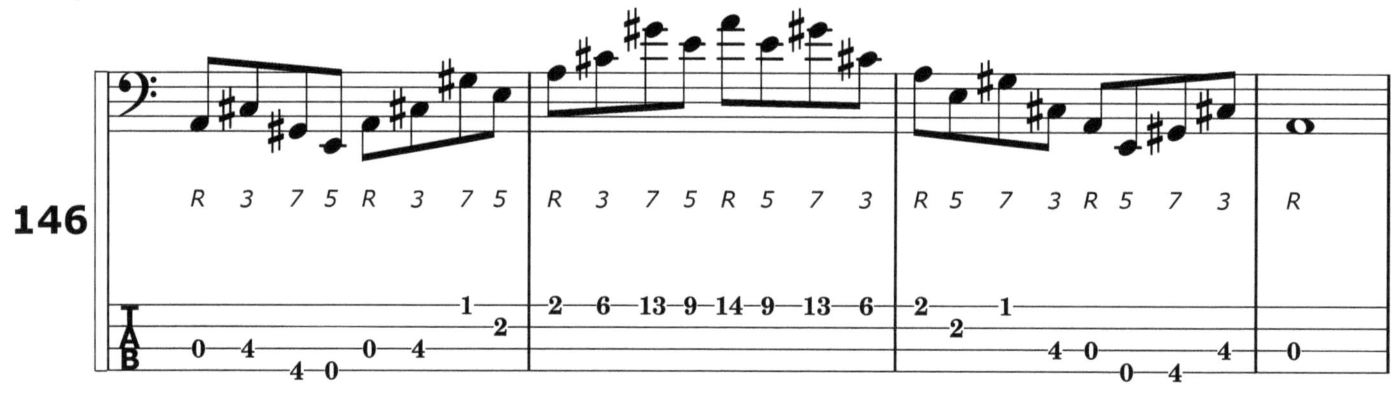

A Major - Root Pattern 3

147

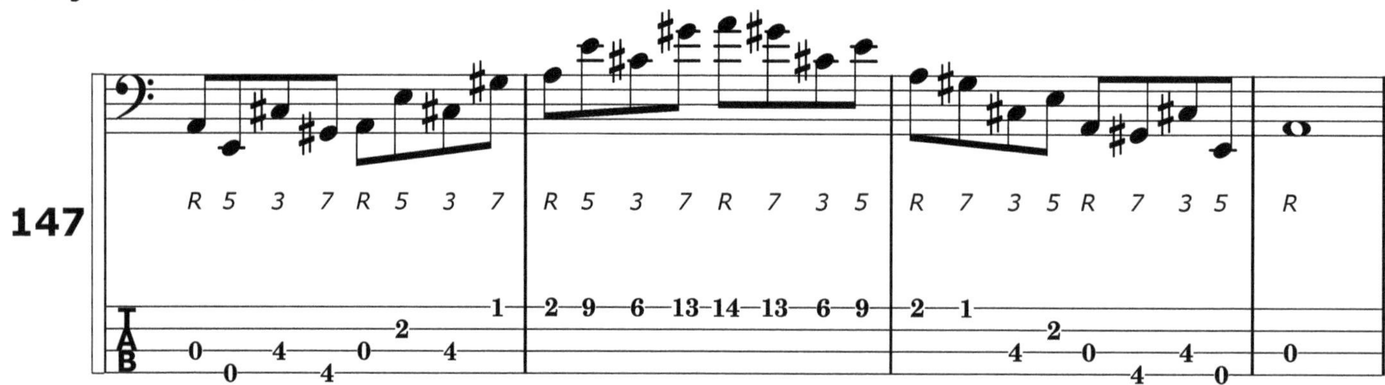

A Major - Root Pattern 4

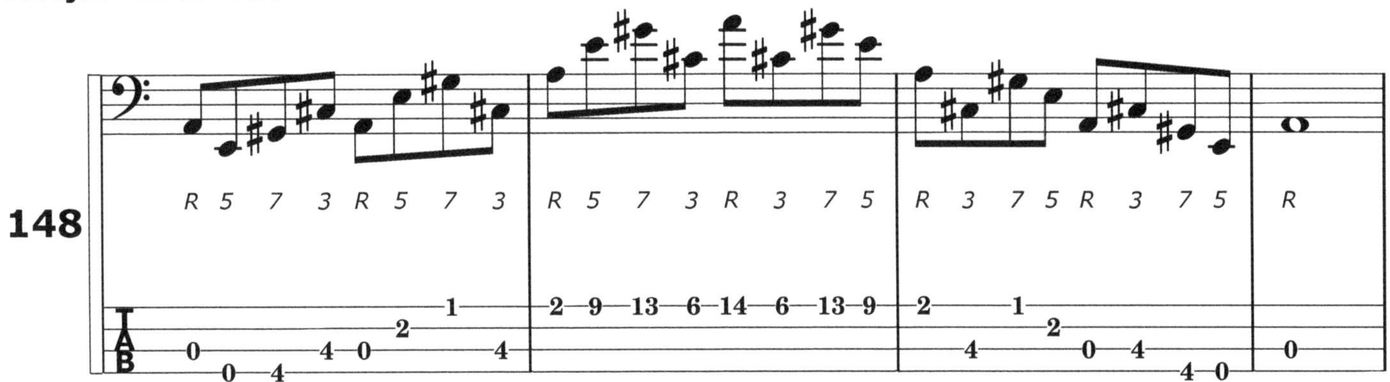

A Major - Root Pattern 5

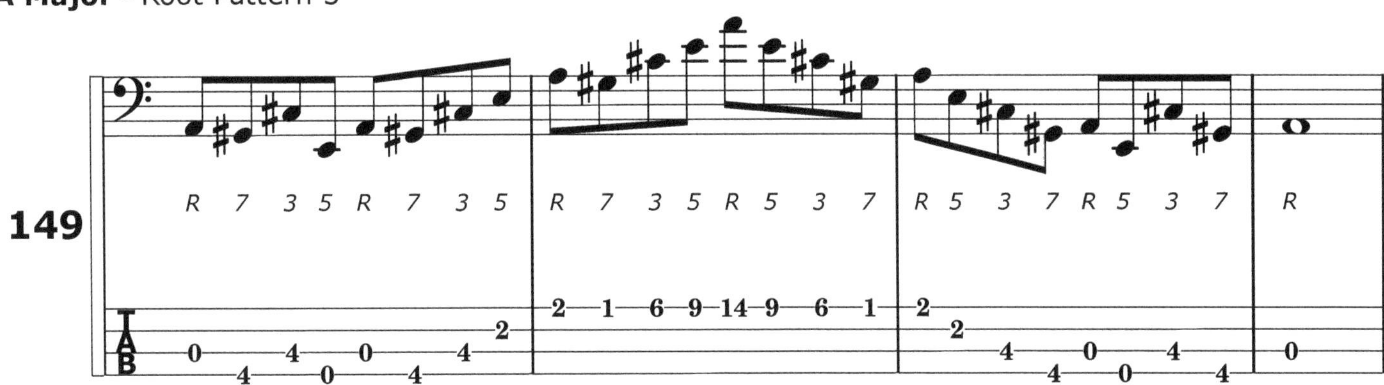

A Major - Root Pattern 6

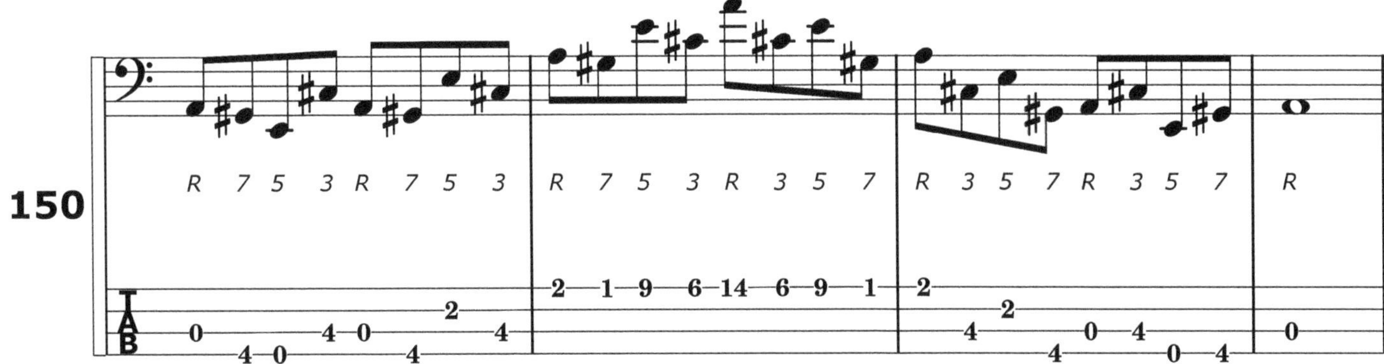

A Major - Third Pattern 1

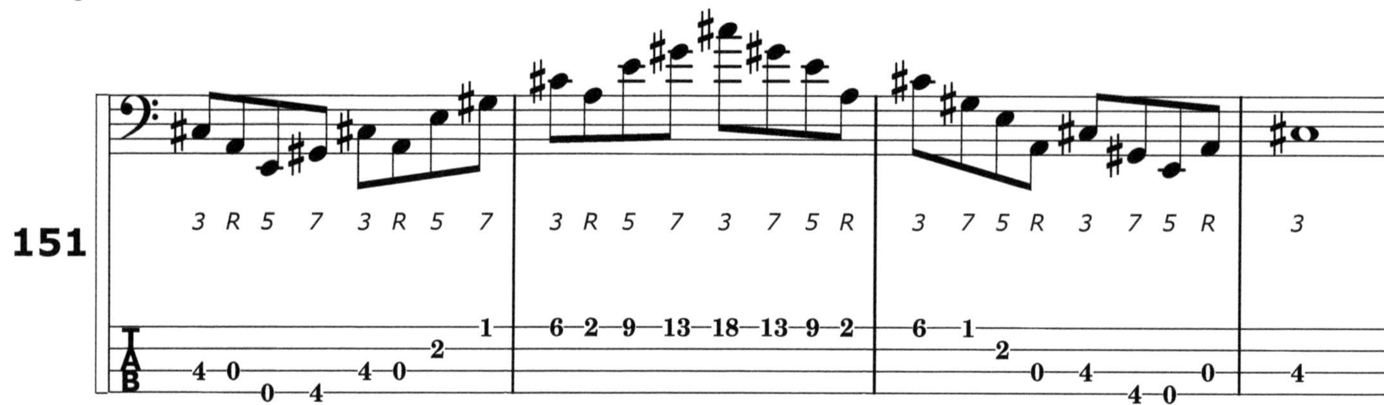

A Major - Third Pattern 2

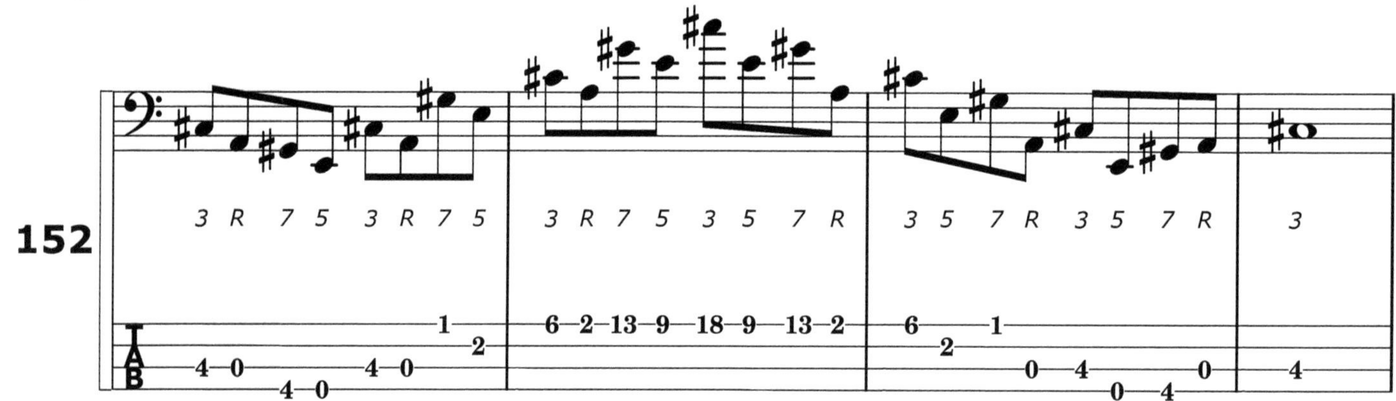

A Major - Third Pattern 3

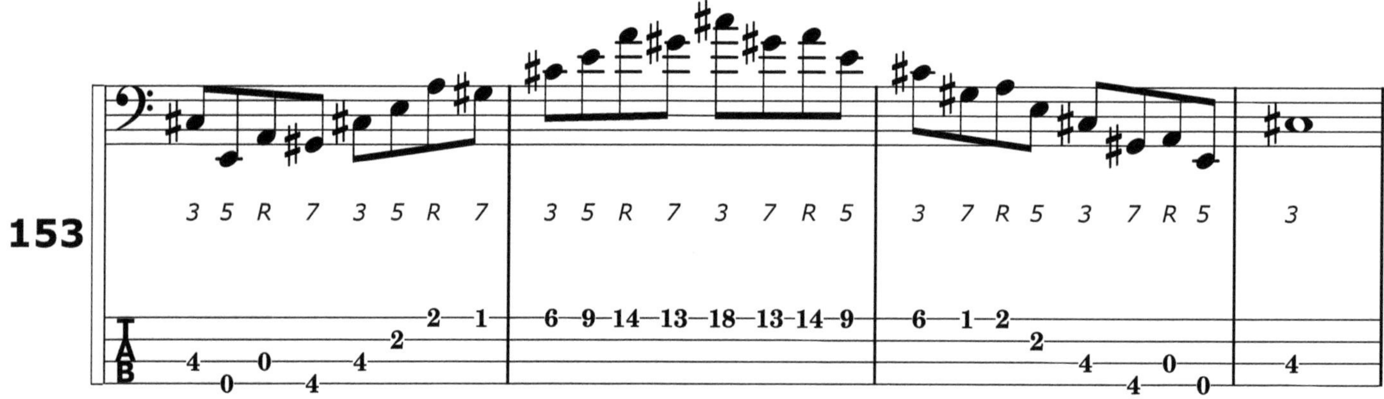

A Major - Third Pattern 4

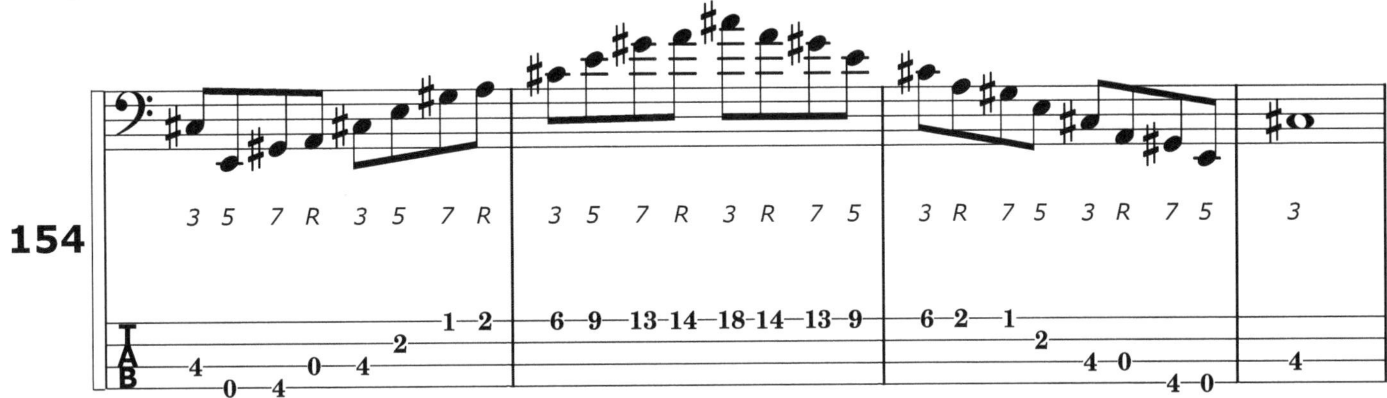

A Major - Third Pattern 5

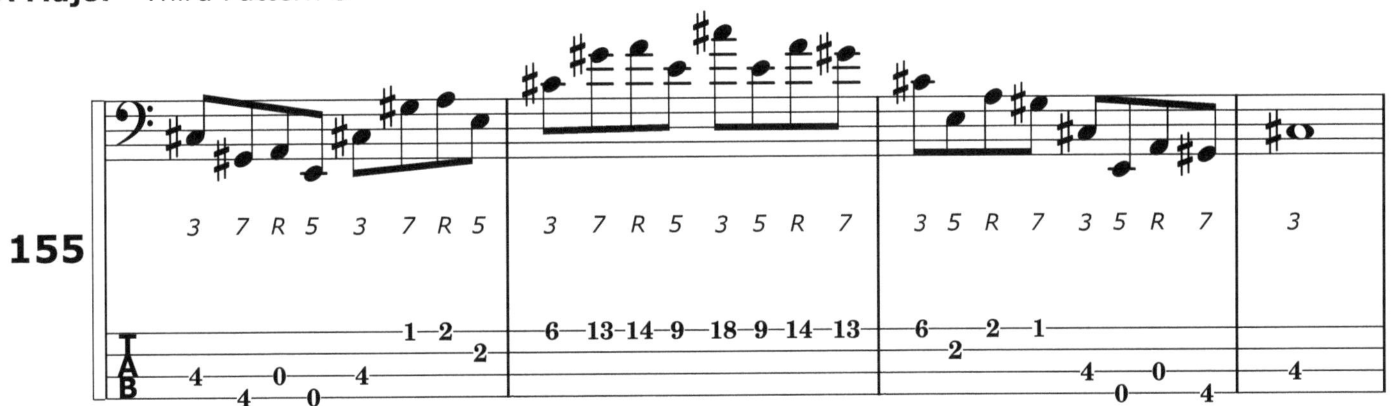

A Major - Third Pattern 6

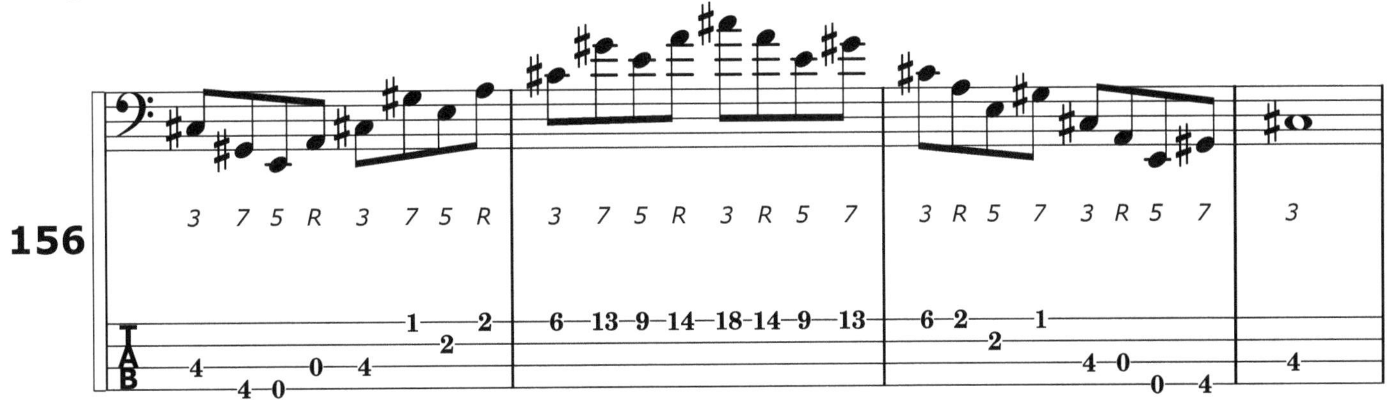

A Major - Fifth Pattern 1

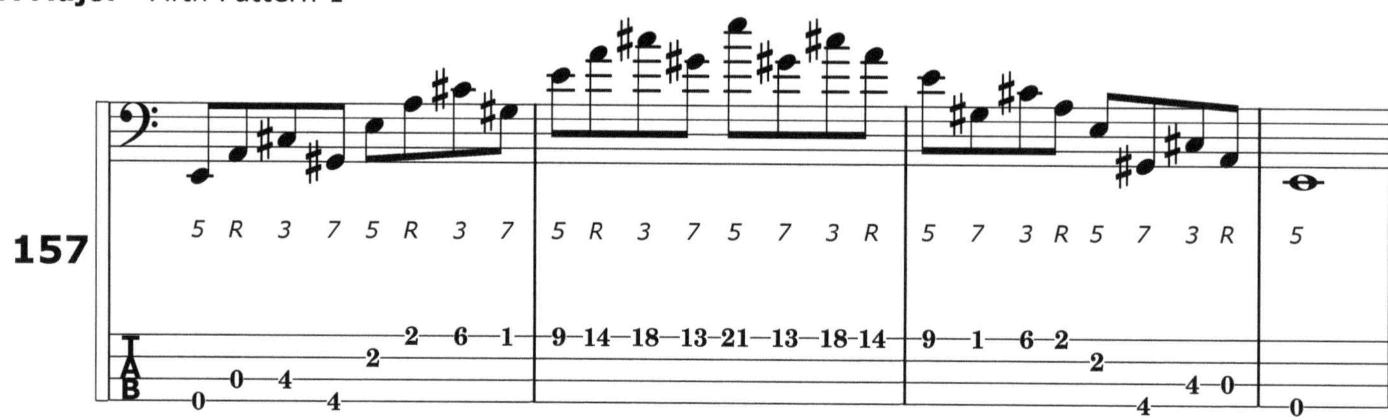

A Major - Fifth Pattern 2

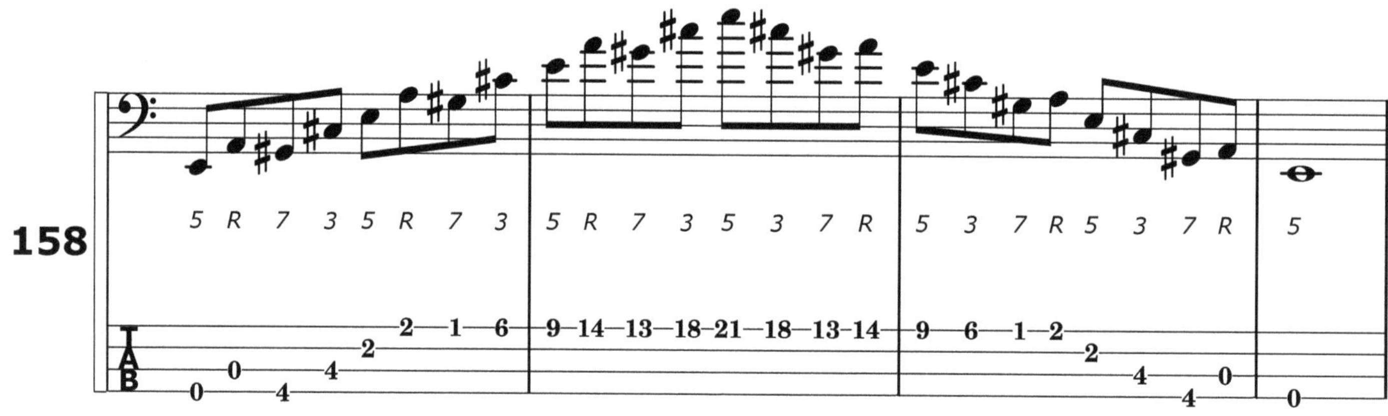

A Major - Fifth Pattern 3

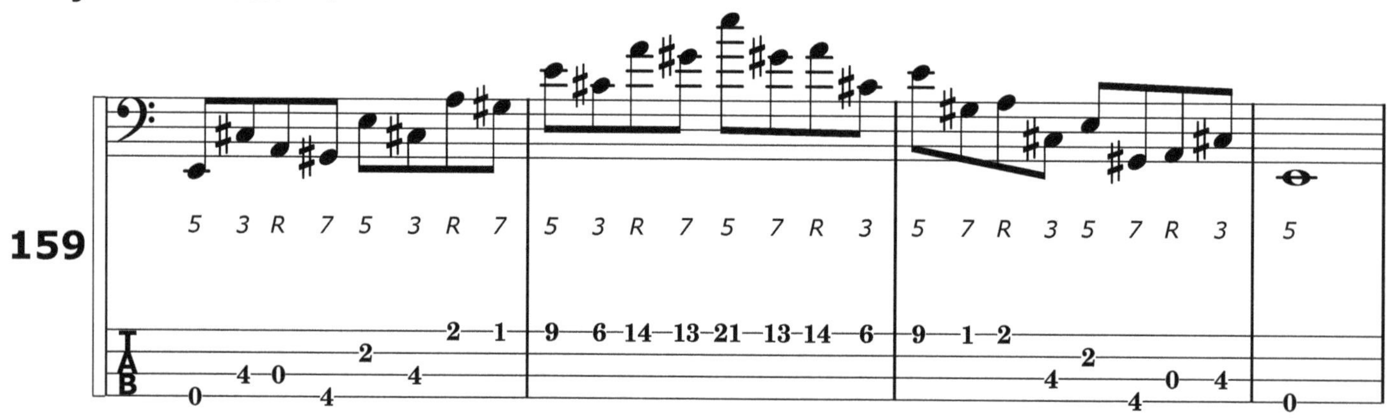

A Major - Fifth Pattern 4

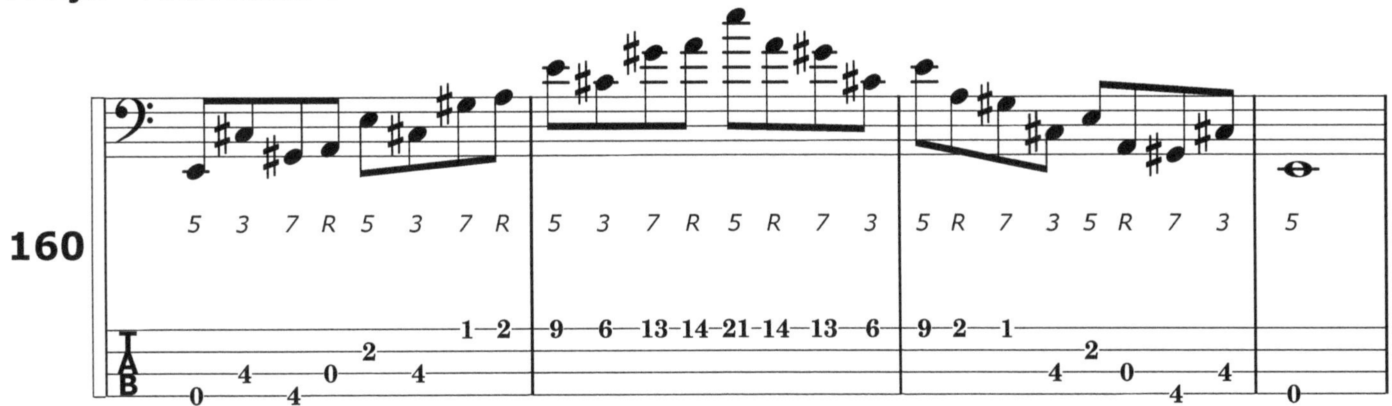

A Major - Fifth Pattern 5

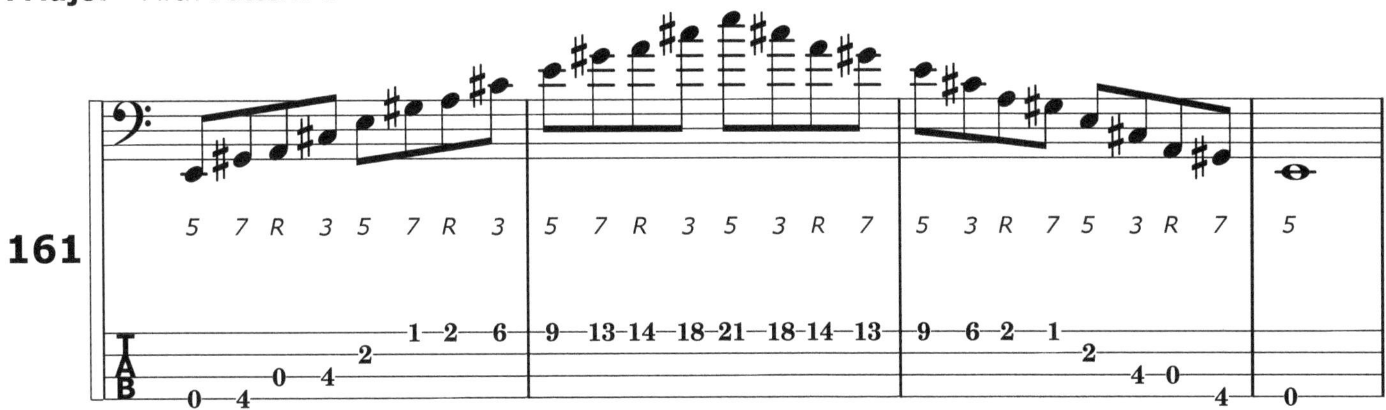

A Major - Fifth Pattern 6

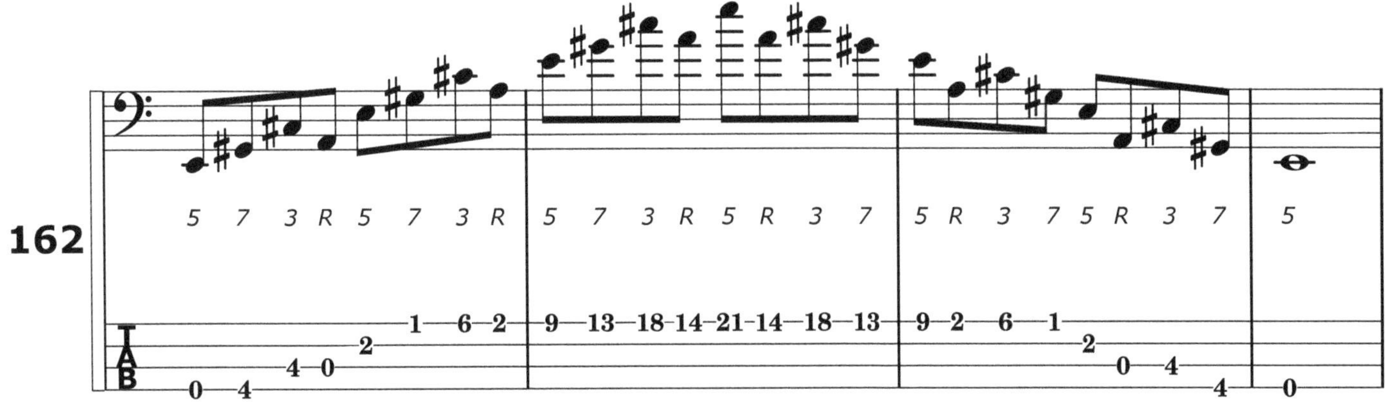

A Major - Seventh Pattern 1

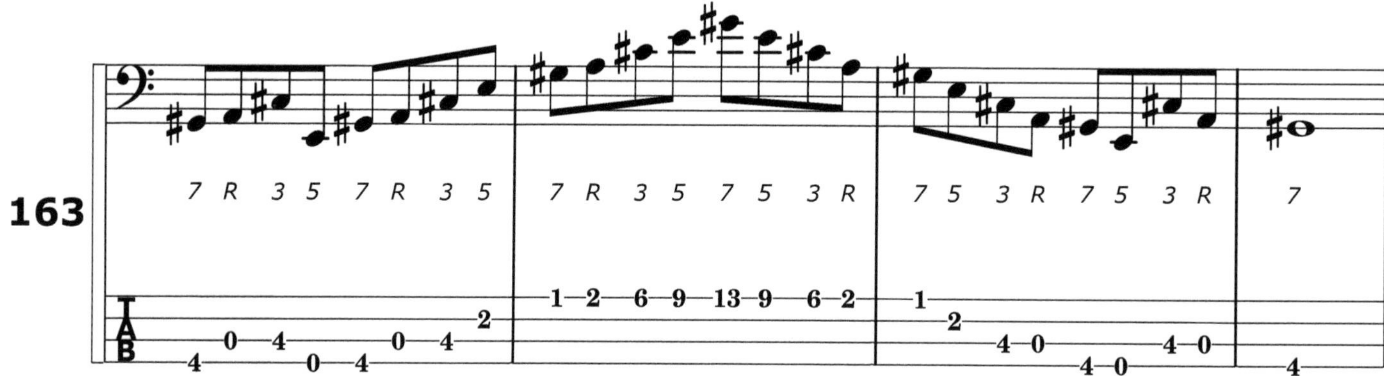

A Major - Seventh Pattern 2

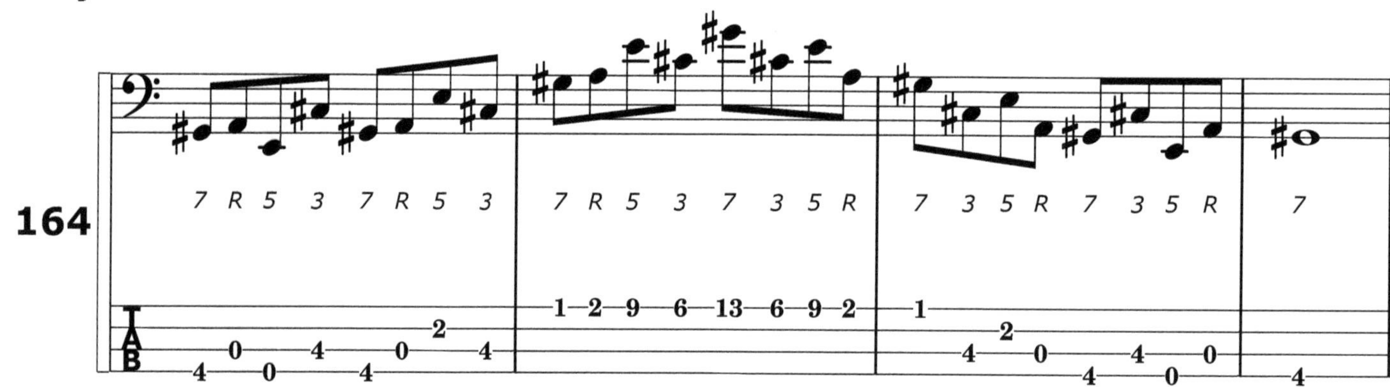

A Major - Seventh Pattern 3

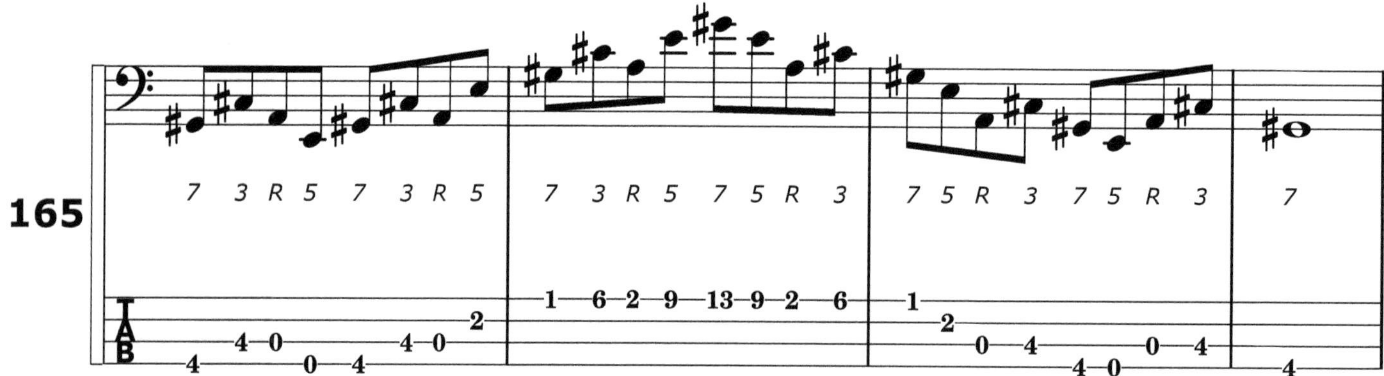

A Major - Seventh Pattern 4

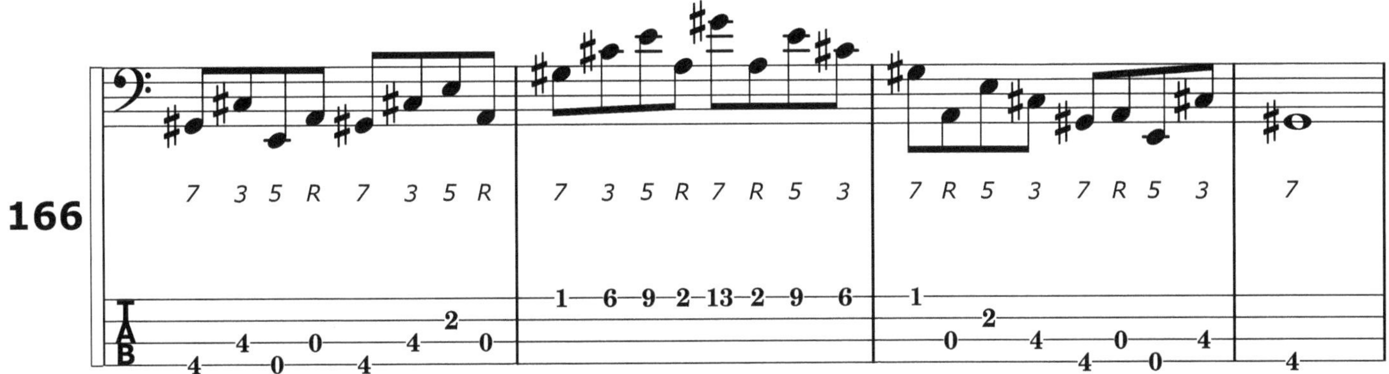

A Major - Seventh Pattern 5

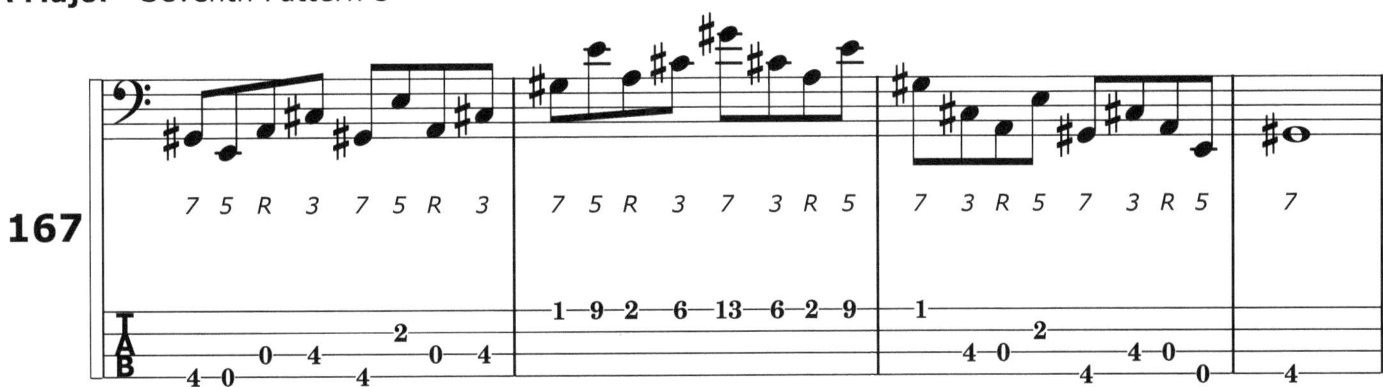

A Major - Seventh Pattern 6

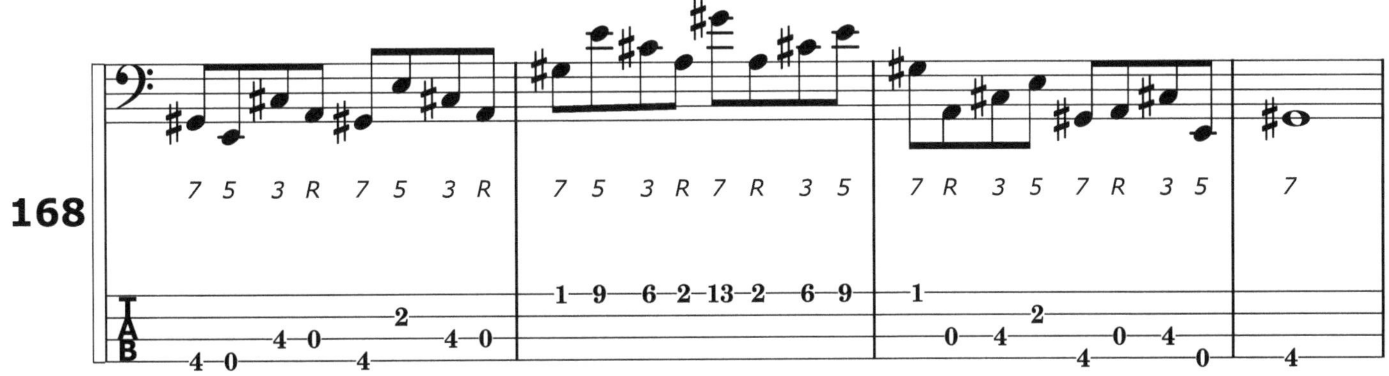

A♭ Major - Root Pattern 1

169

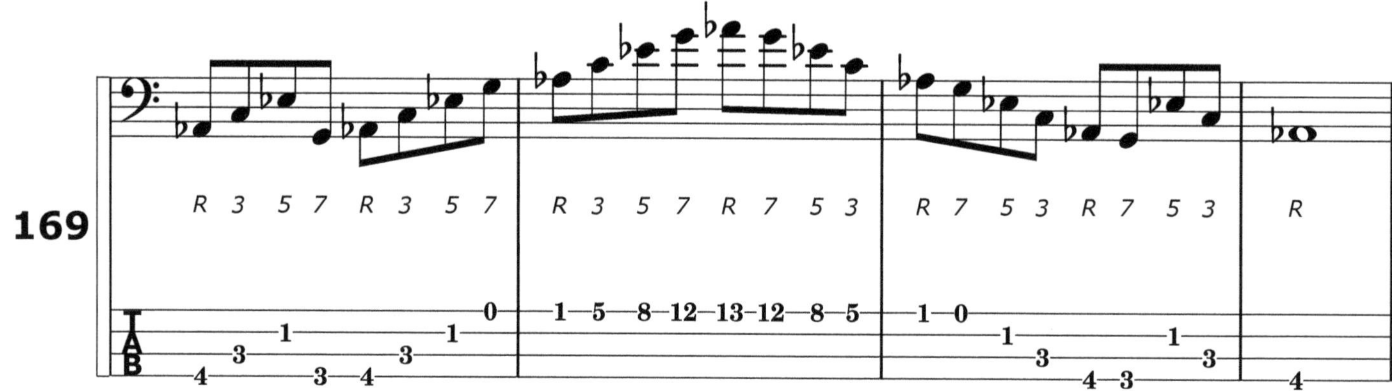

A♭ Major - Root Pattern 2

170

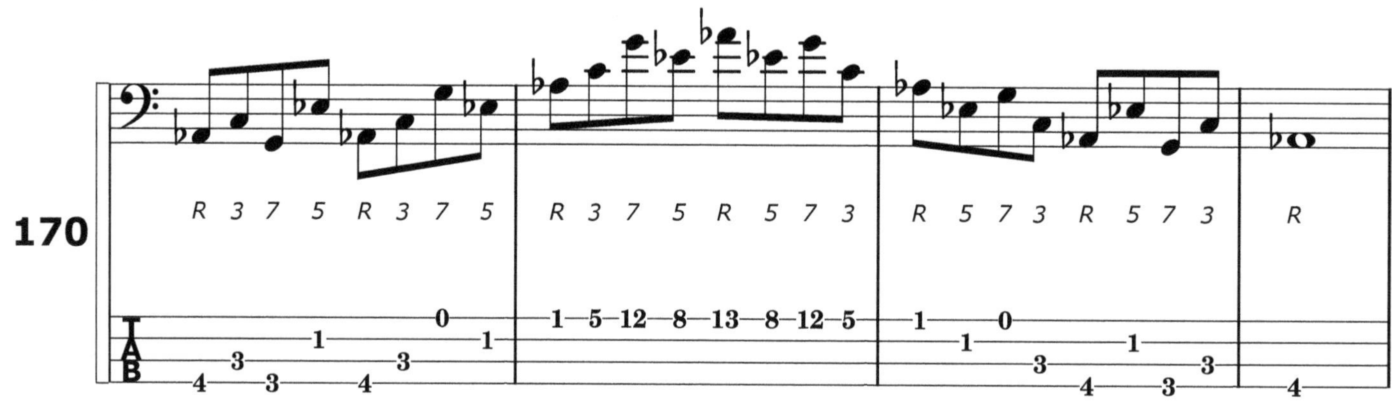

A♭ Major - Root Pattern 3

171

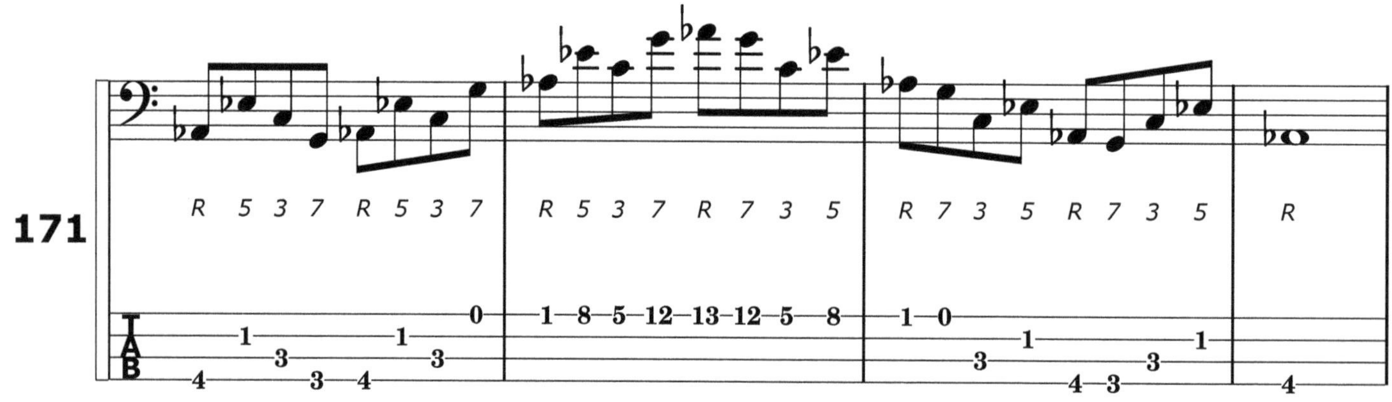

A♭ Major - Root Pattern 4

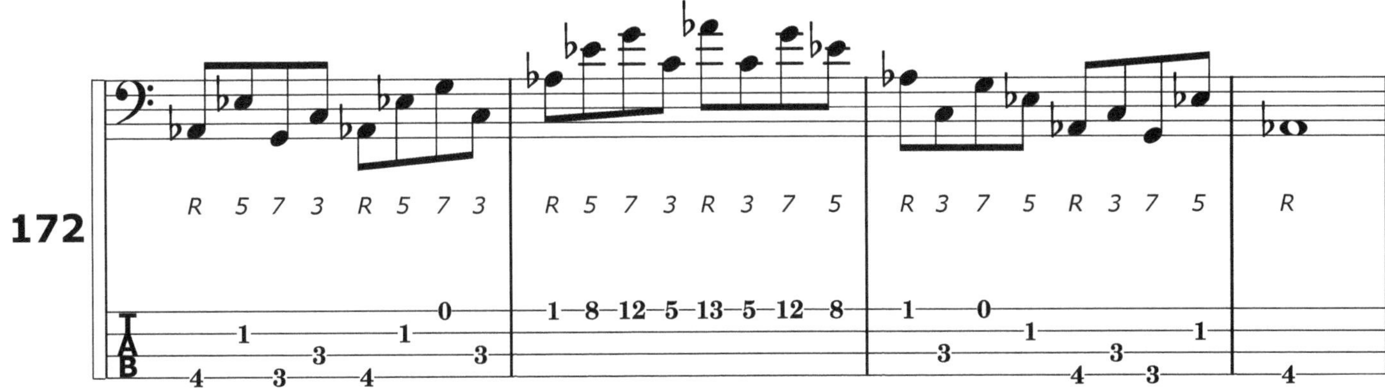

A♭ Major - Root Pattern 5

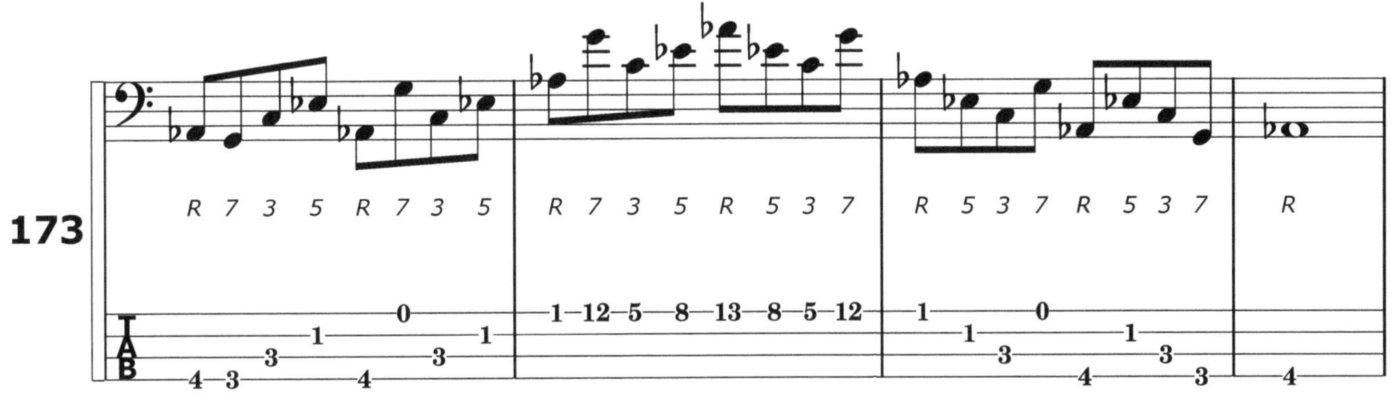

A♭ Major - Root Pattern 6

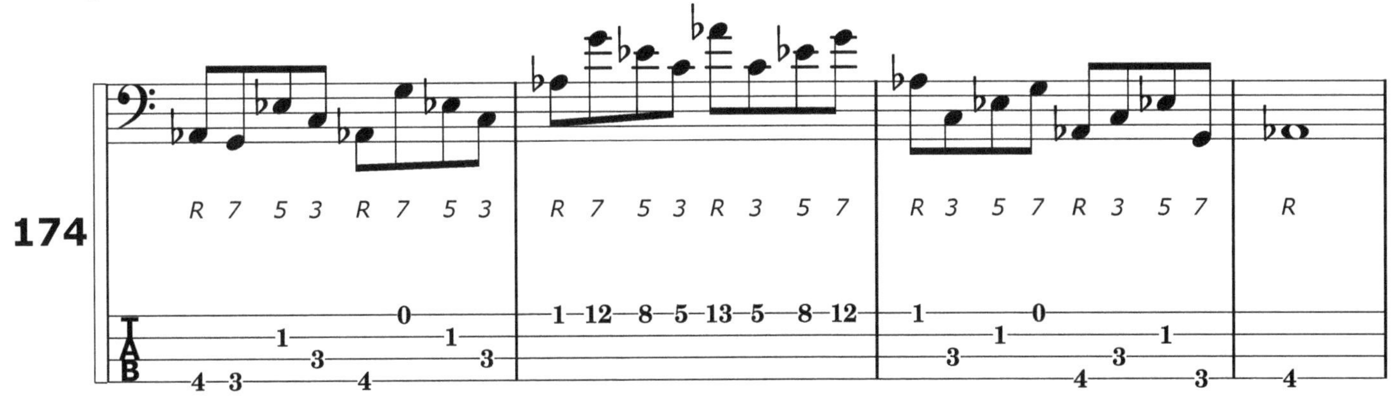

A♭ Major - Third Pattern 1

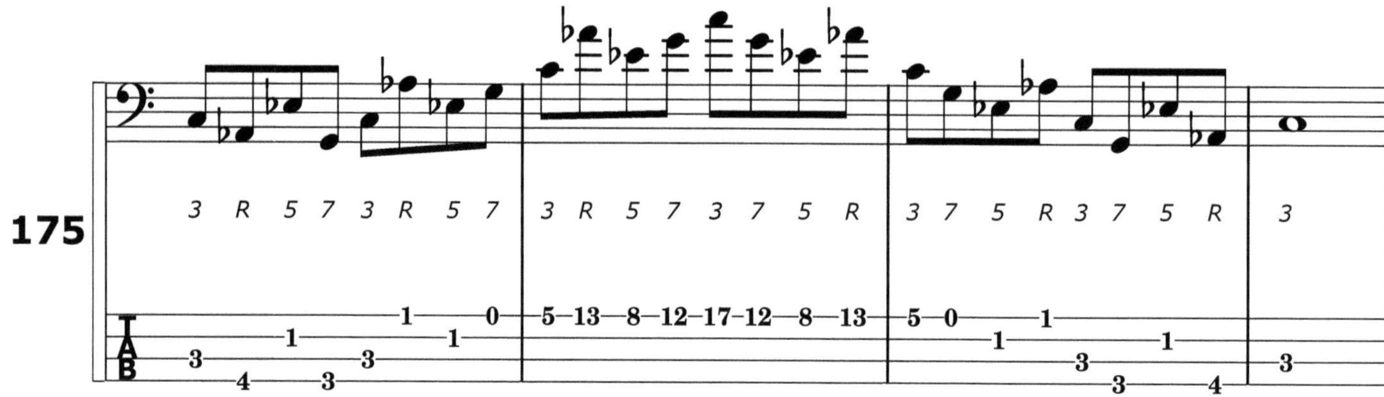

A♭ Major - Third Pattern 2

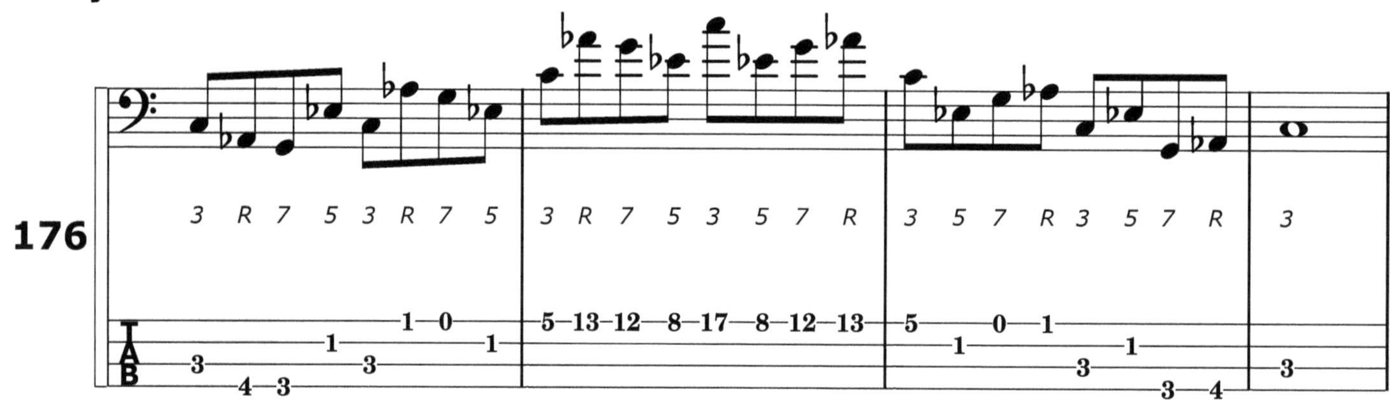

A♭ Major - Third Pattern 3

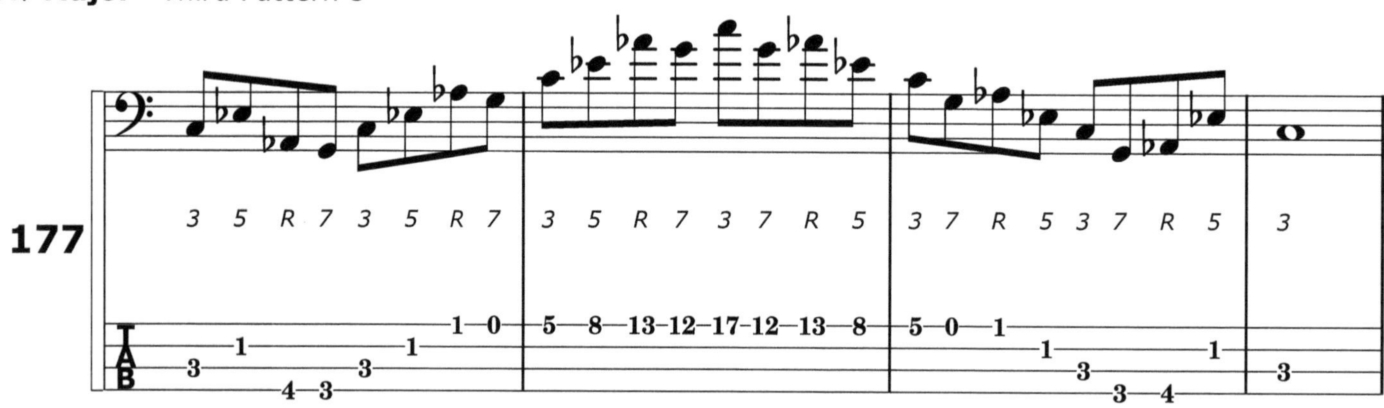

A♭ Major - Third Pattern 4

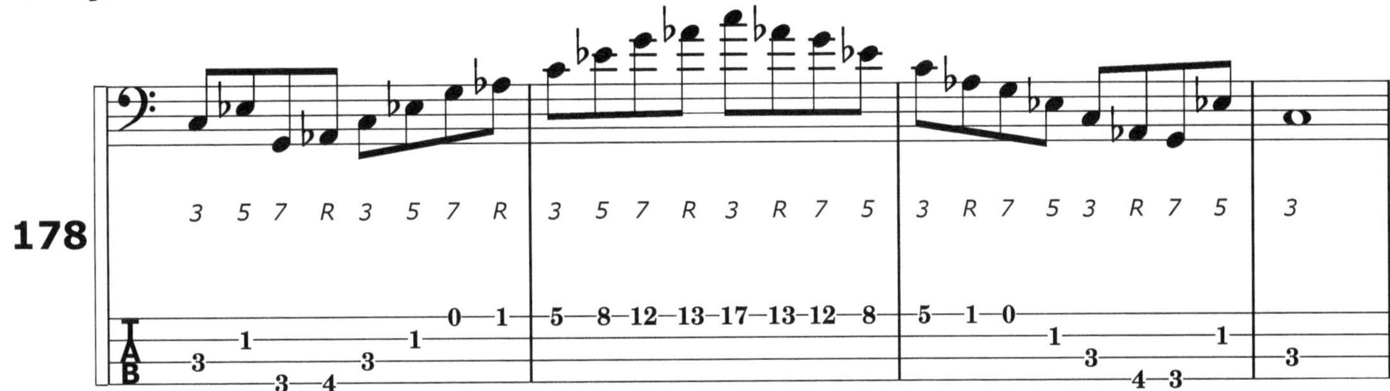

A♭ Major - Third Pattern 5

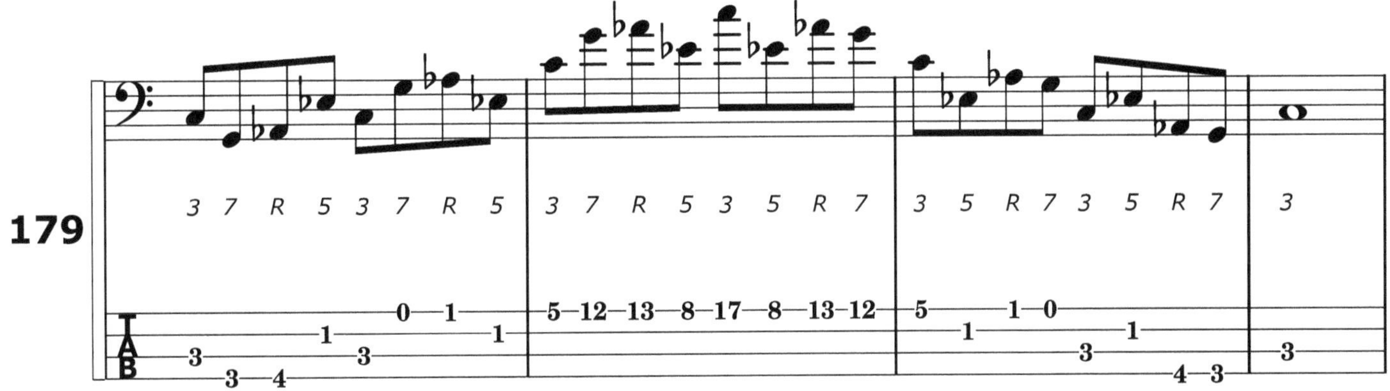

A♭ Major - Third Pattern 6

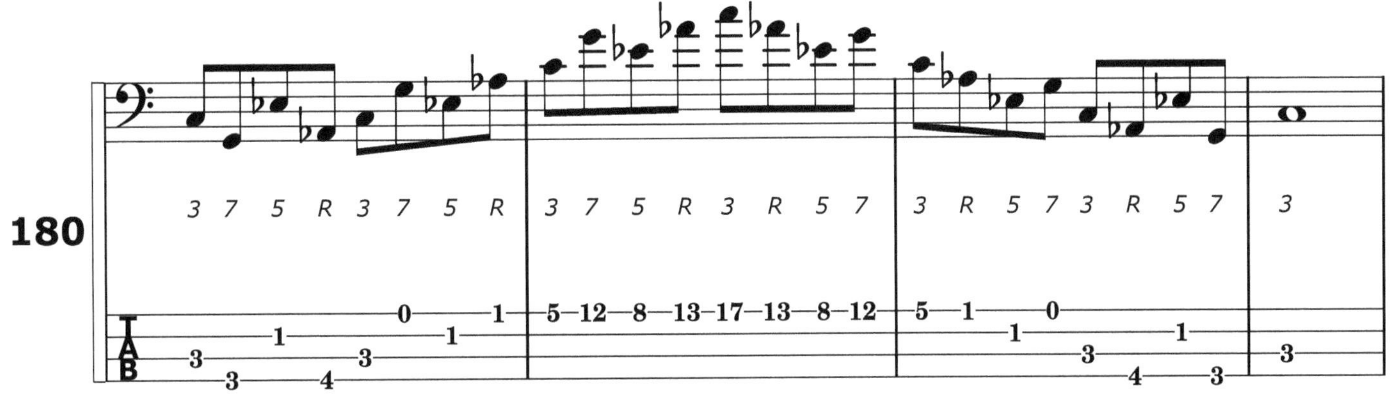

A♭ Major - Fifth Pattern 1

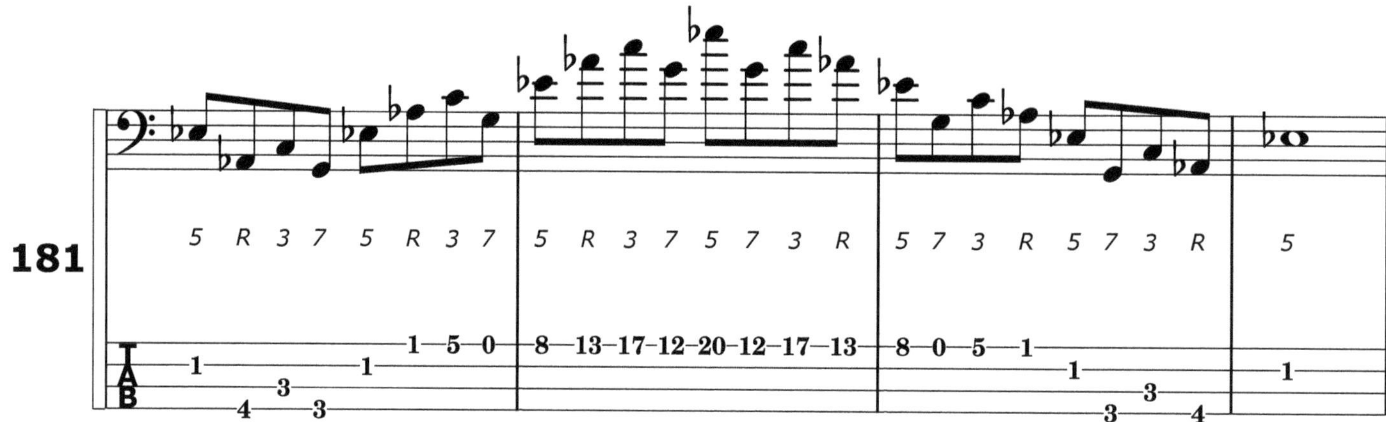

A♭ Major - Fifth Pattern 2

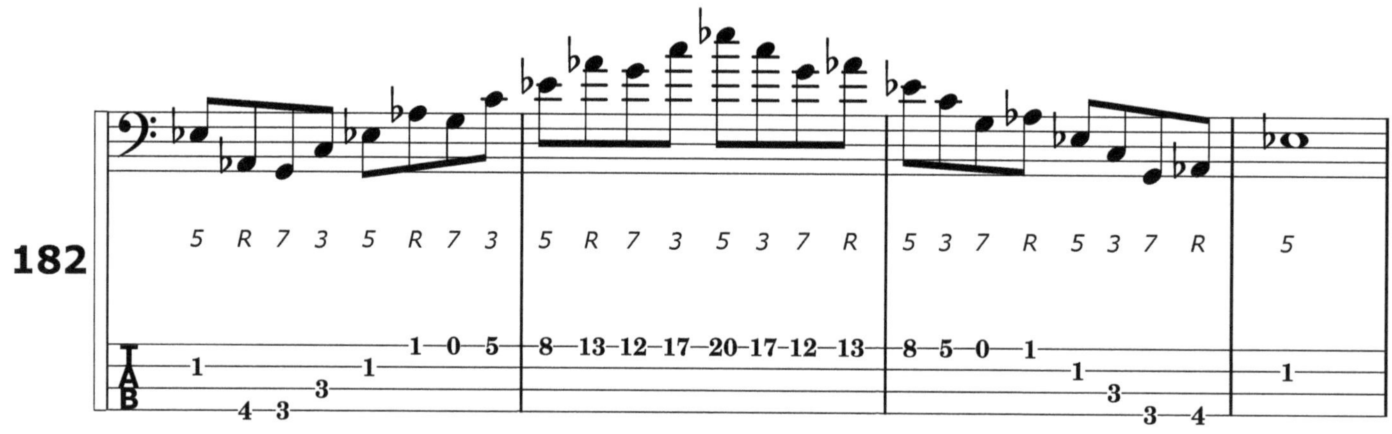

A♭ Major - Fifth Pattern 3

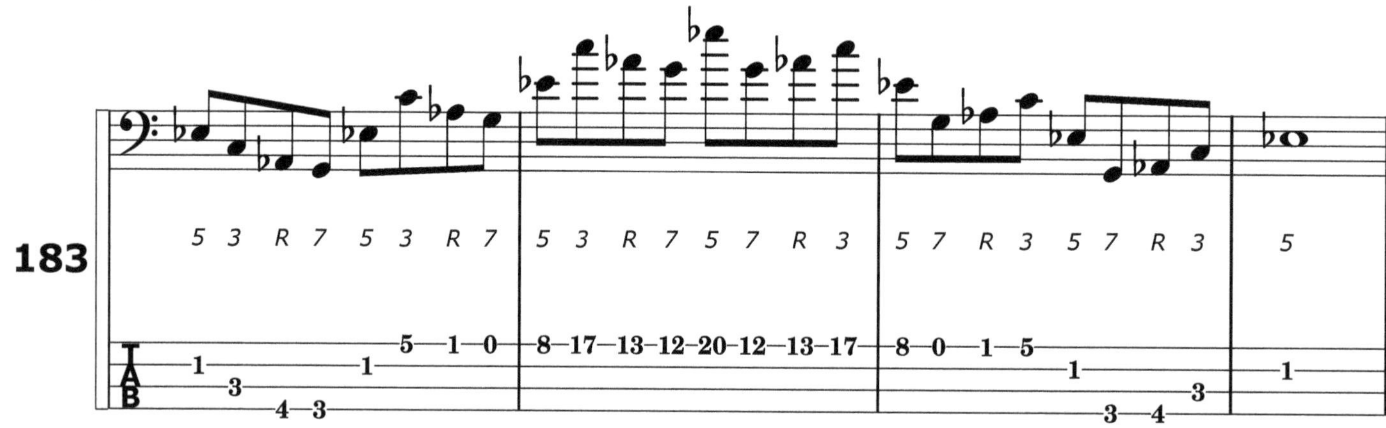

A♭ Major - Third Pattern 4

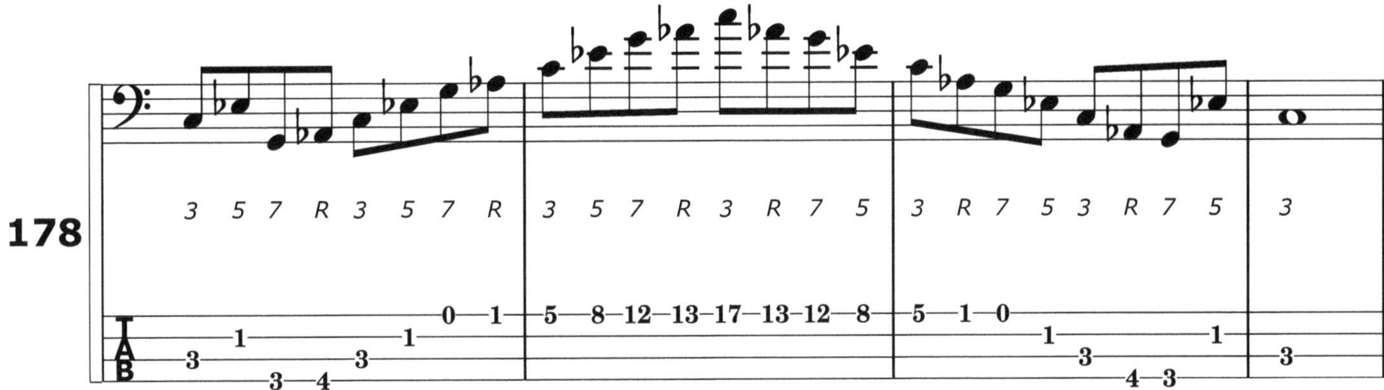

A♭ Major - Third Pattern 5

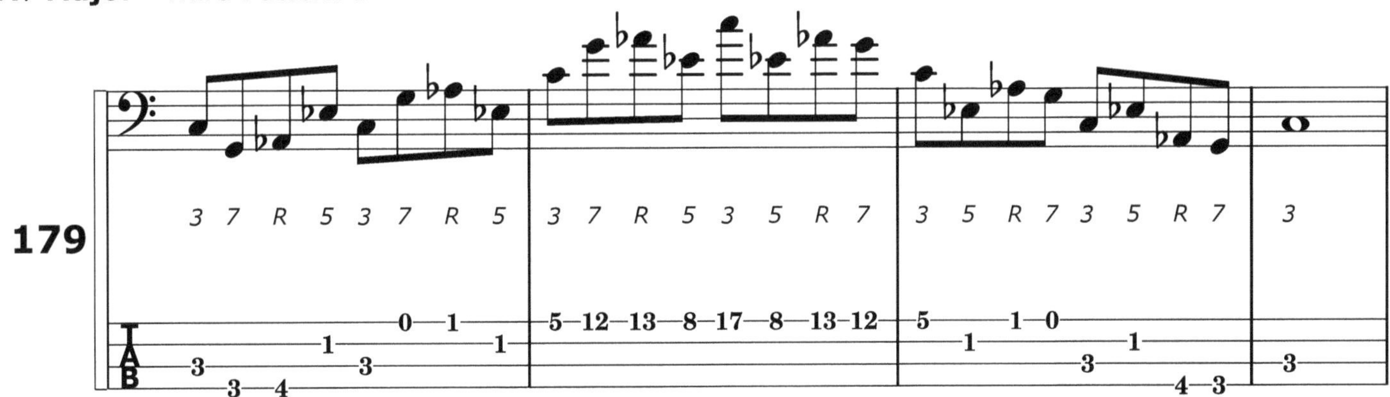

A♭ Major - Third Pattern 6

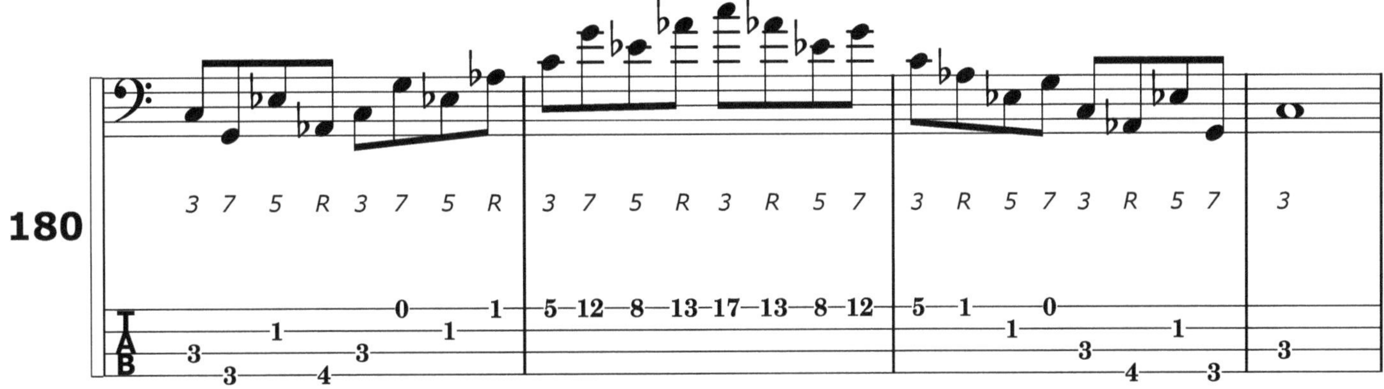

A♭ Major - Fifth Pattern 1

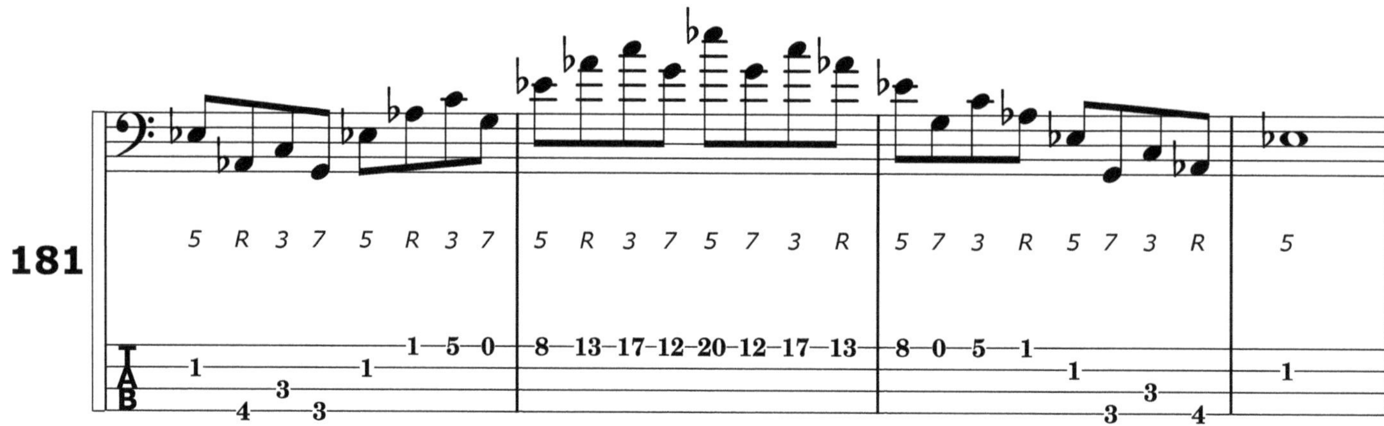

A♭ Major - Fifth Pattern 2

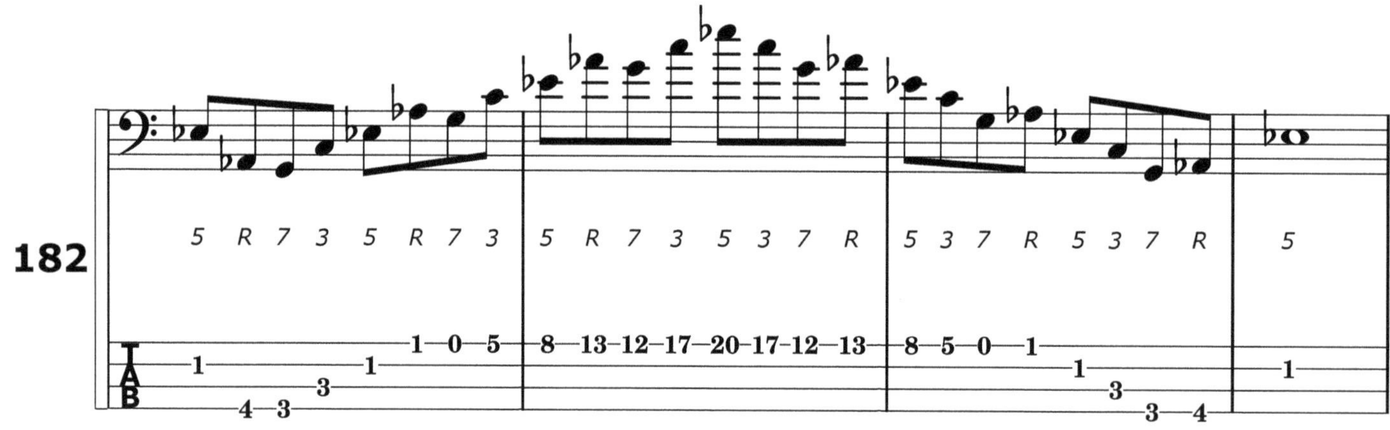

A♭ Major - Fifth Pattern 3

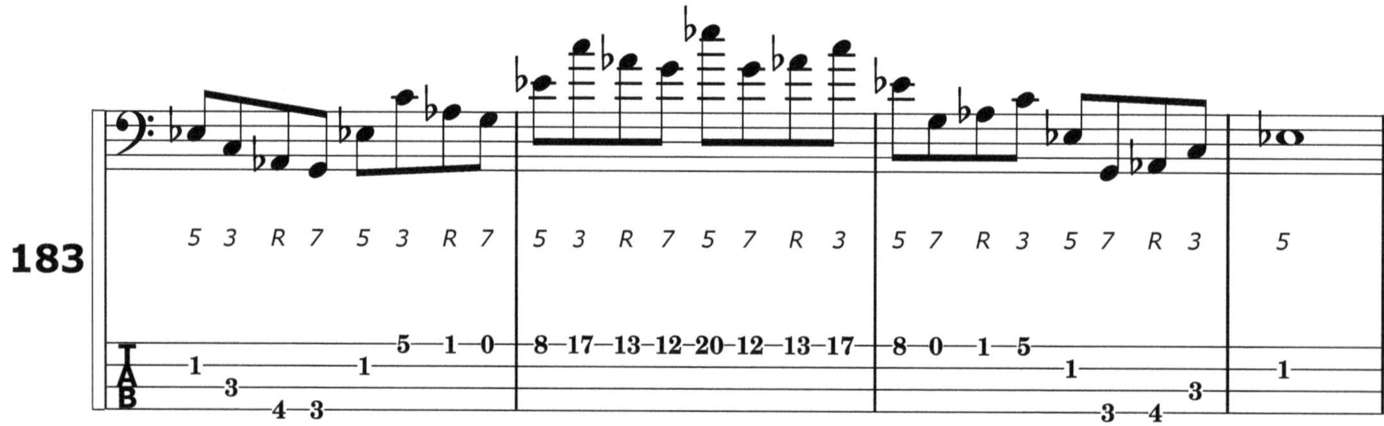

A♭ Major - Fifth Pattern 4

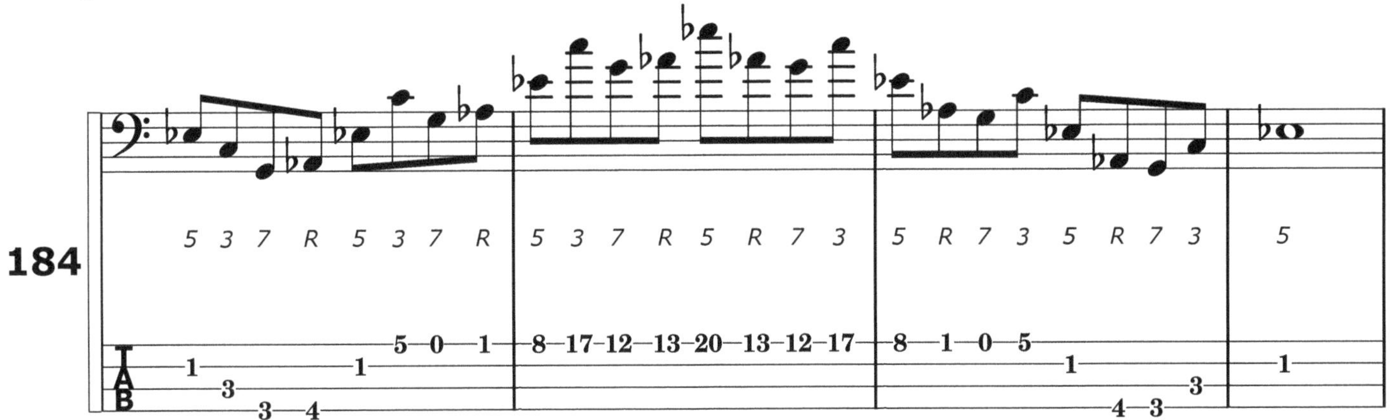

A♭ Major - Fifth Pattern 5

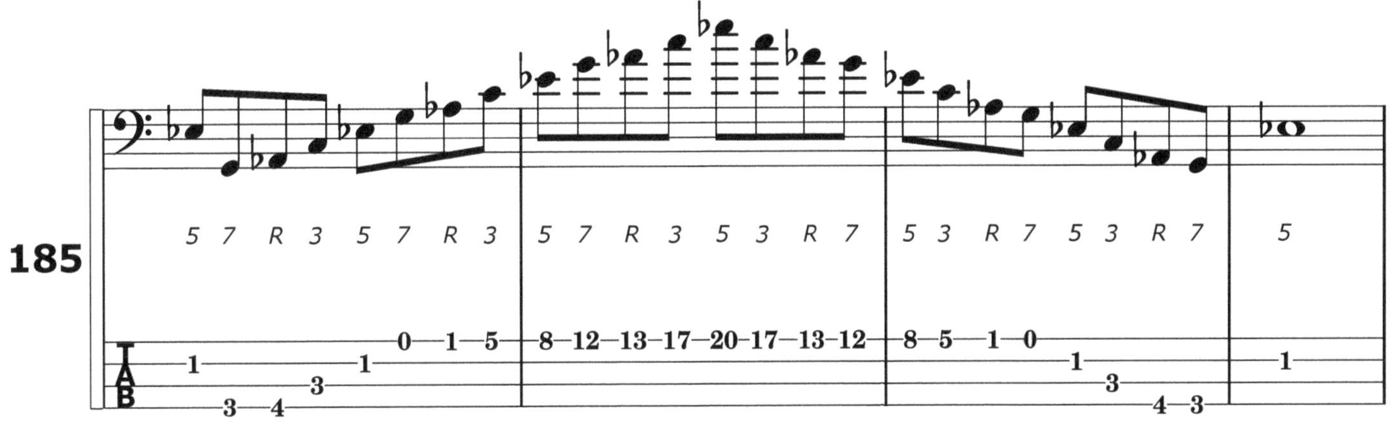

A♭ Major - Fifth Pattern 6

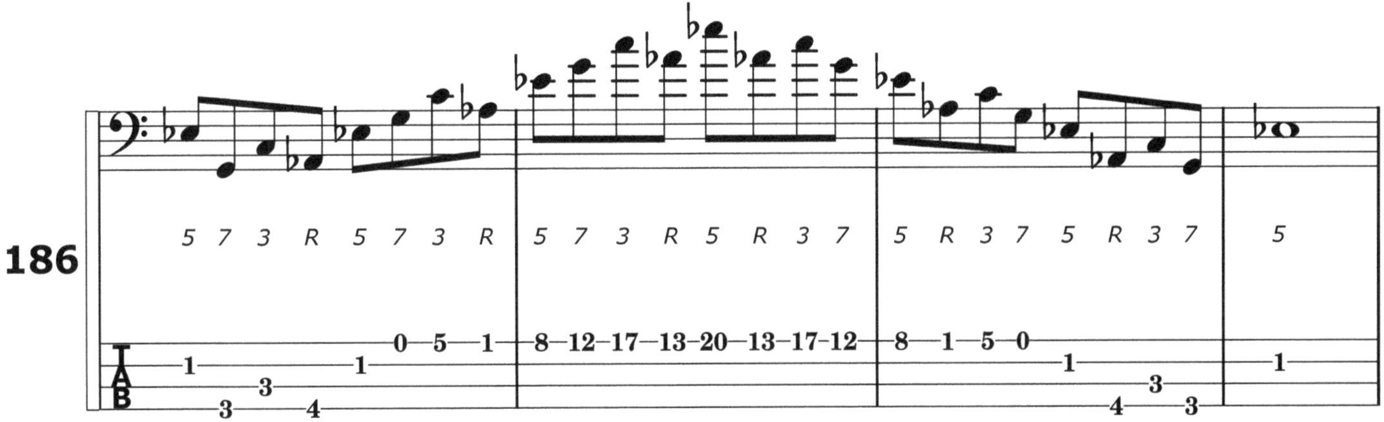

A♭ Major - Seventh Pattern 1

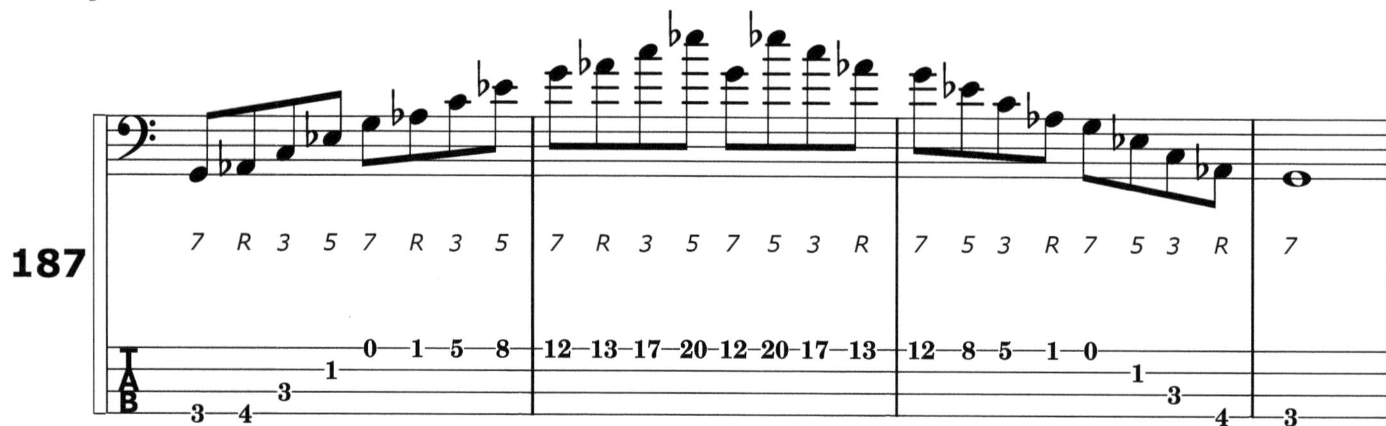

A♭ Major - Seventh Pattern 2

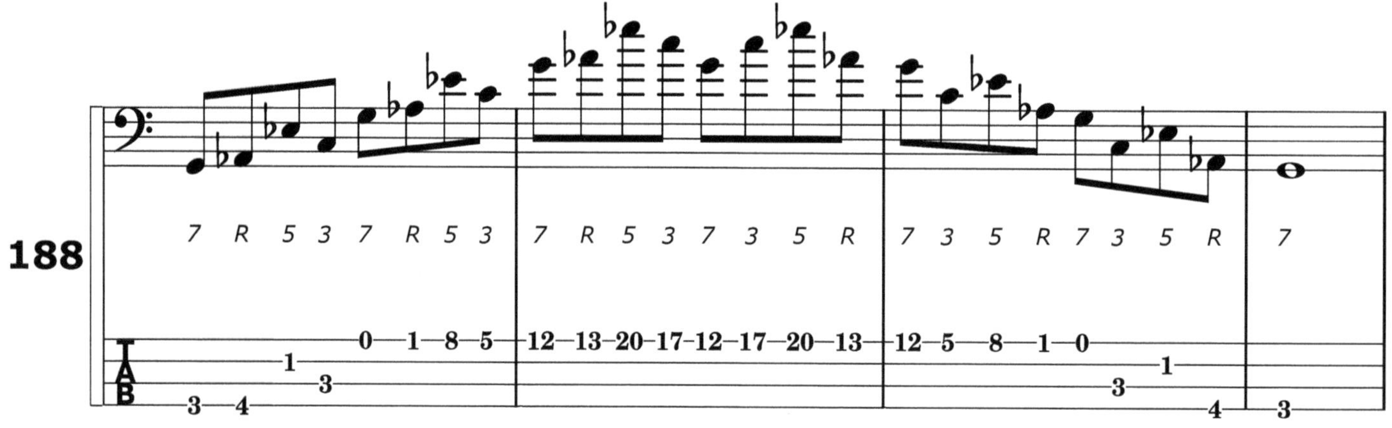

A♭ Major - Seventh Pattern 3

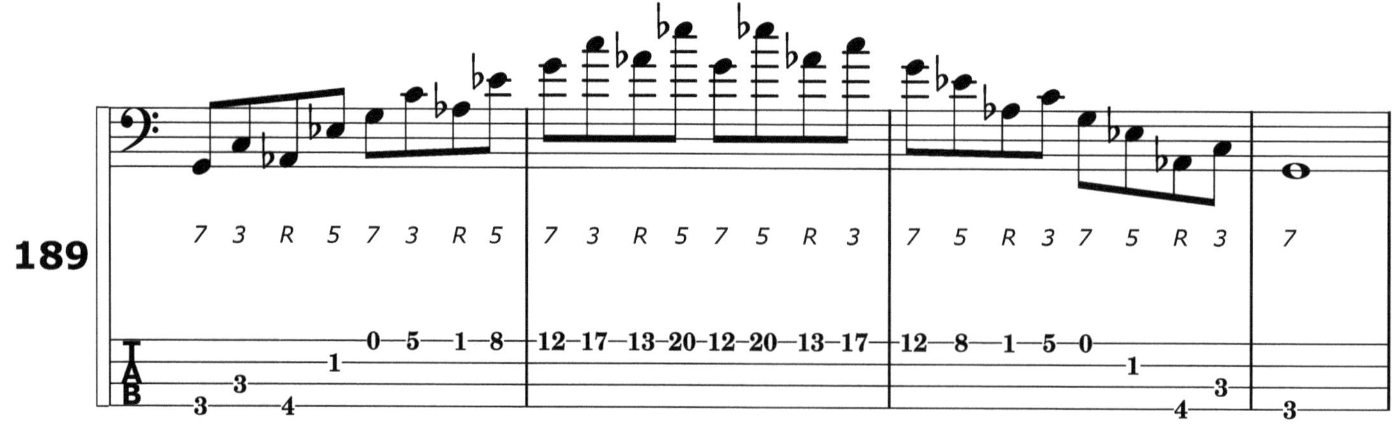

A♭ Major - Seventh Pattern 4

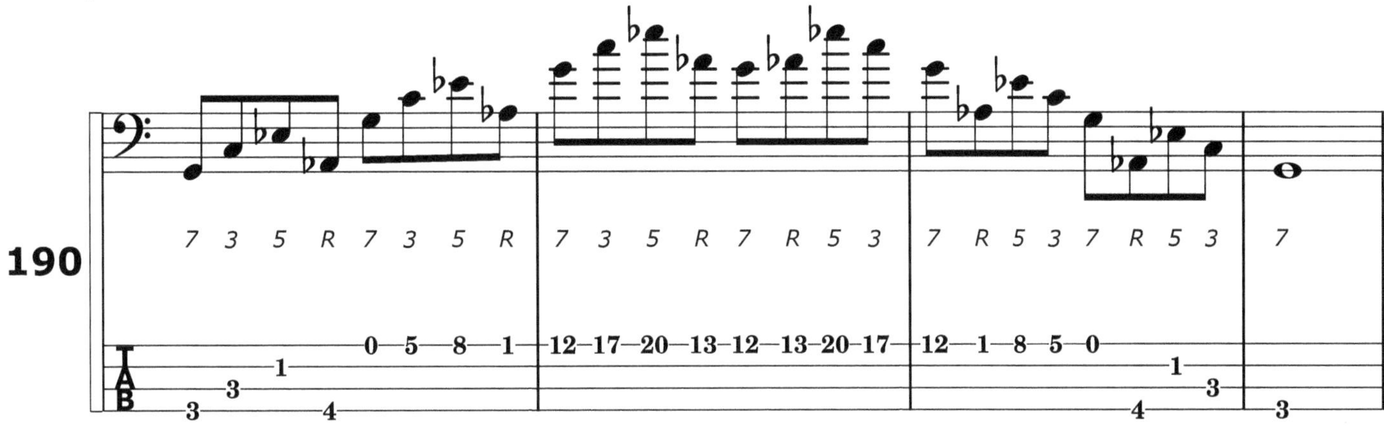

A♭ Major - Seventh Pattern 5

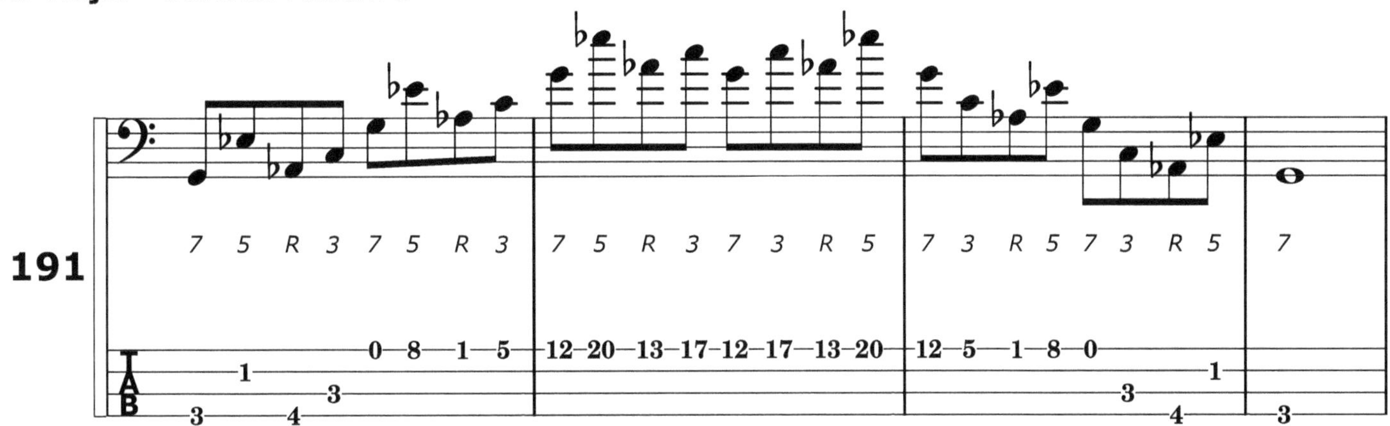

A♭ Major - Seventh Pattern 6

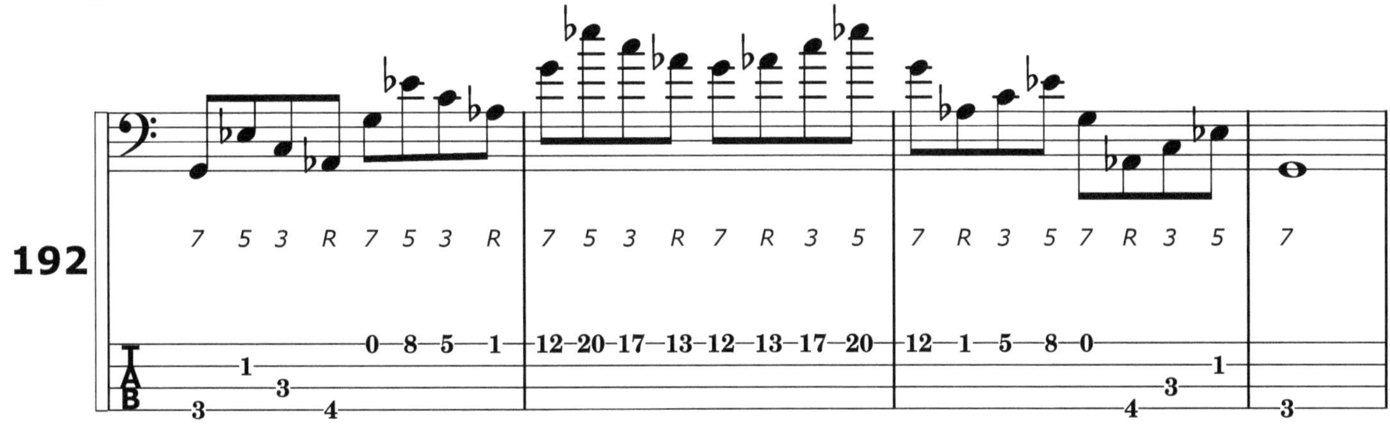

E Major - Root Pattern 1

193

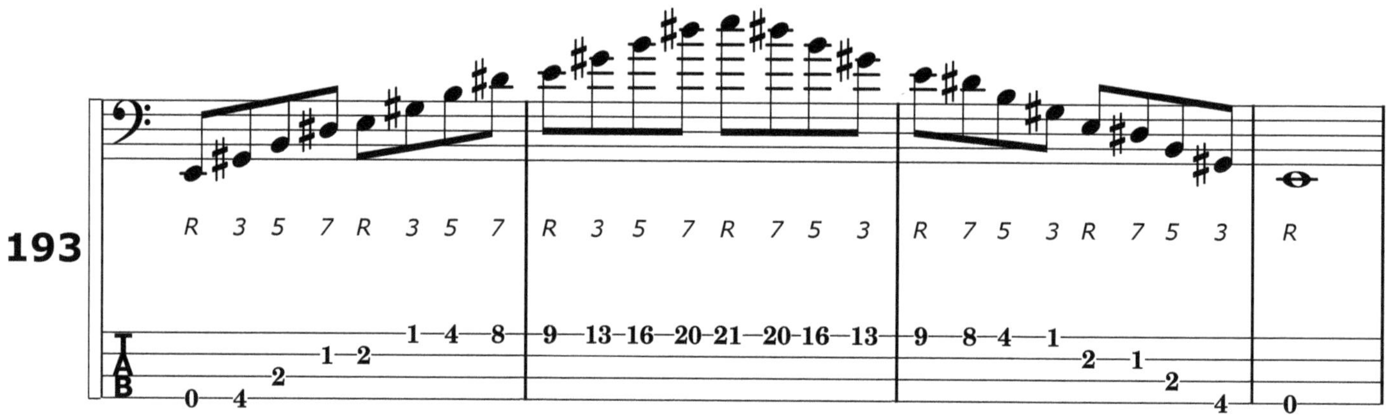

E Major - Root Pattern 2

194

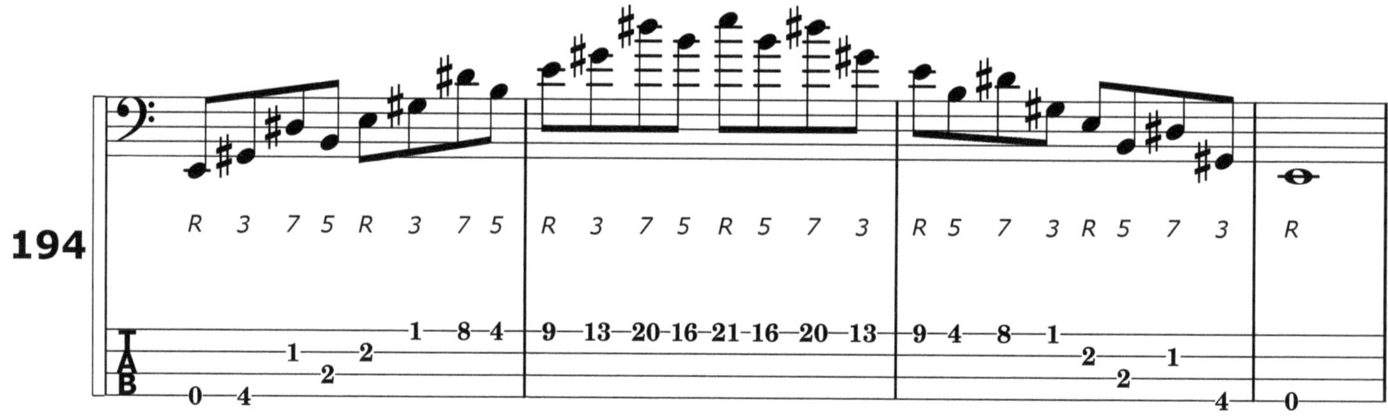

E Major - Root Pattern 3

195

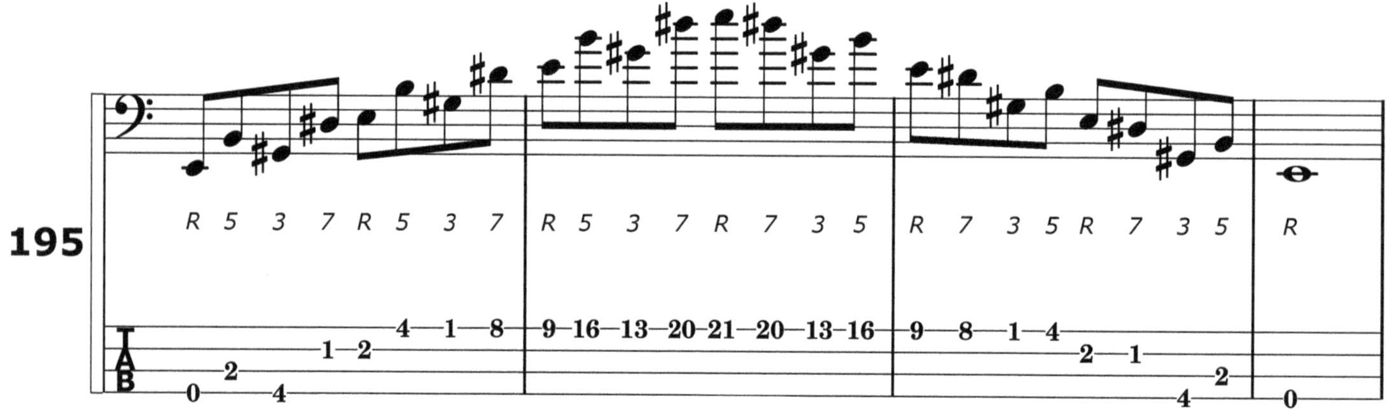

E Major - Root Pattern 4

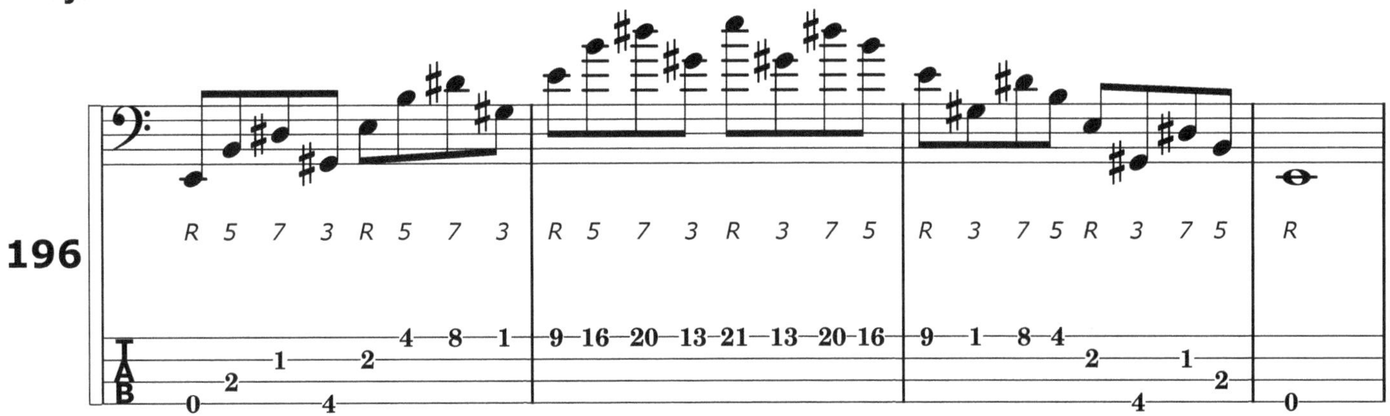

E Major - Root Pattern 5

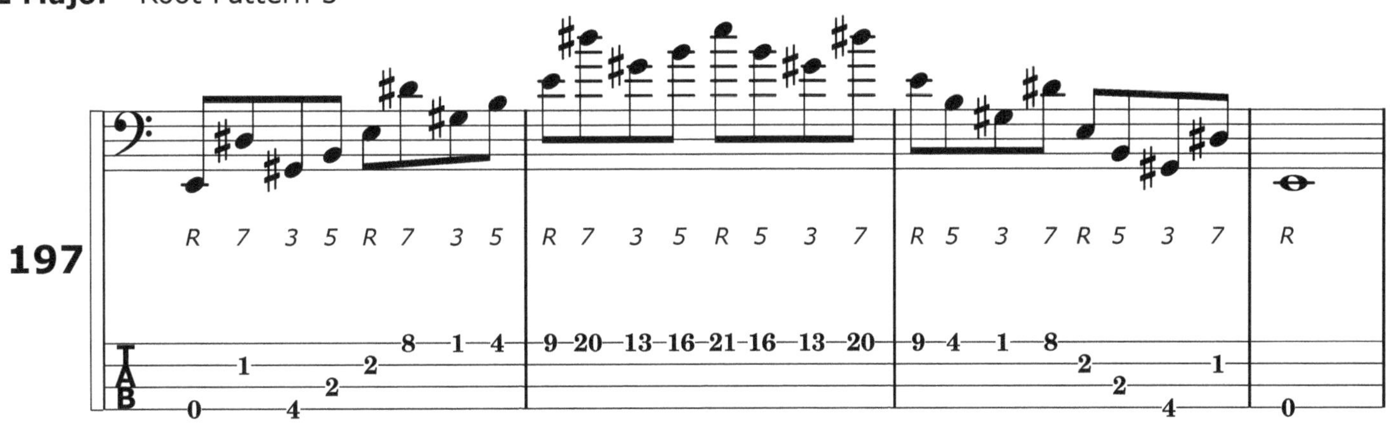

E Major - Root Pattern 6

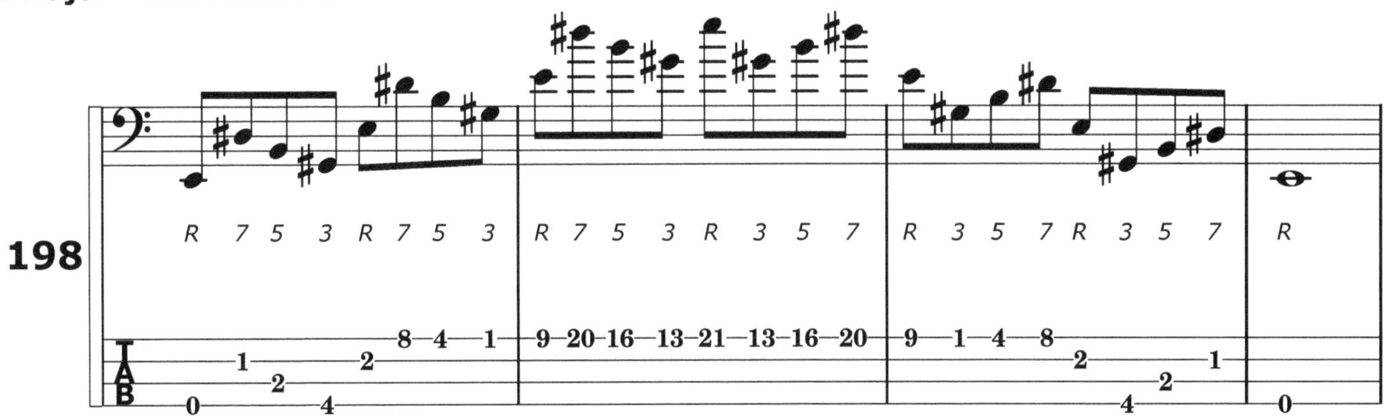

E Major - Third Pattern 1

199 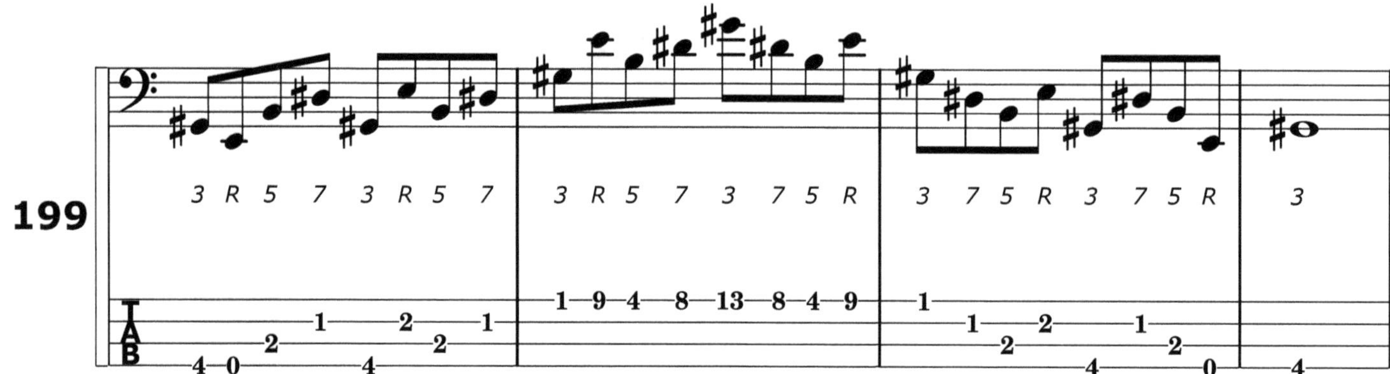

E Major - Third Pattern 2

200 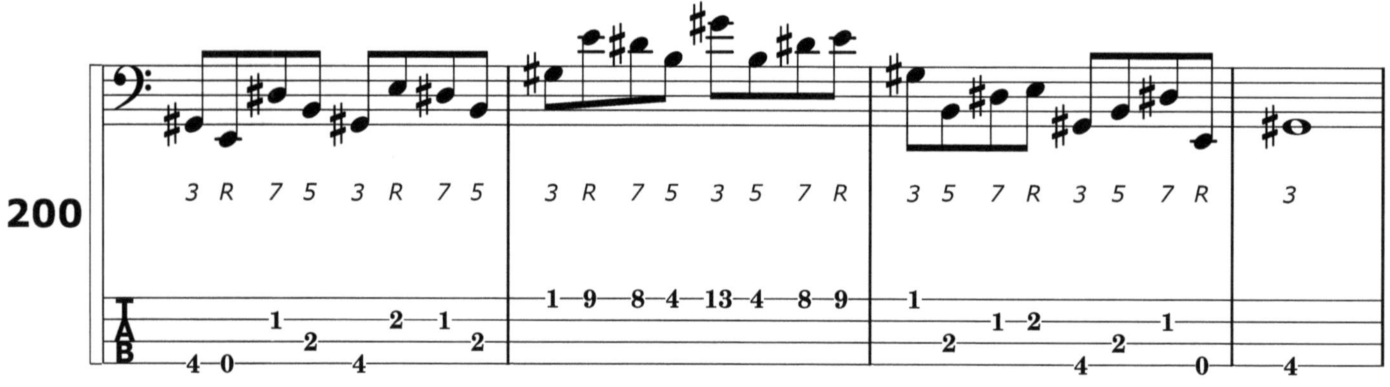

E Major - Third Pattern 3

201 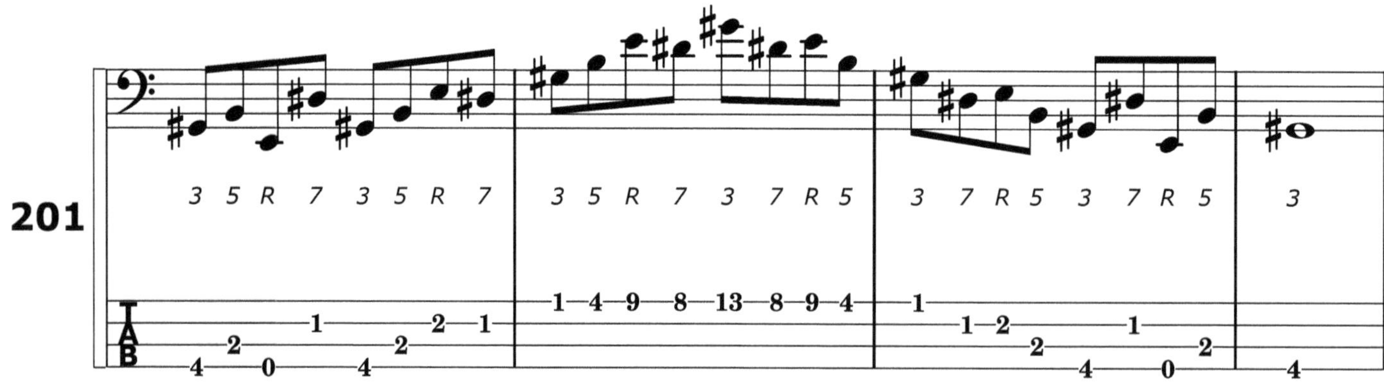

E Major - Third Pattern 4

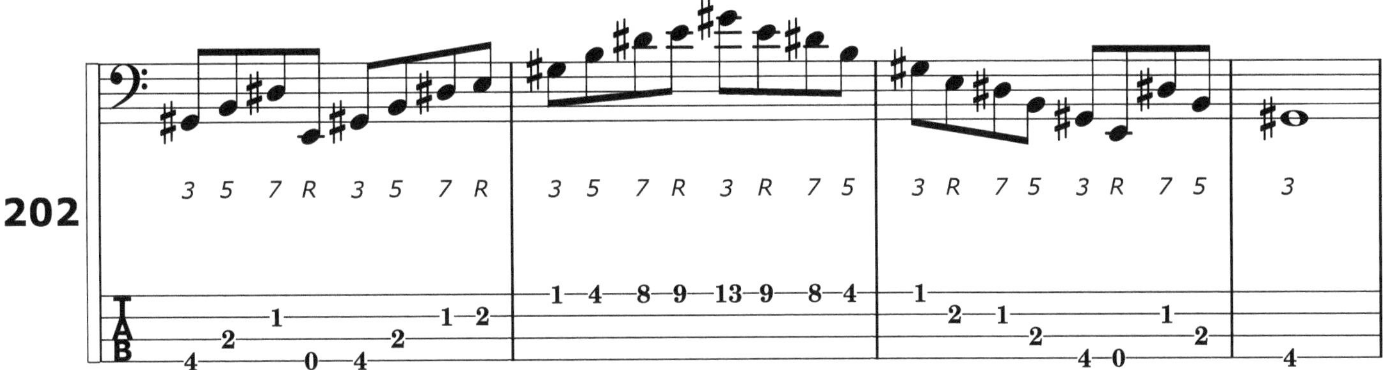

E Major - Third Pattern 5

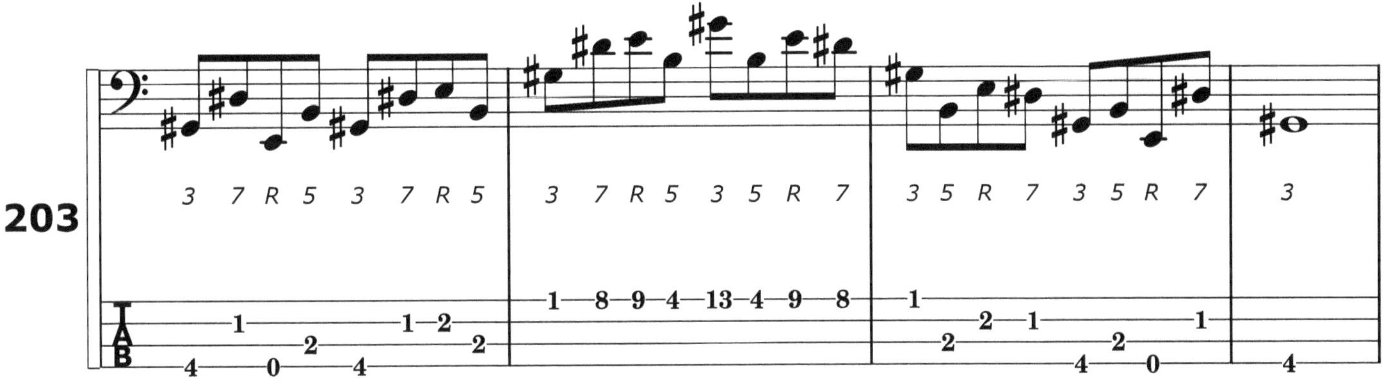

E Major - Third Pattern 6

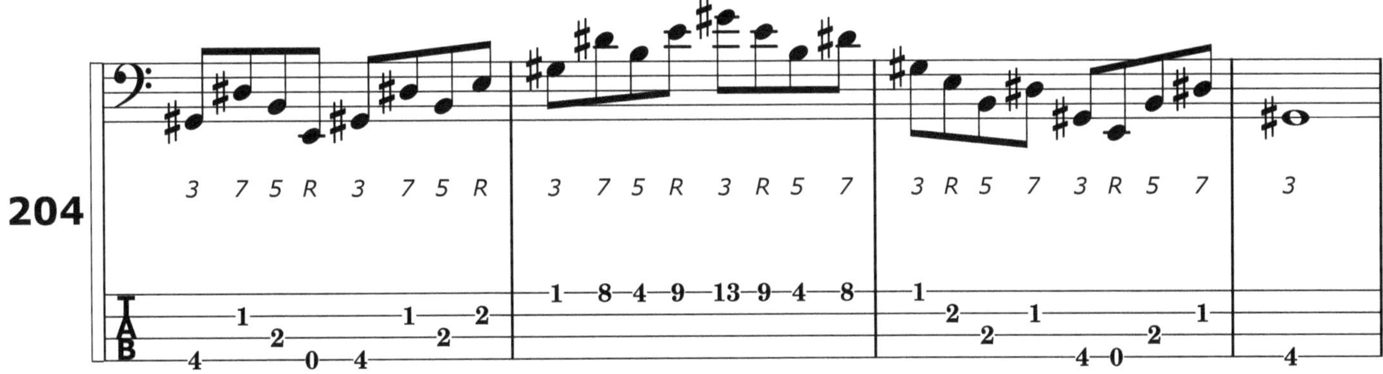

E Major - Fifth Pattern 1

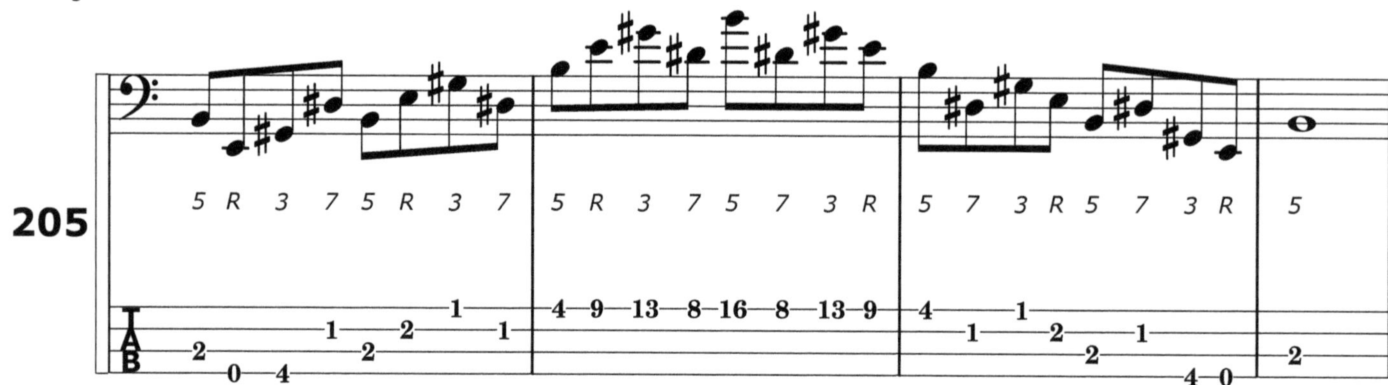

E Major - Fifth Pattern 2

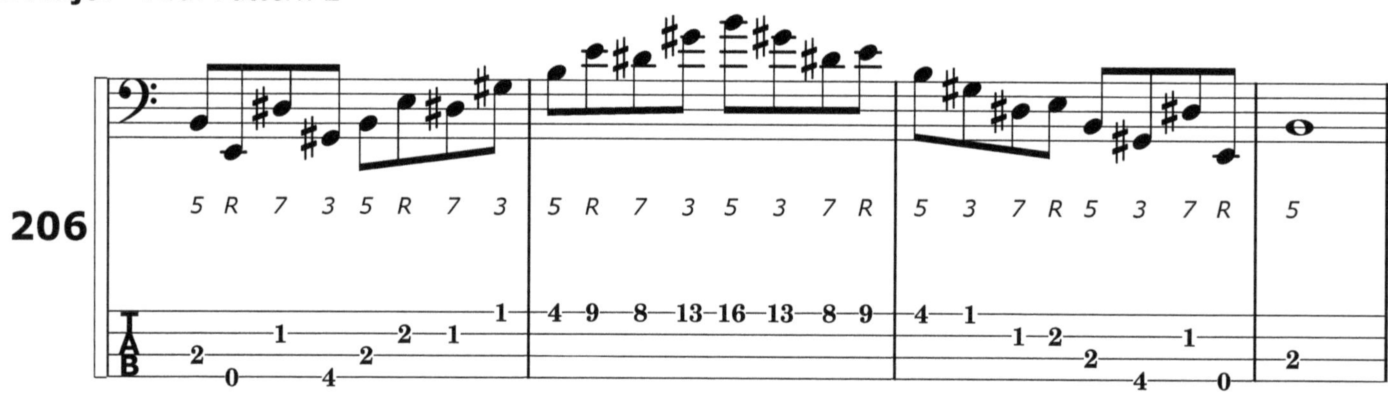

E Major - Fifth Pattern 3

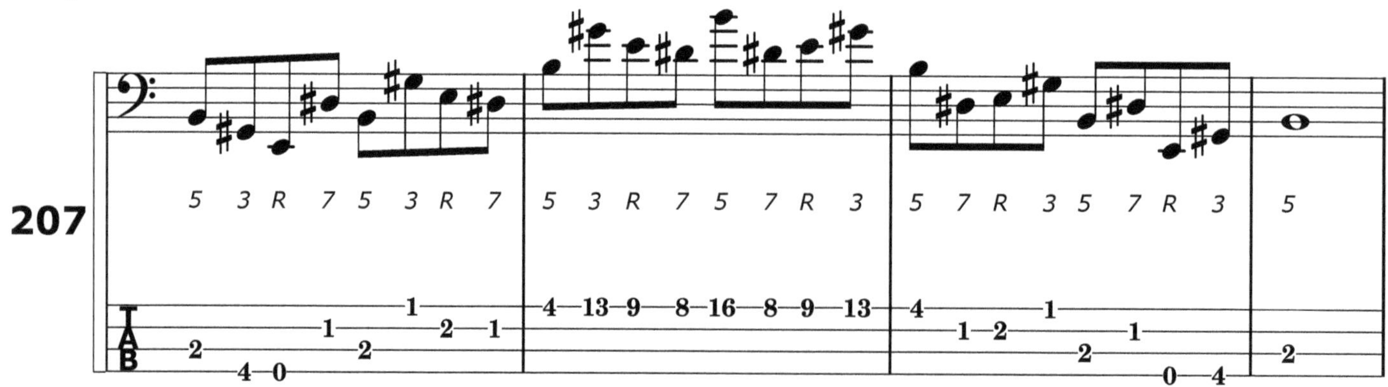

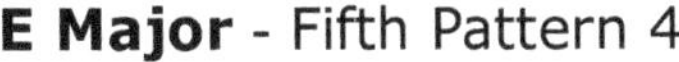

E Major - Fifth Pattern 4

208

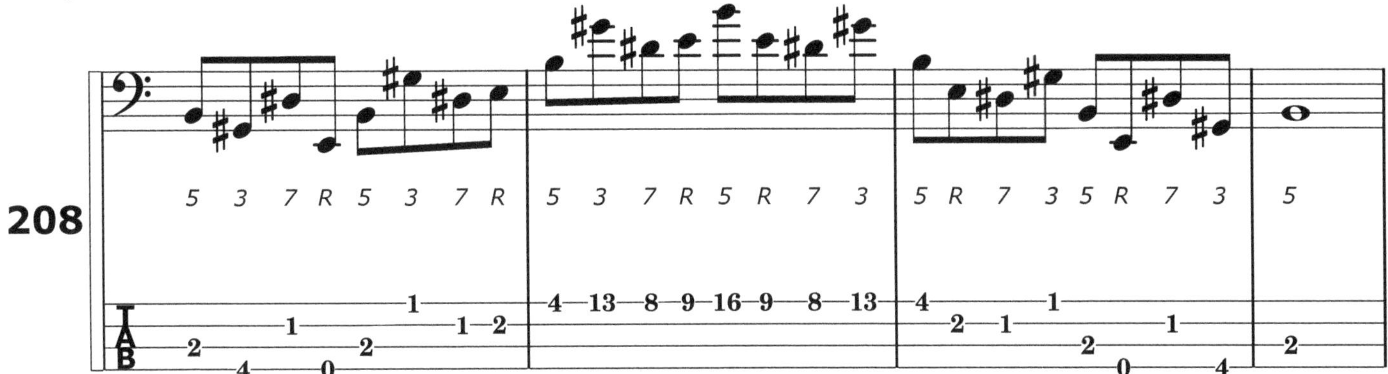

E Major - Fifth Pattern 5

209

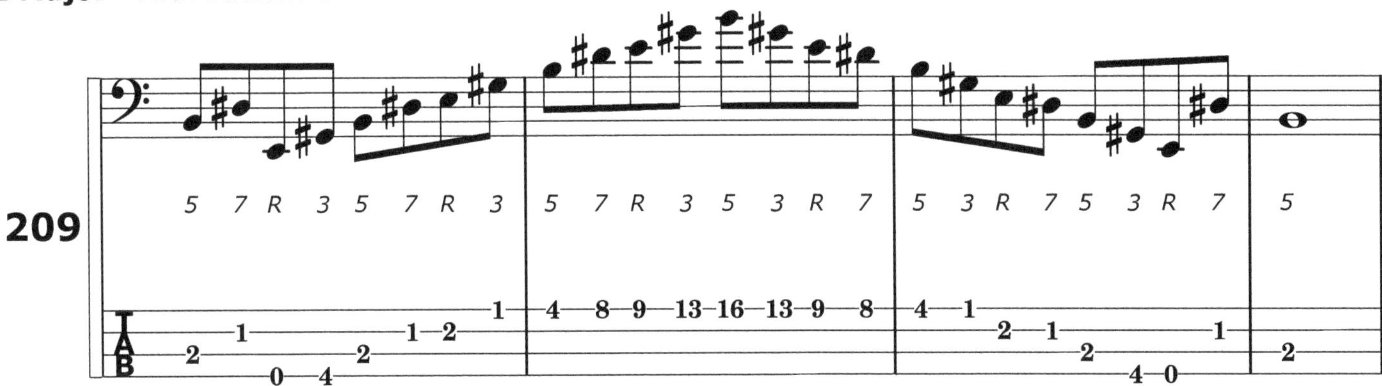

E Major - Fifth Pattern 6

210

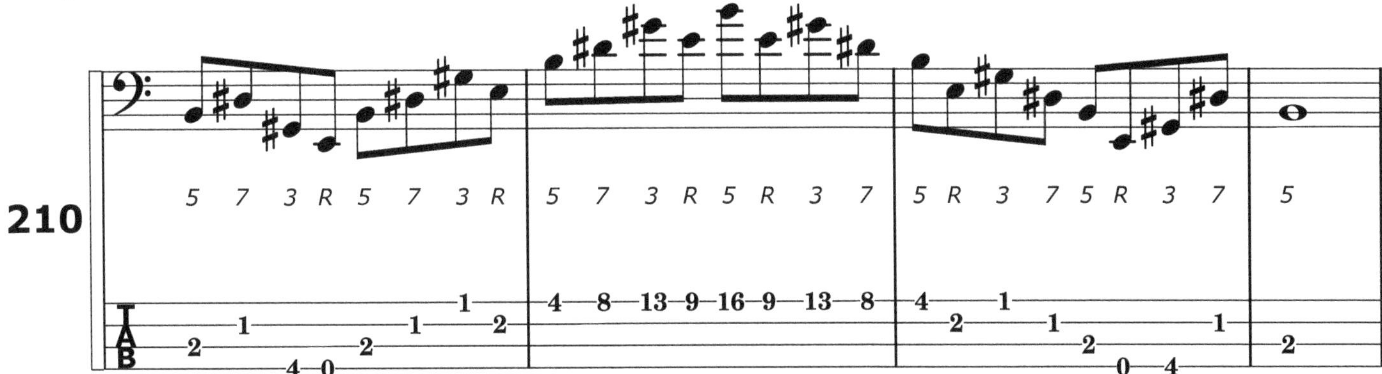

E Major - Seventh Pattern 1

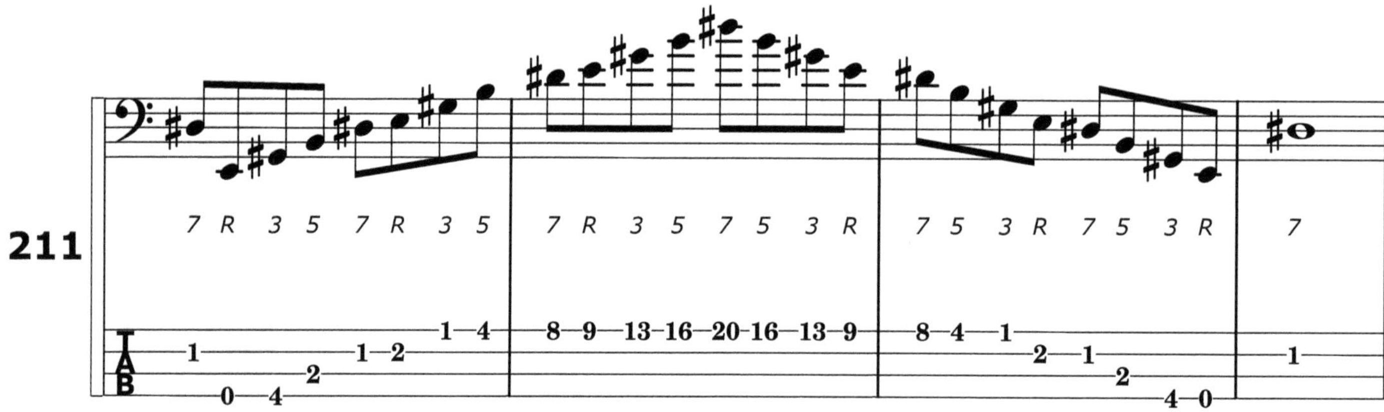

E Major - Seventh Pattern 2

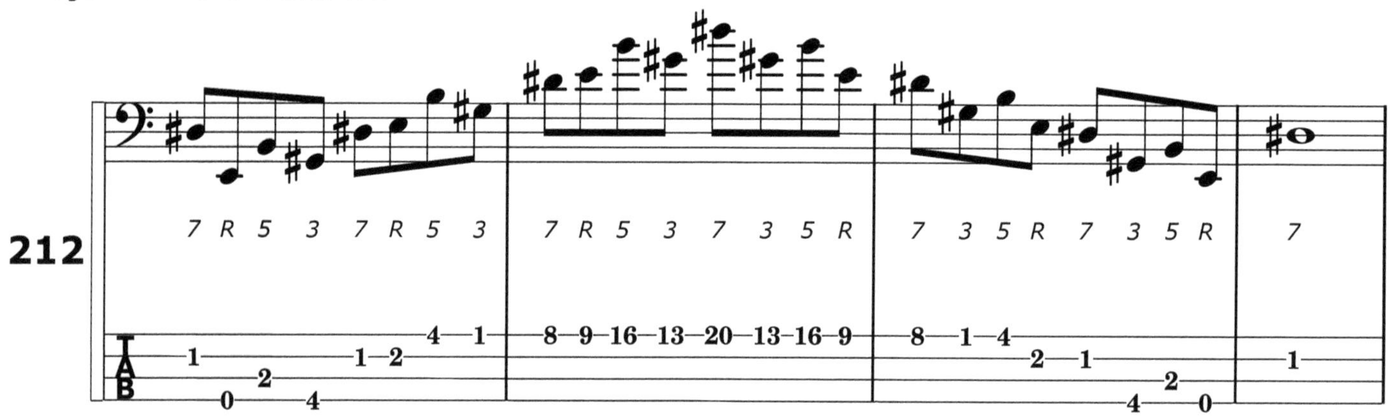

E Major - Seventh Pattern 3

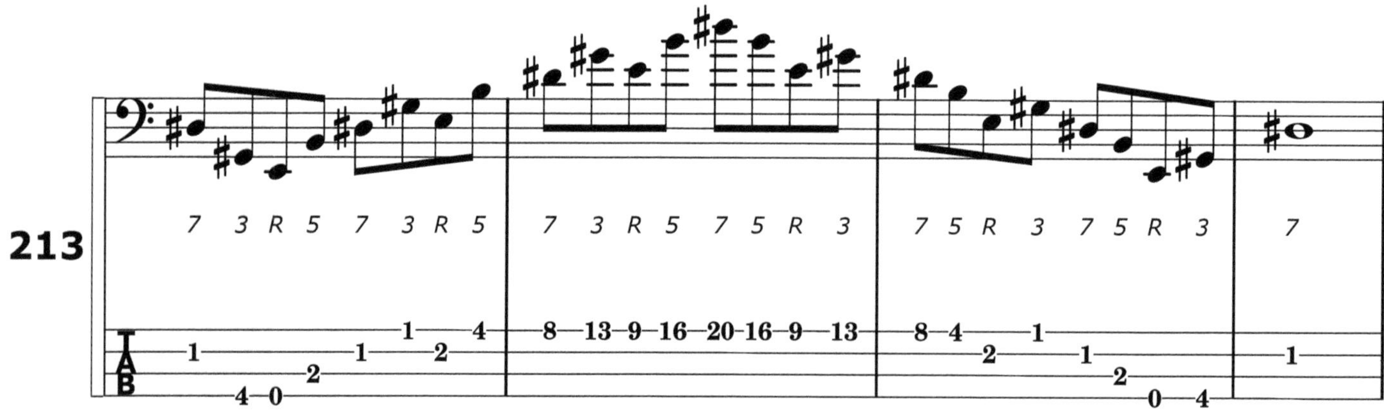

E Major - Seventh Pattern 4

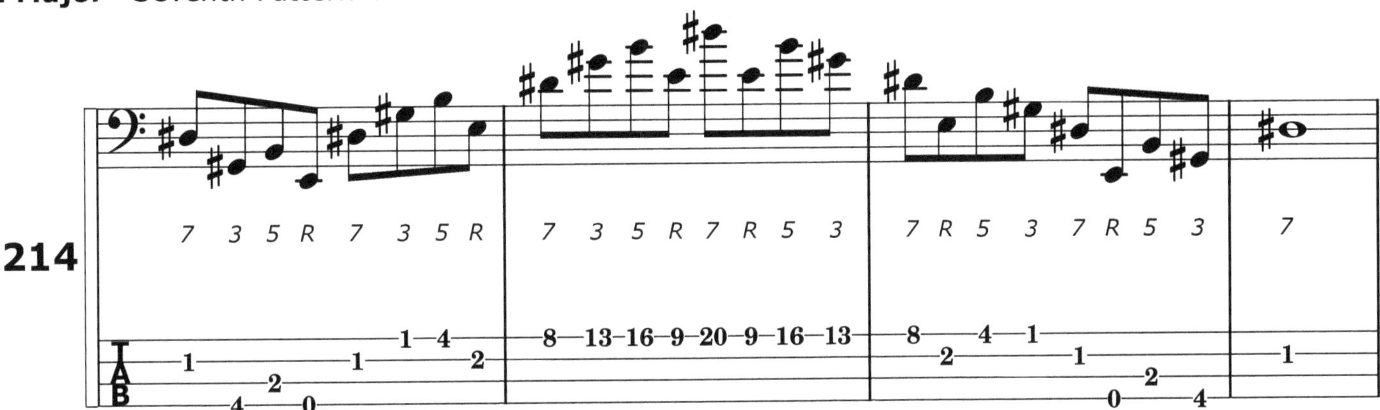

E Major - Seventh Pattern 5

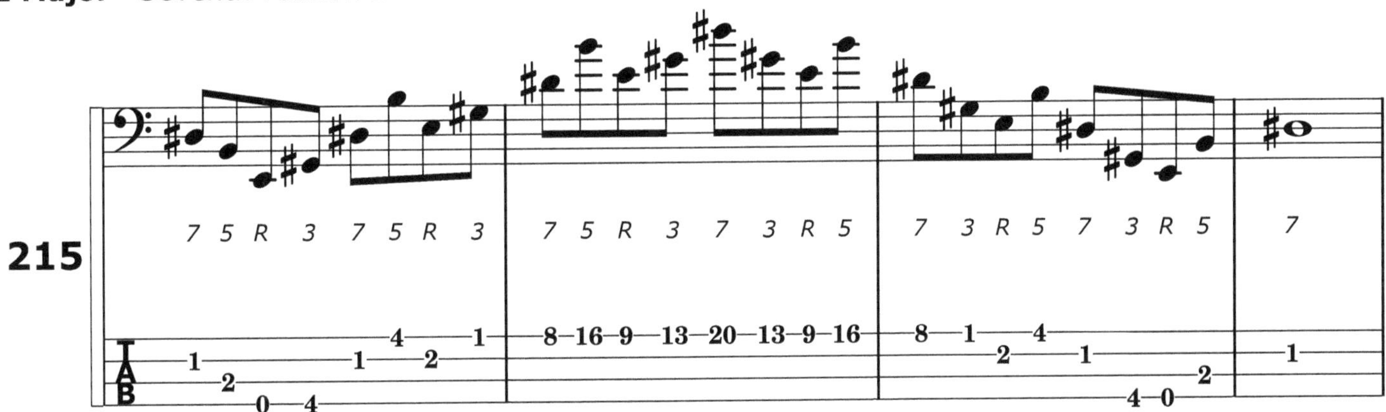

E Major - Seventh Pattern 6

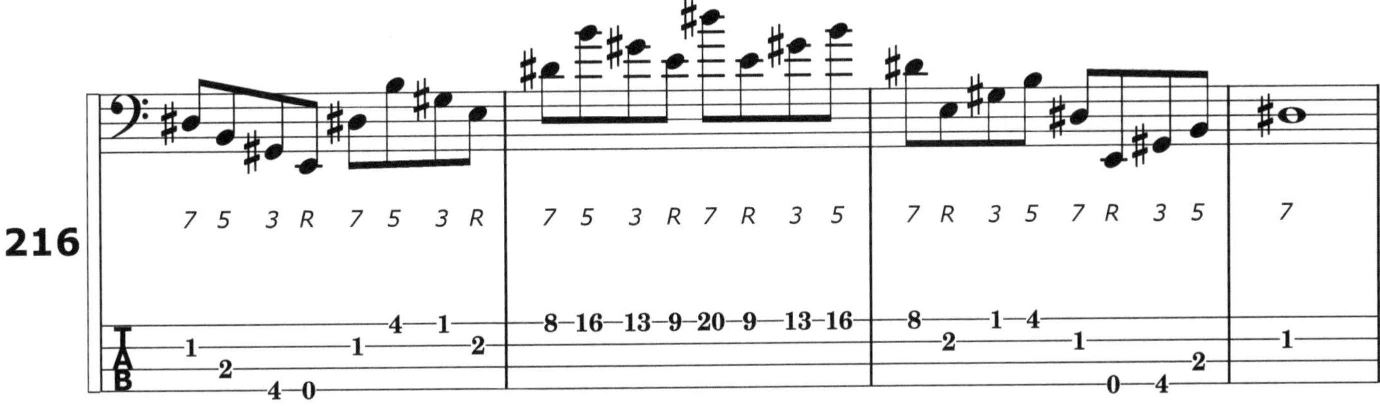

D♭ Major - Root Pattern 1

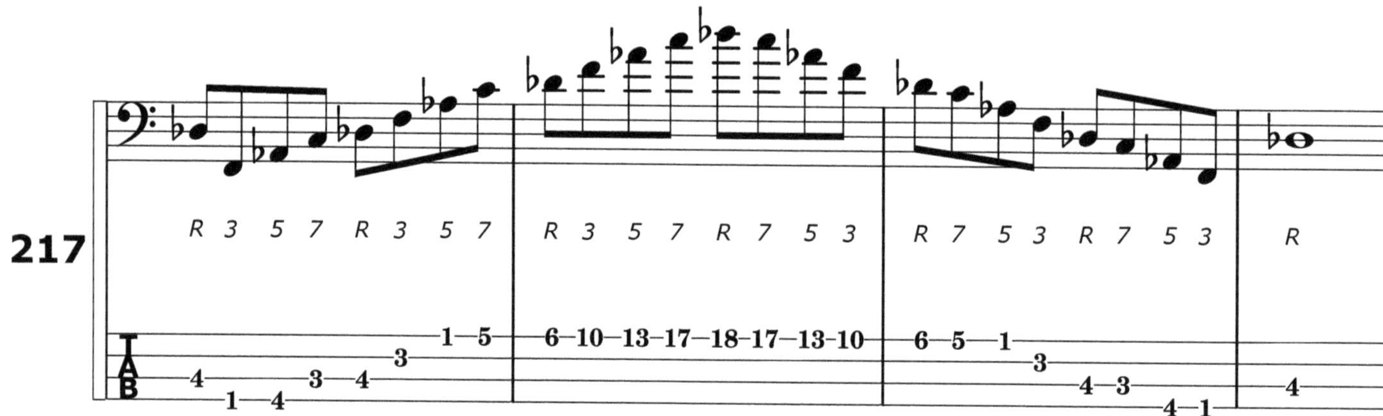

D♭ Major - Root Pattern 2

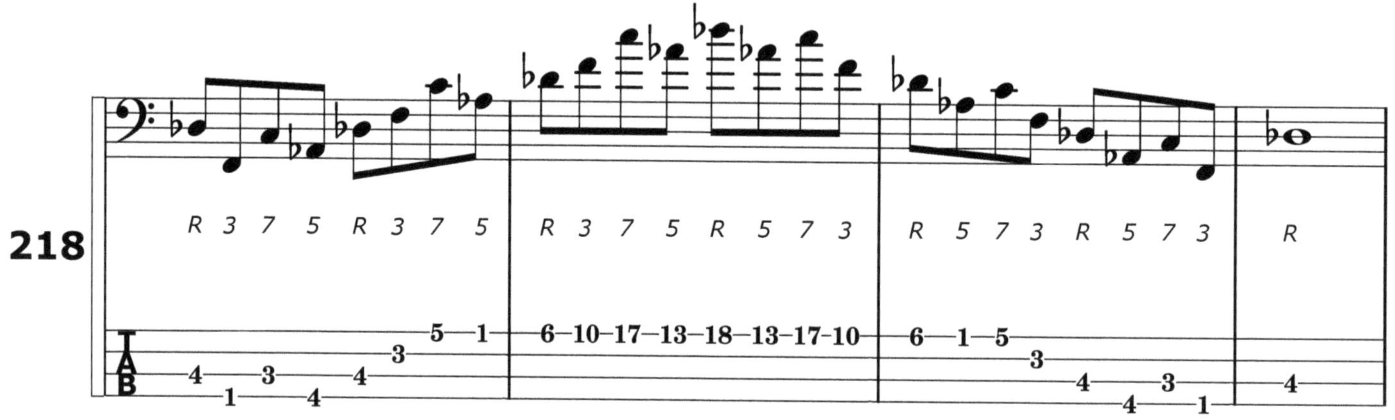

D♭ Major - Root Pattern 3

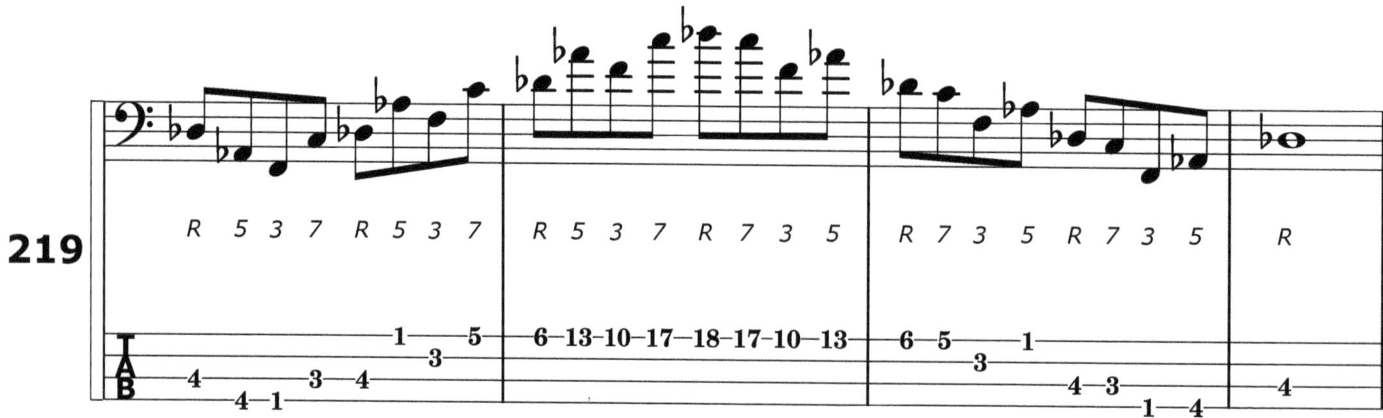

D♭ Major - Root Pattern 4

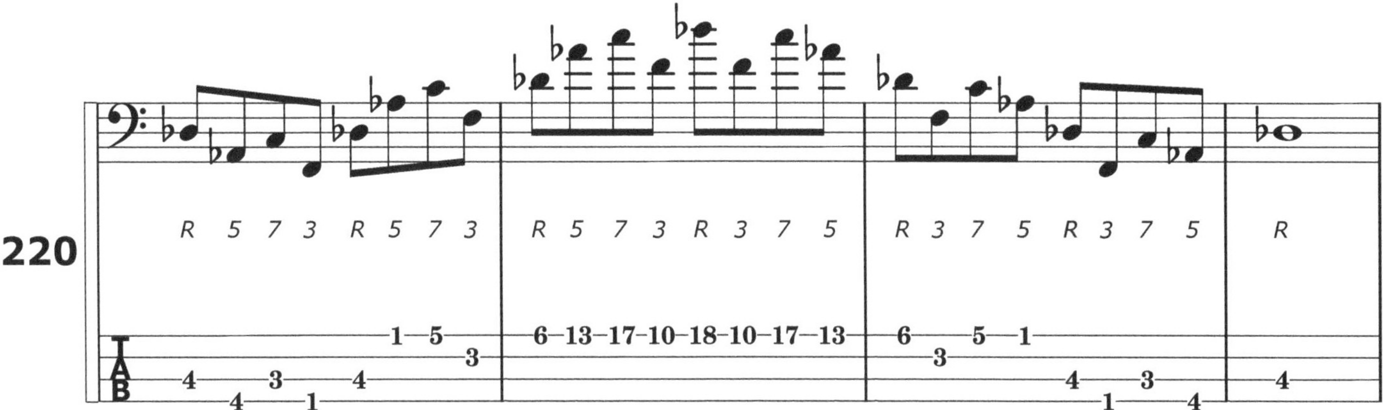

D♭ Major - Root Pattern 5

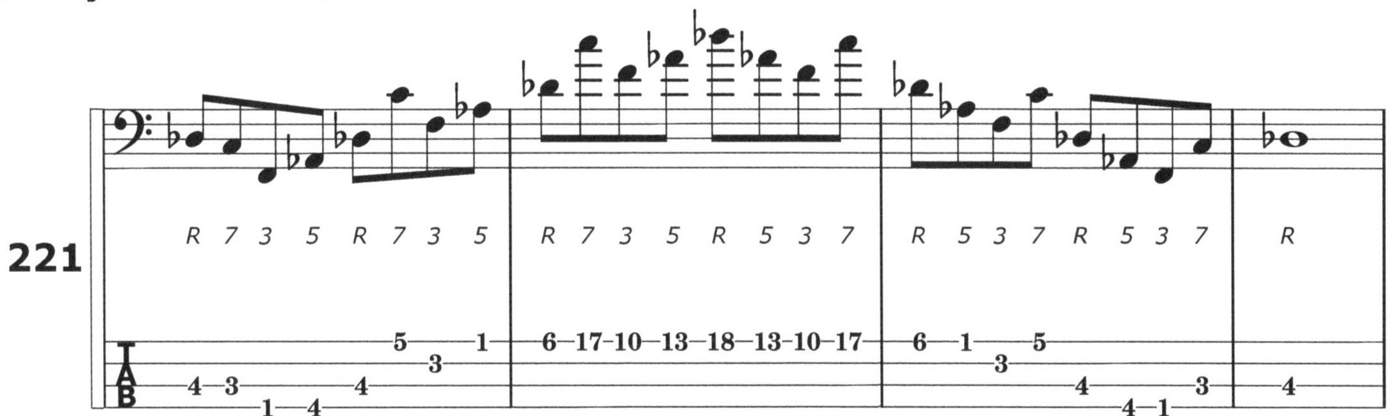

D♭ Major - Root Pattern 6

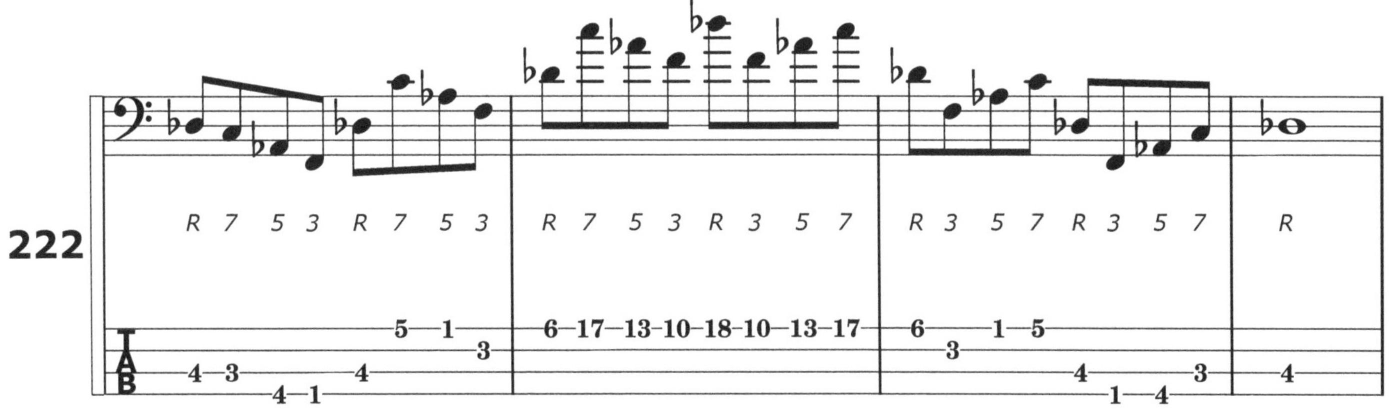

D♭ Major - Third Pattern 1

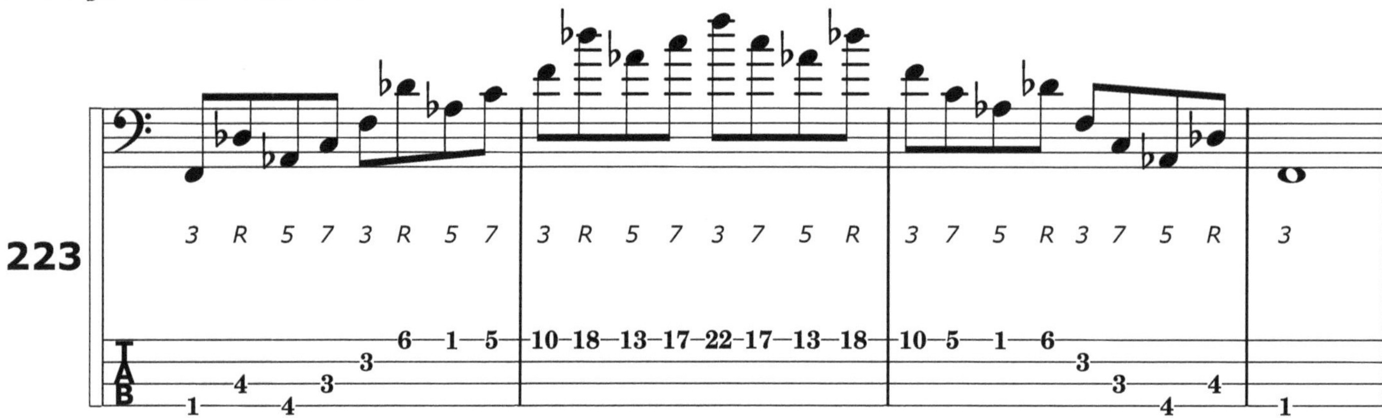

D♭ Major - Third Pattern 2

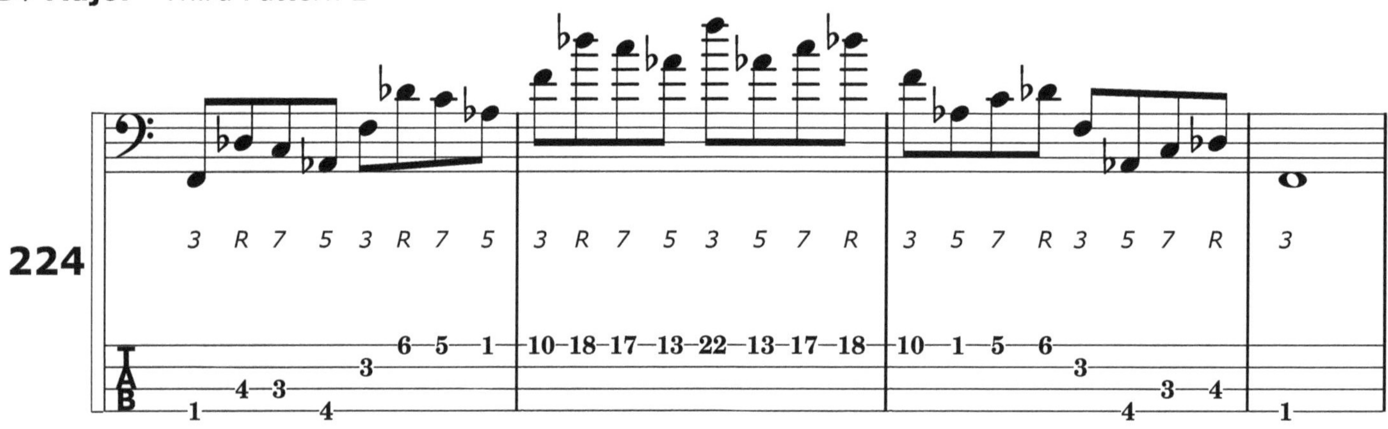

D♭ Major - Third Pattern 3

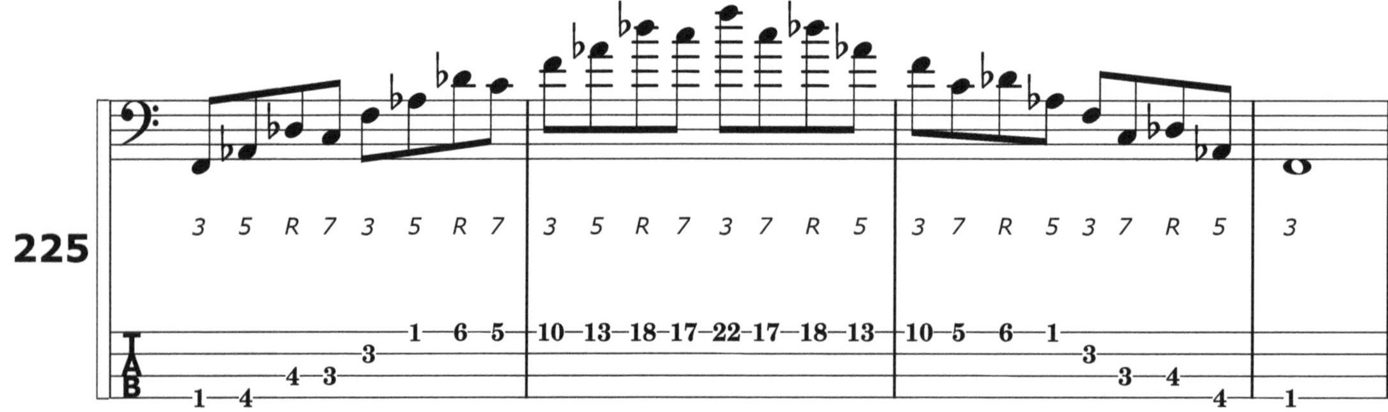

D♭ Major - Third Pattern 4

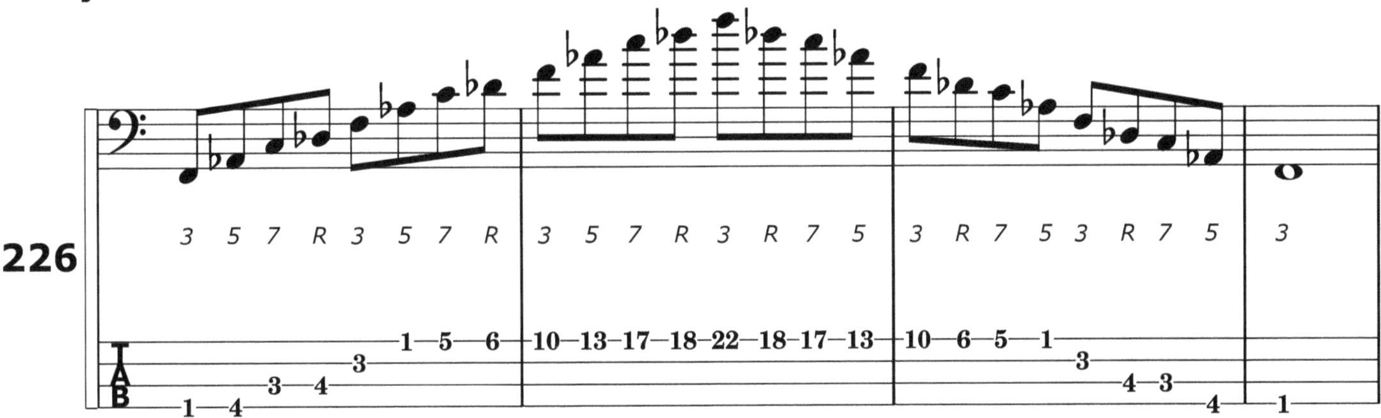

D♭ Major - Third Pattern 5

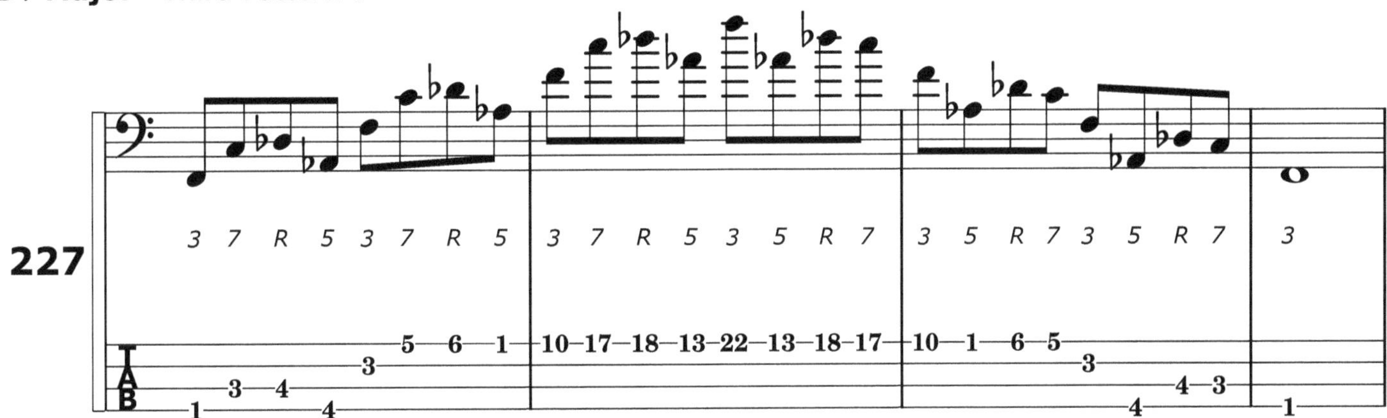

D♭ Major - Third Pattern 6

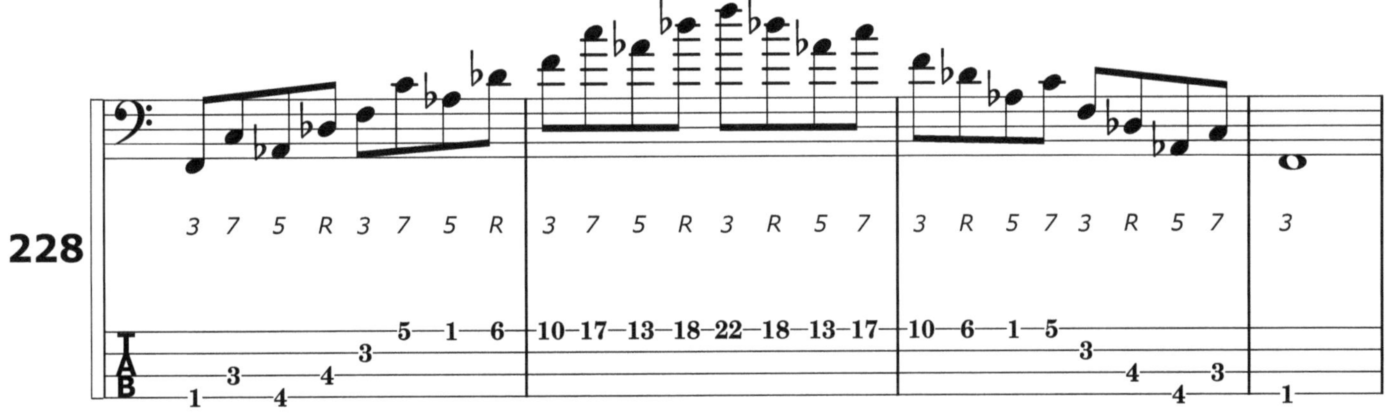

D♭ Major - Fifth Pattern 1

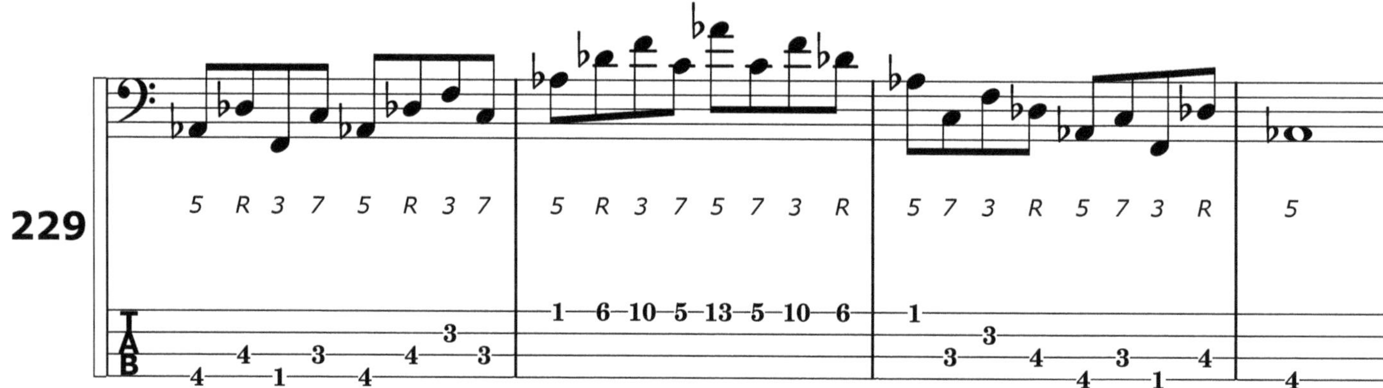

D♭ Major - Fifth Pattern 2

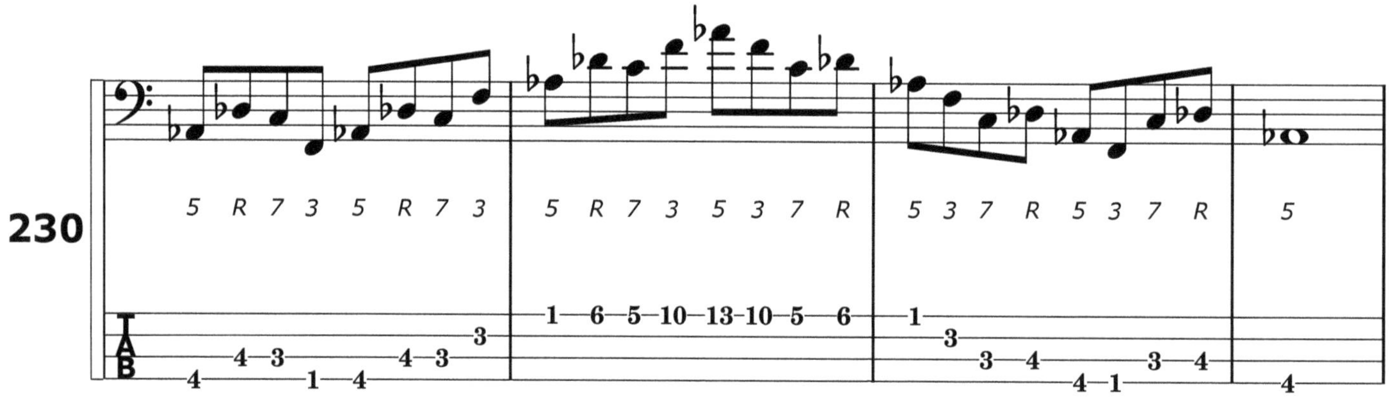

D♭ Major - Fifth Pattern 3

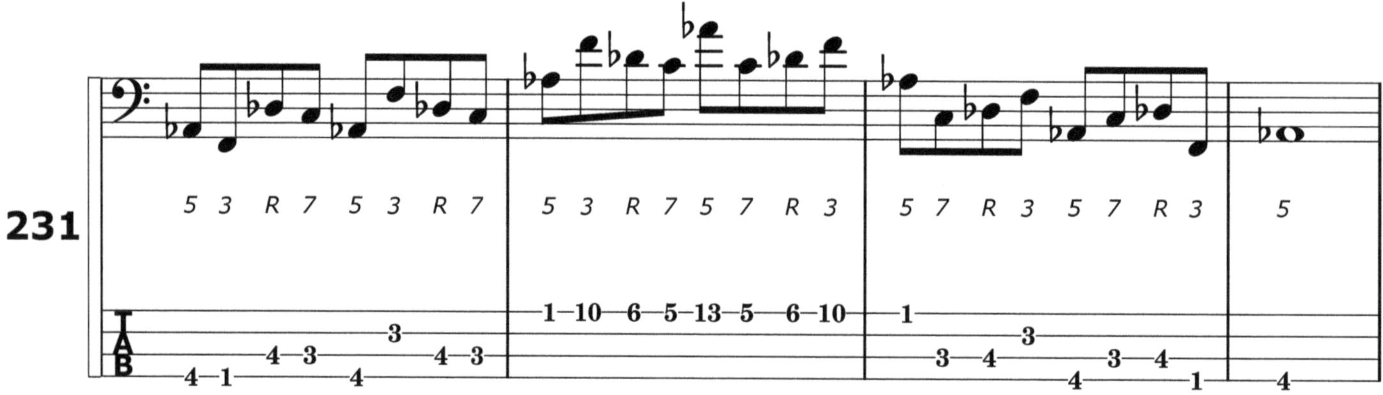

D♭ **Major** - Fifth Pattern 4

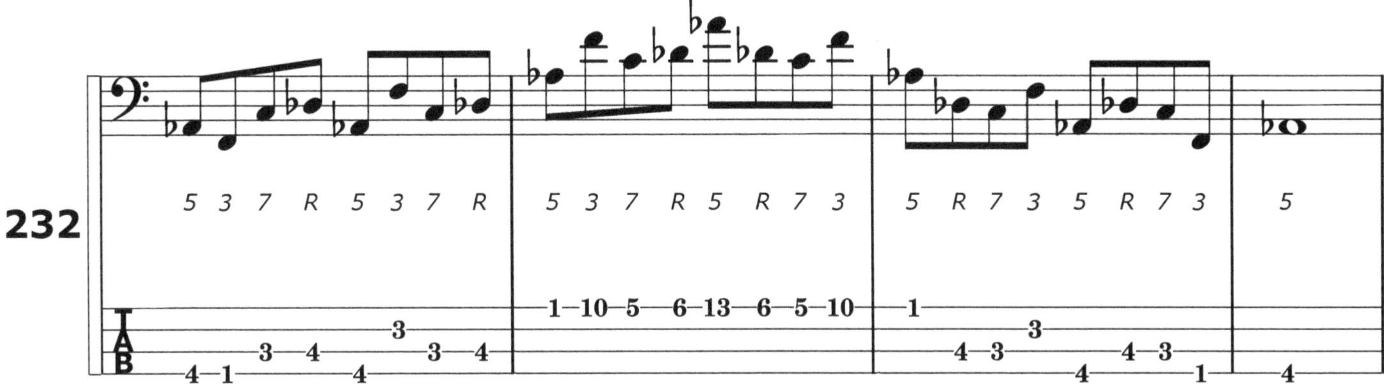

D♭ **Major** - Fifth Pattern 5

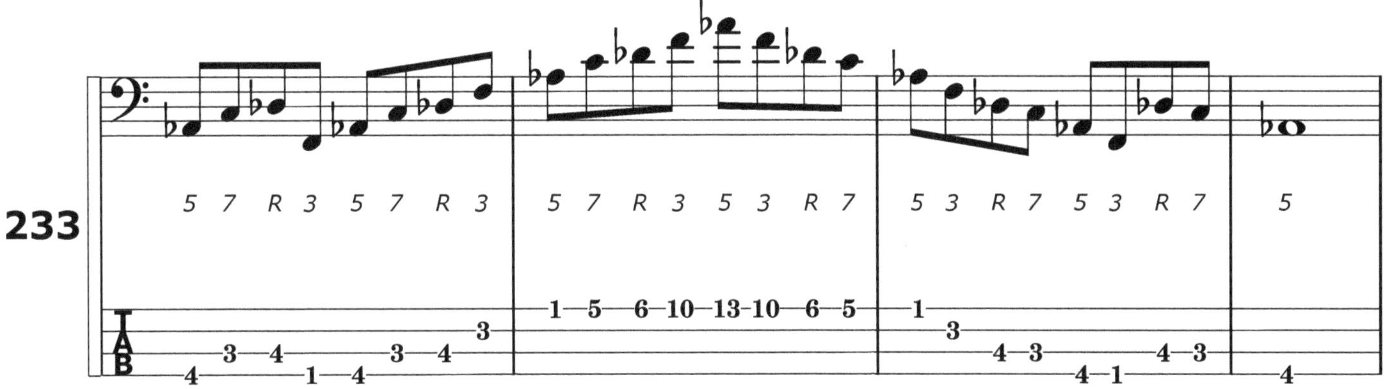

D♭ **Major** - Fifth Pattern 6

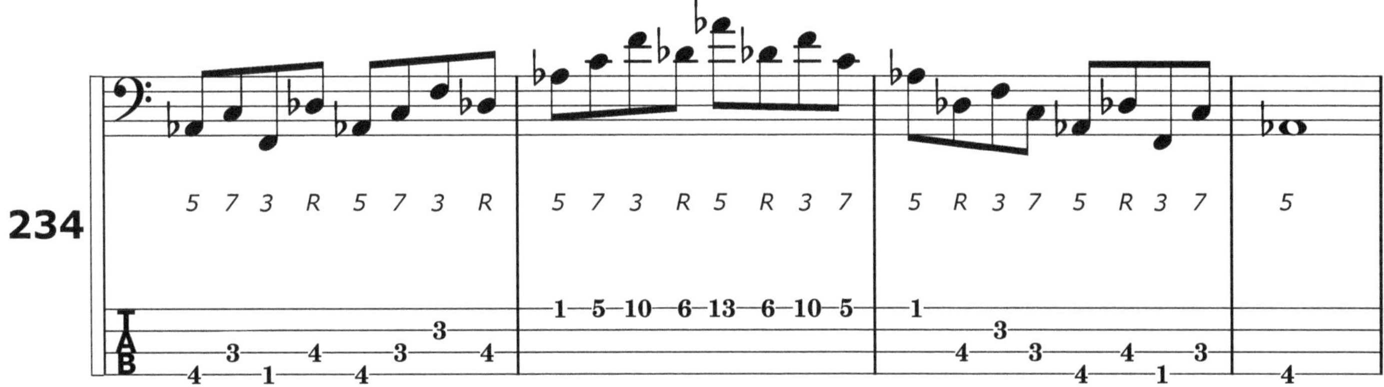

D♭ Major - Seventh Pattern 1

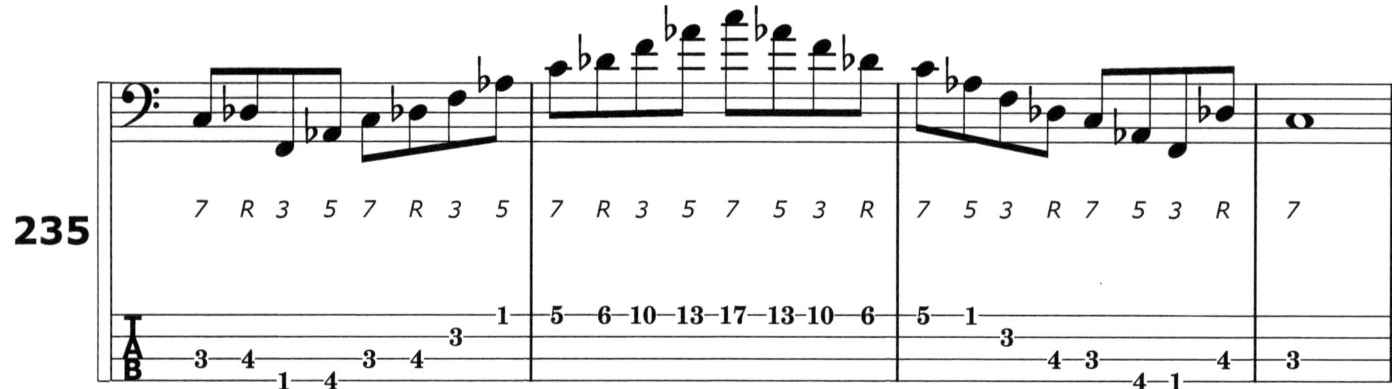

D♭ Major - Seventh Pattern 2

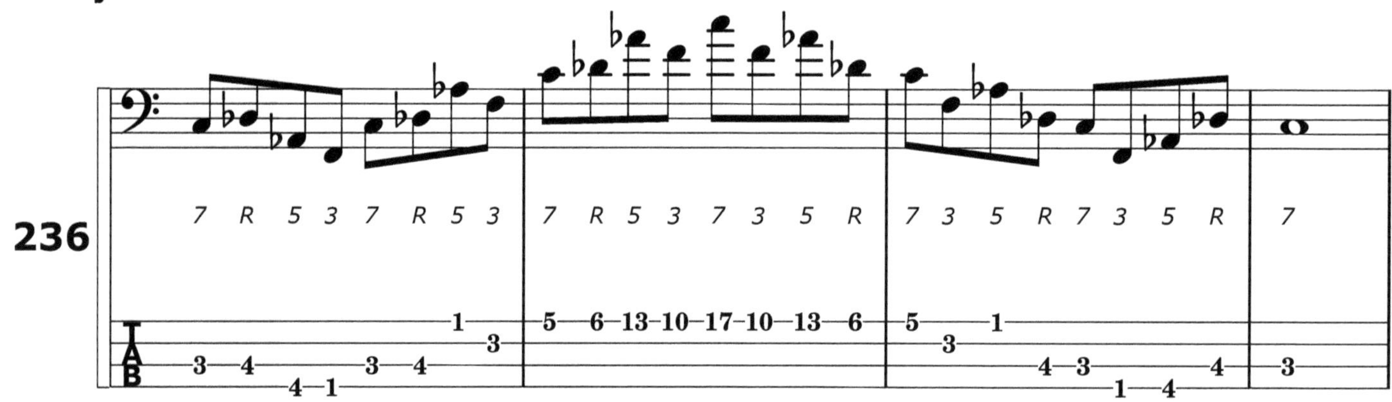

D♭ Major - Seventh Pattern 3

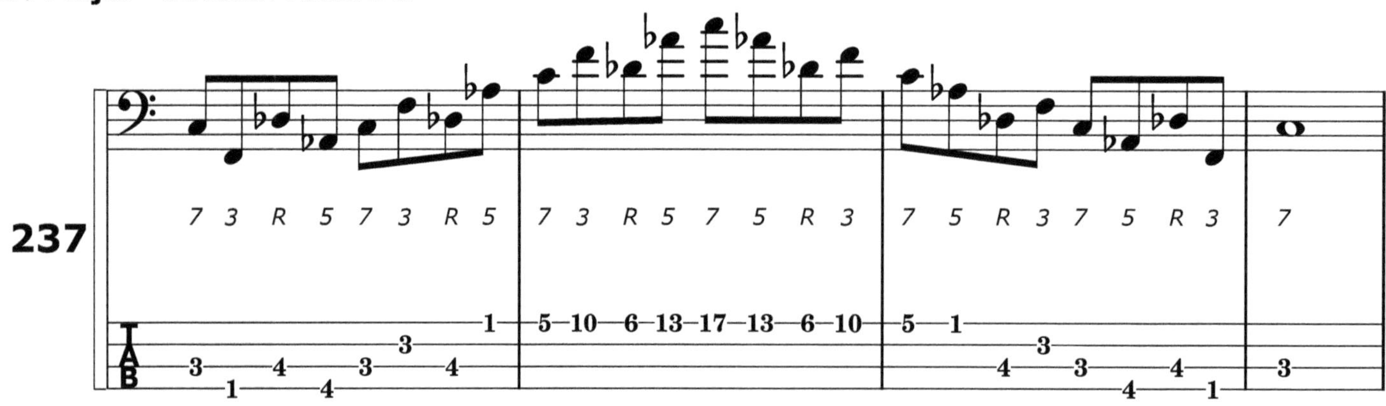

D♭ Major - Seventh Pattern 4

238
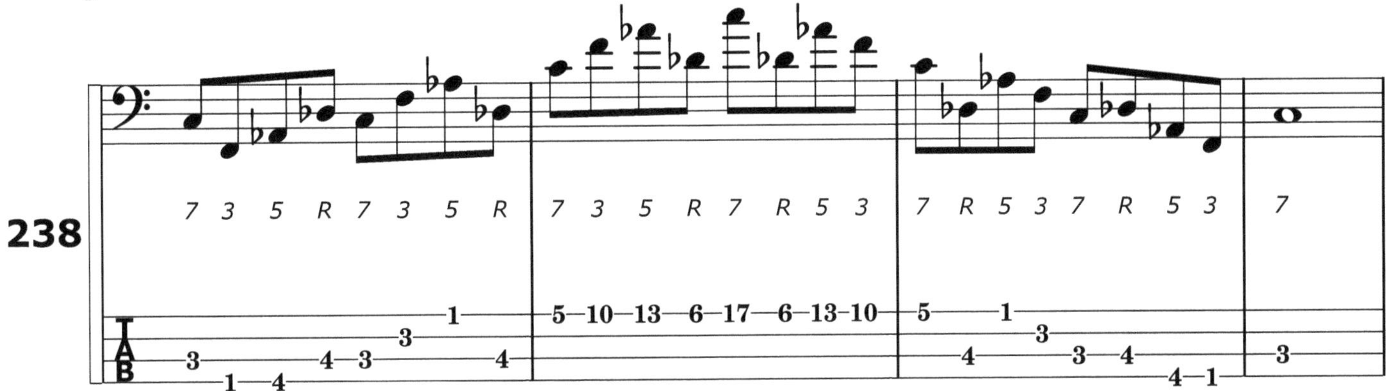

D♭ Major - Seventh Pattern 5

239
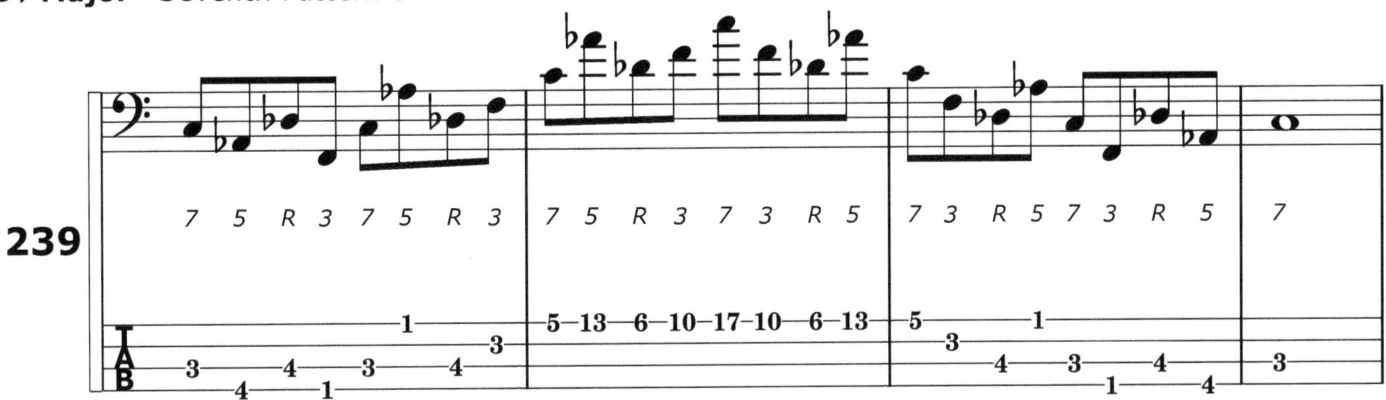

D♭ Major - Seventh Pattern 6

240
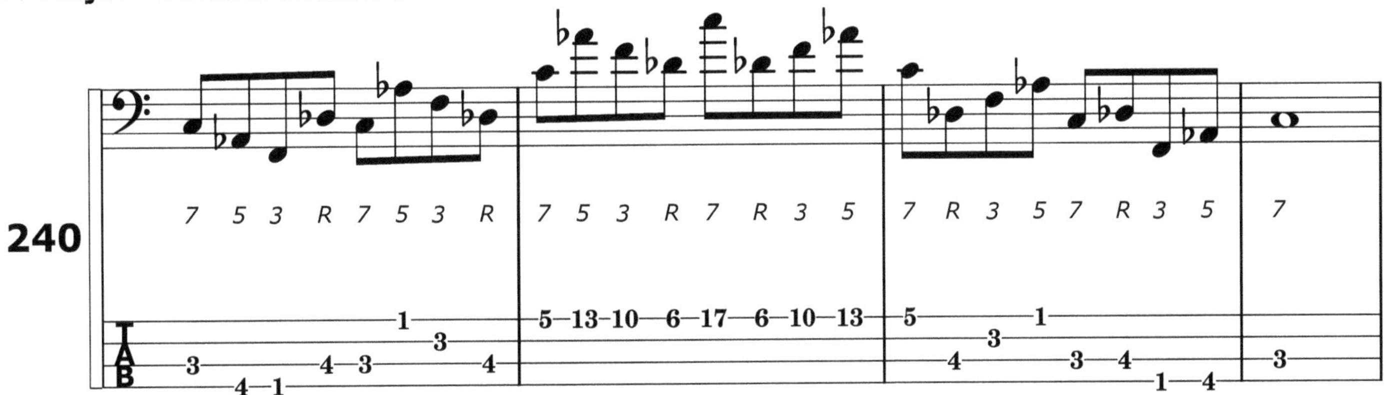

B Major - Root Pattern 1

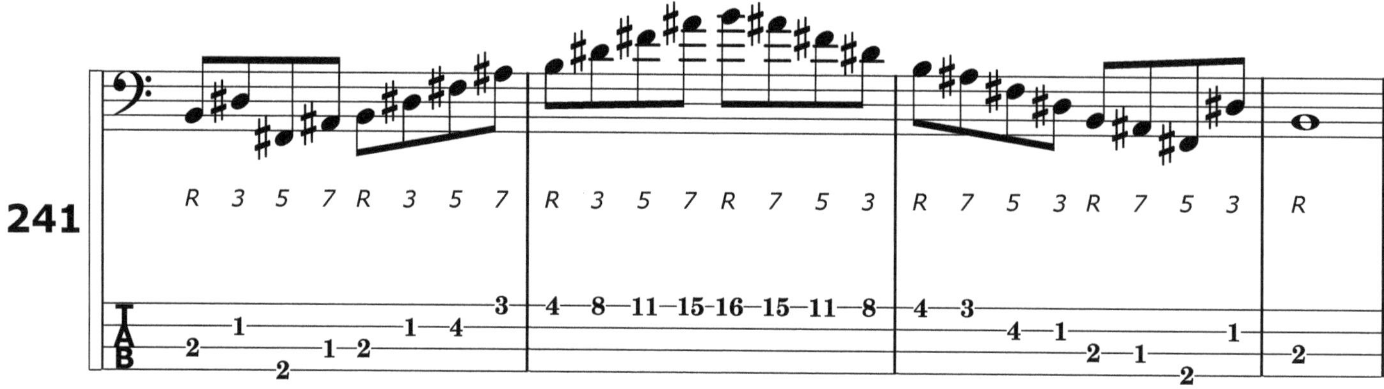

B Major - Root Pattern 2

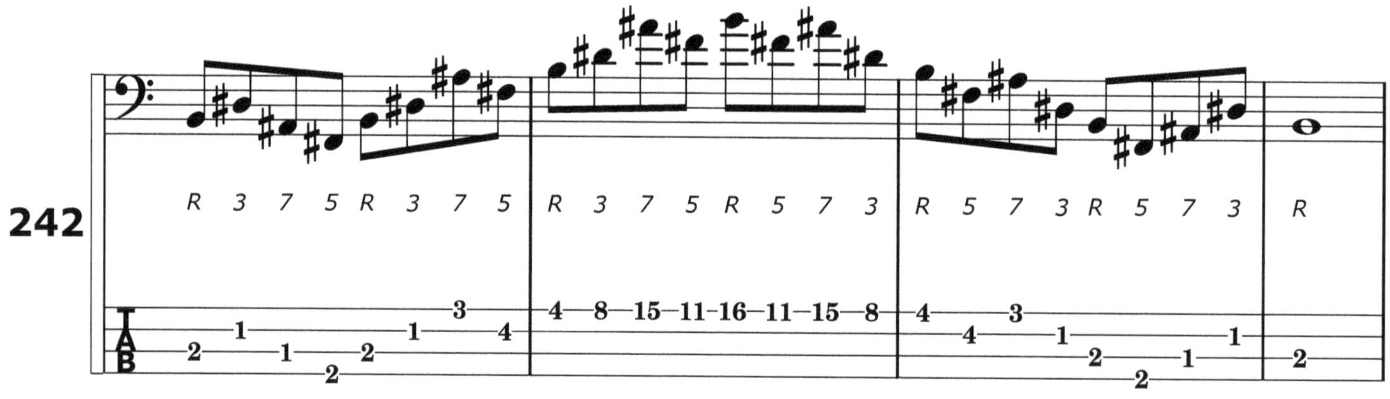

B Major - Root Pattern 3

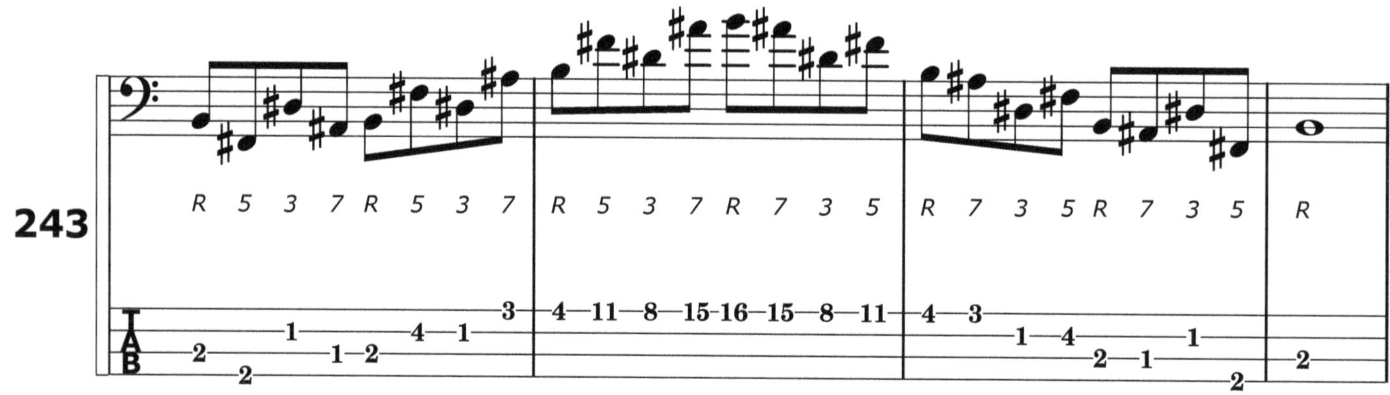

B Major - Root Pattern 4

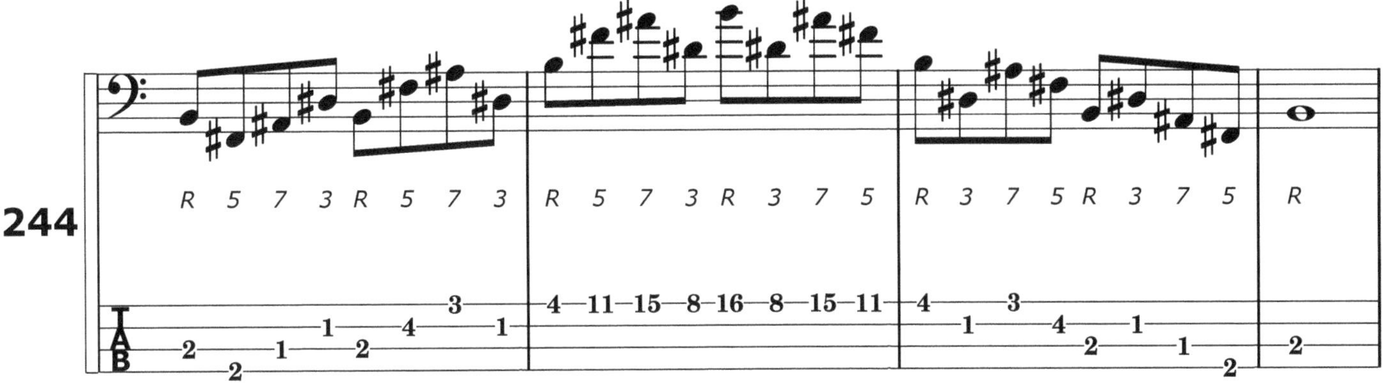

B Major - Root Pattern 5

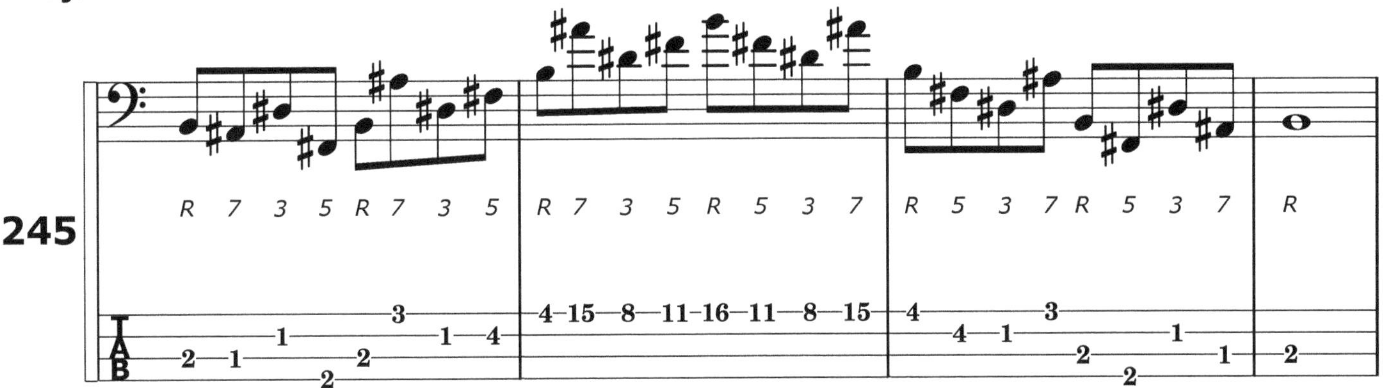

B Major - Root Pattern 6

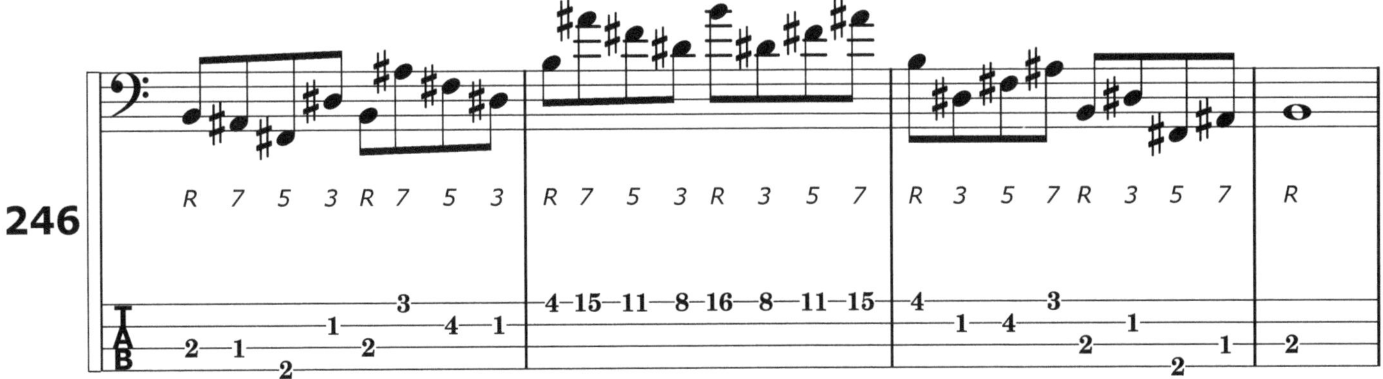

B Major - Third Pattern 1

247 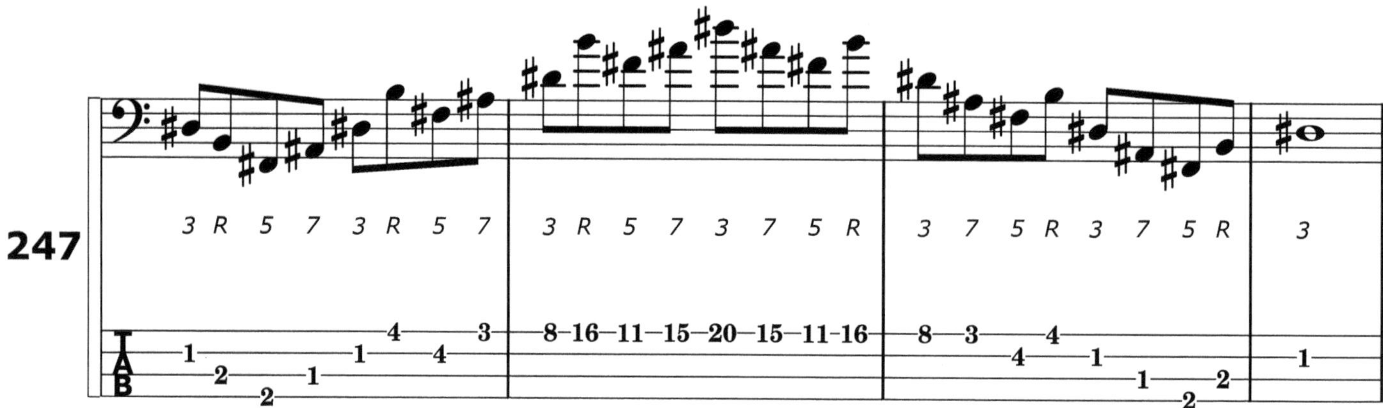

B Major - Third Pattern 2

248 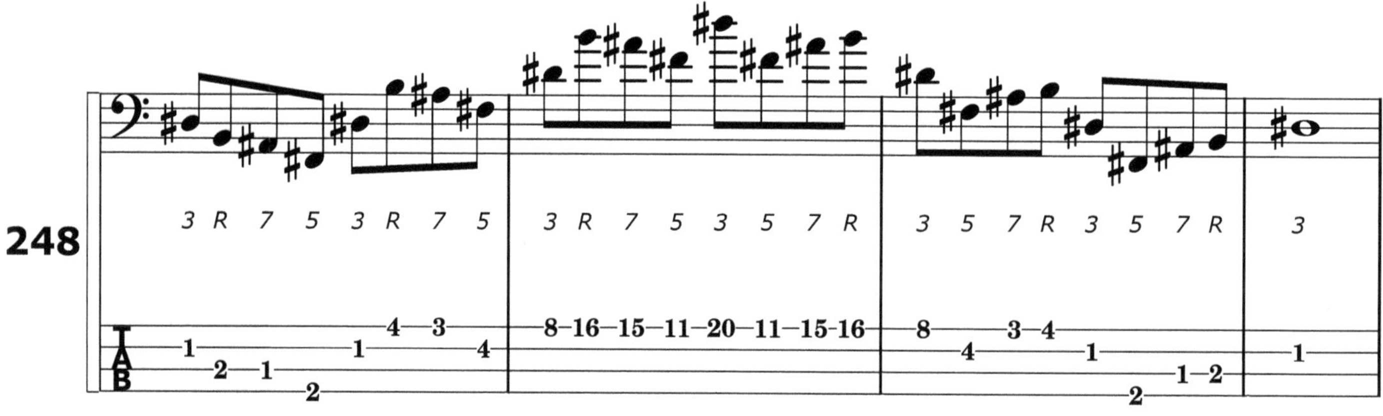

B Major - Third Pattern 3

249 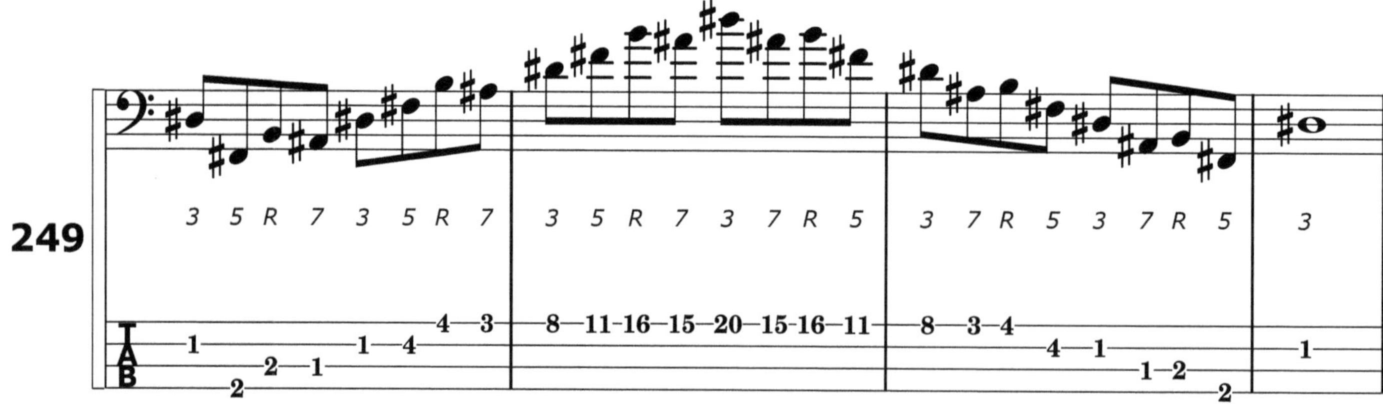

B Major - Third Pattern 4

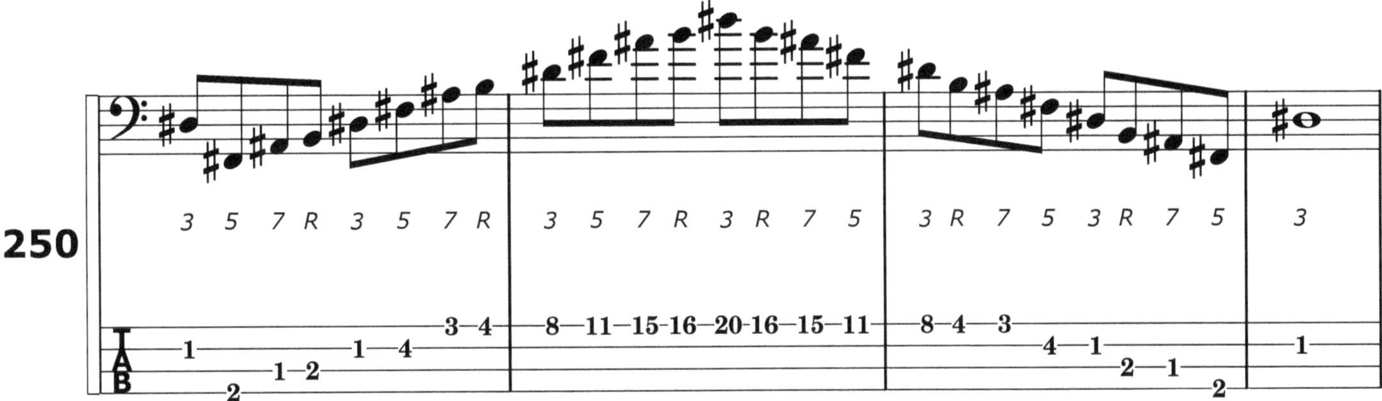

B Major - Third Pattern 5

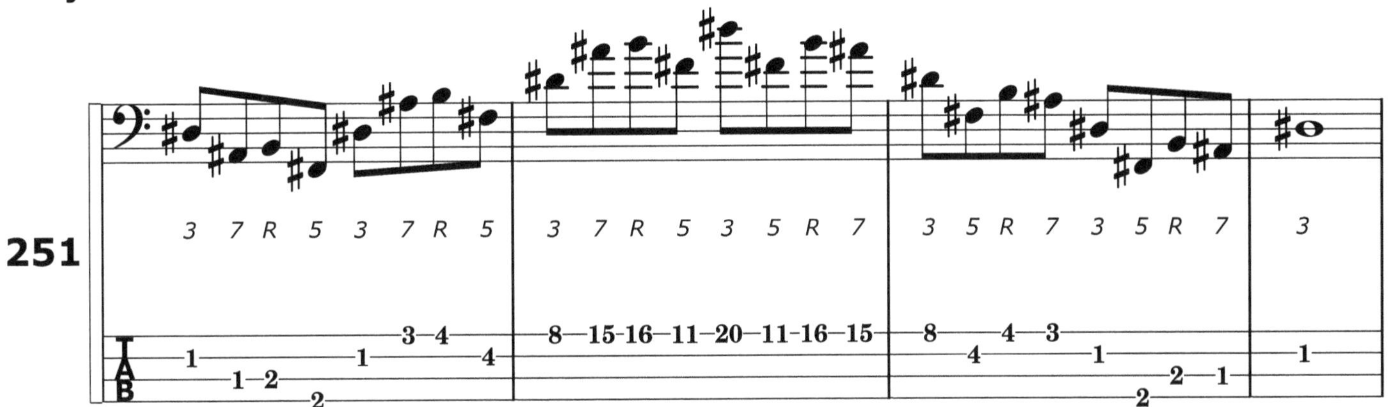

B Major - Third Pattern 6

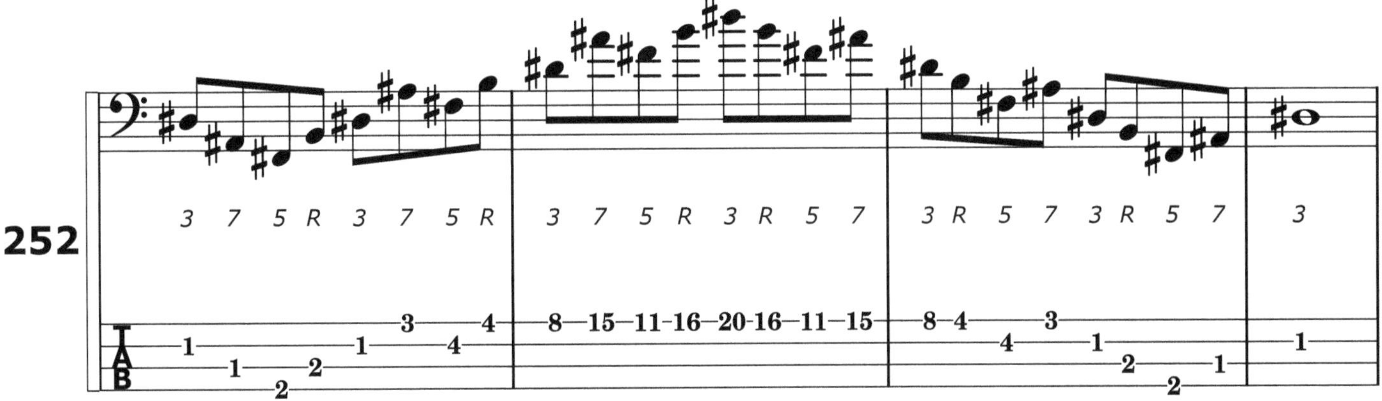

B Major - Fifth Pattern 1

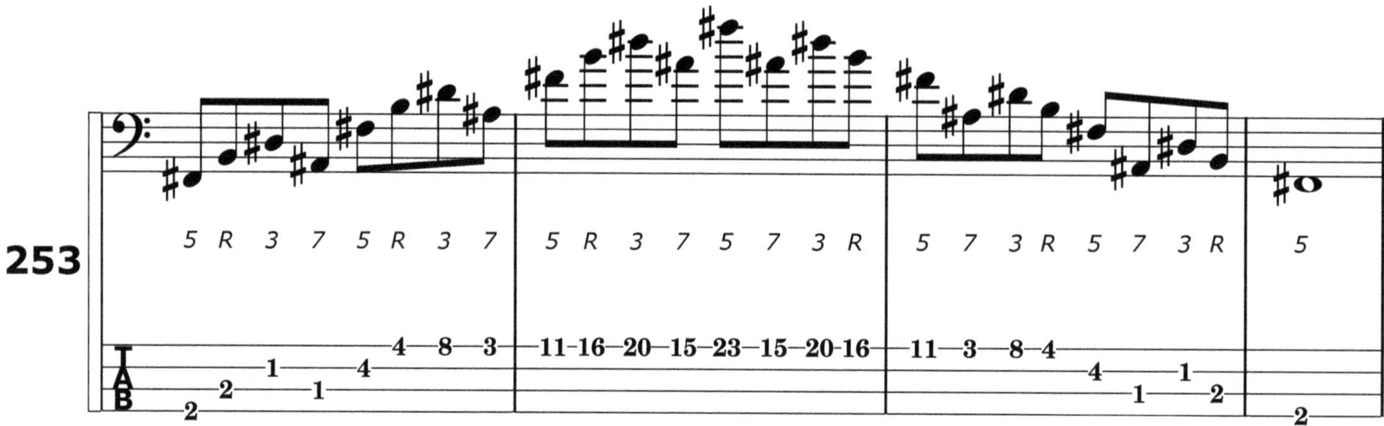

B Major - Fifth Pattern 2

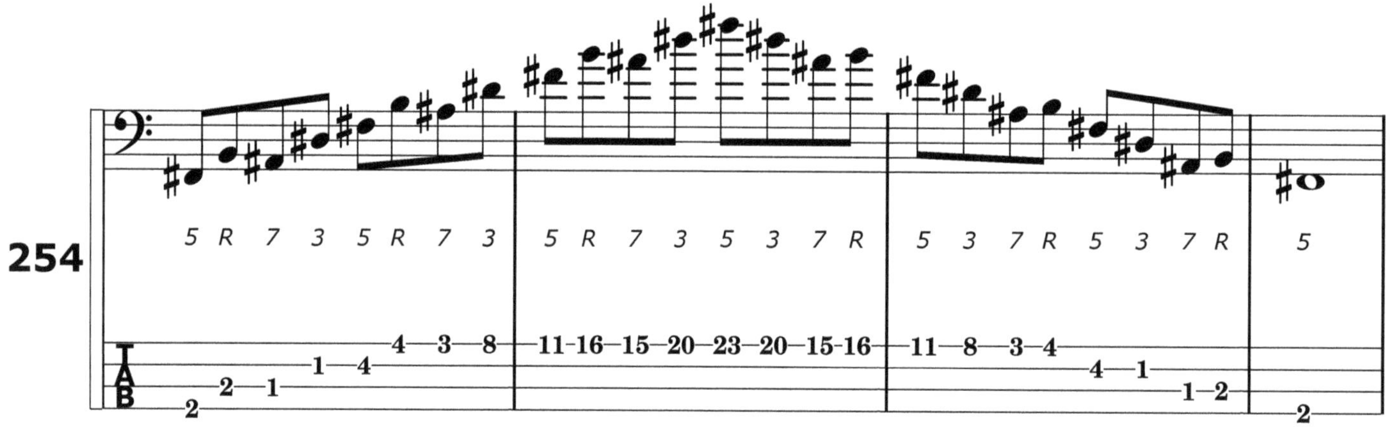

B Major - Fifth Pattern 3

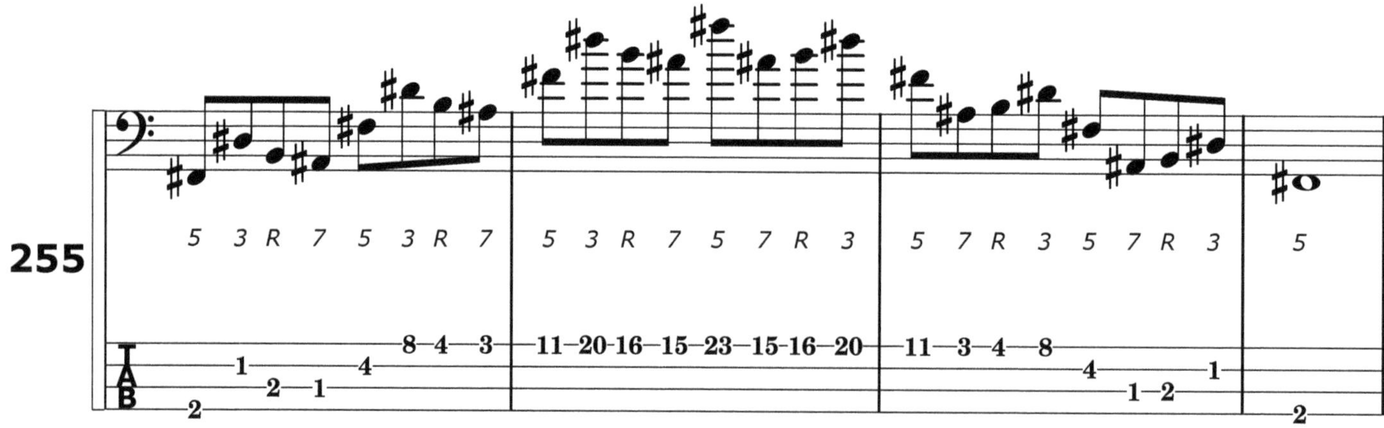

B Major - Fifth Pattern 4

256

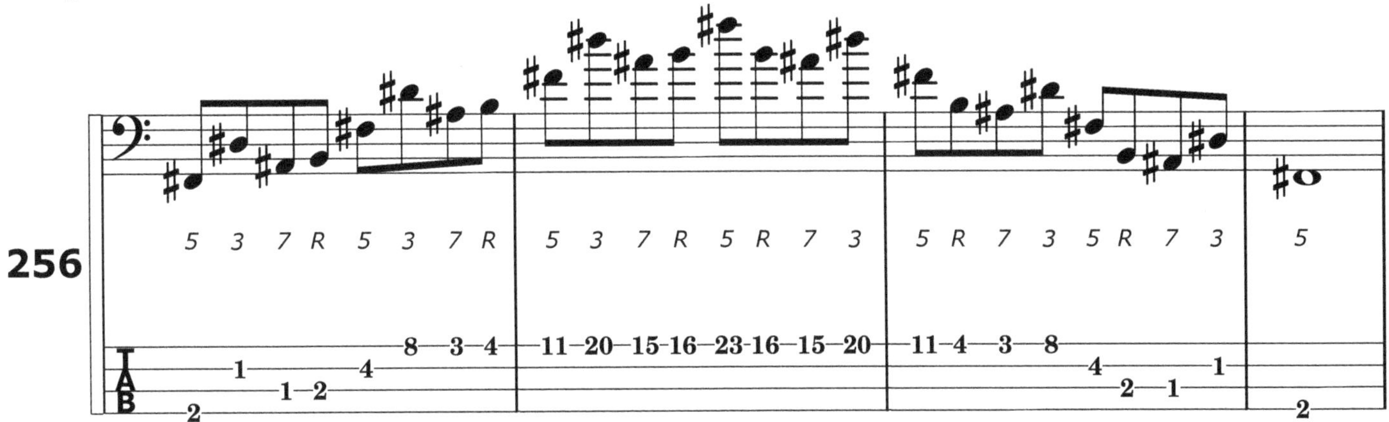

B Major - Fifth Pattern 5

257

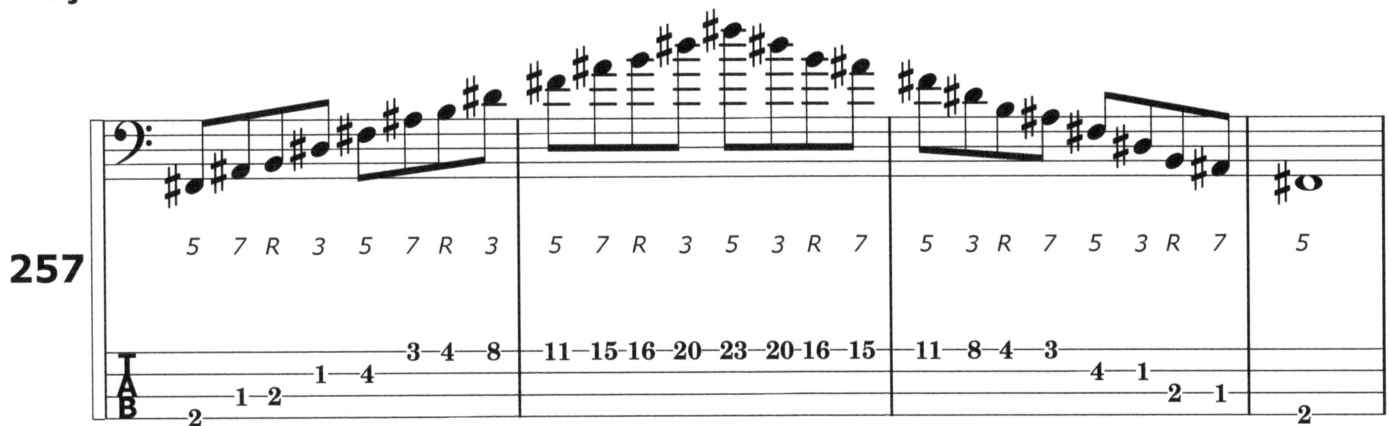

B Major - Fifth Pattern 6

258

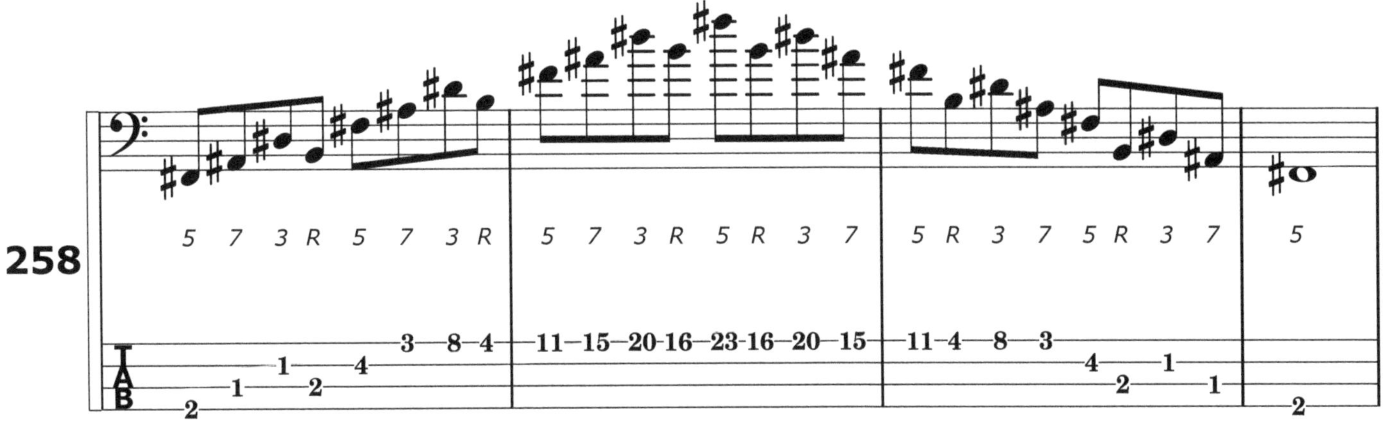

B Major - Seventh Pattern 1

259
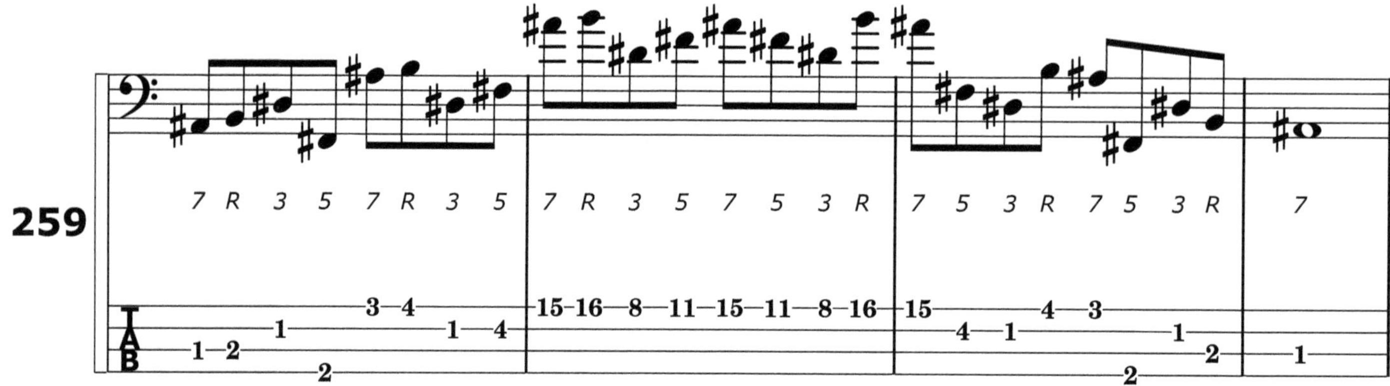

B Major - Seventh Pattern 2

260
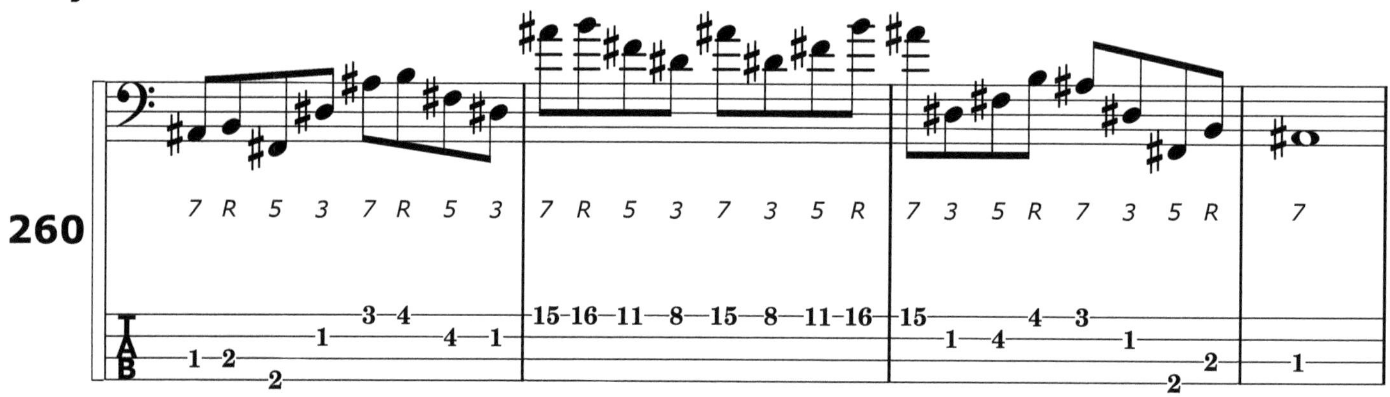

B Major - Seventh Pattern 3

261
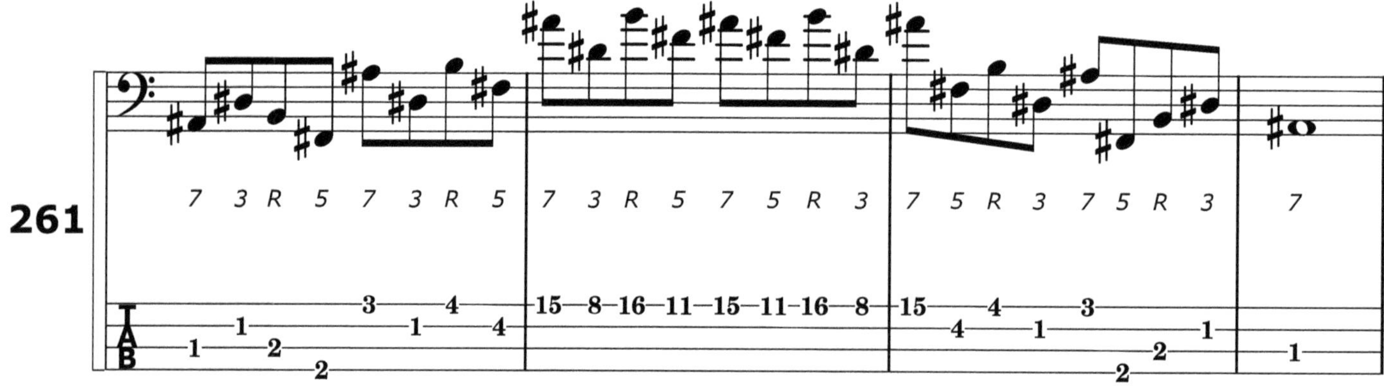

B Major - Seventh Pattern 4

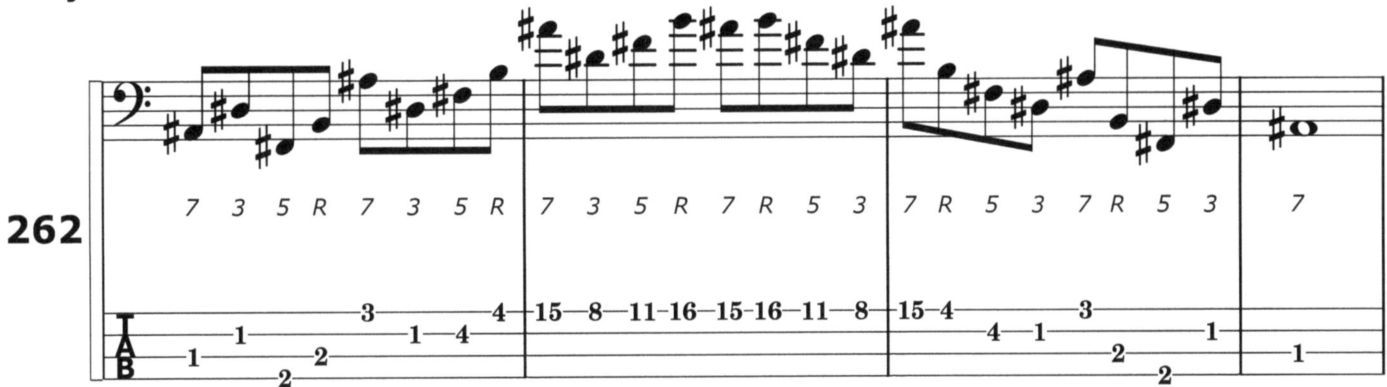

B Major - Seventh Pattern 5

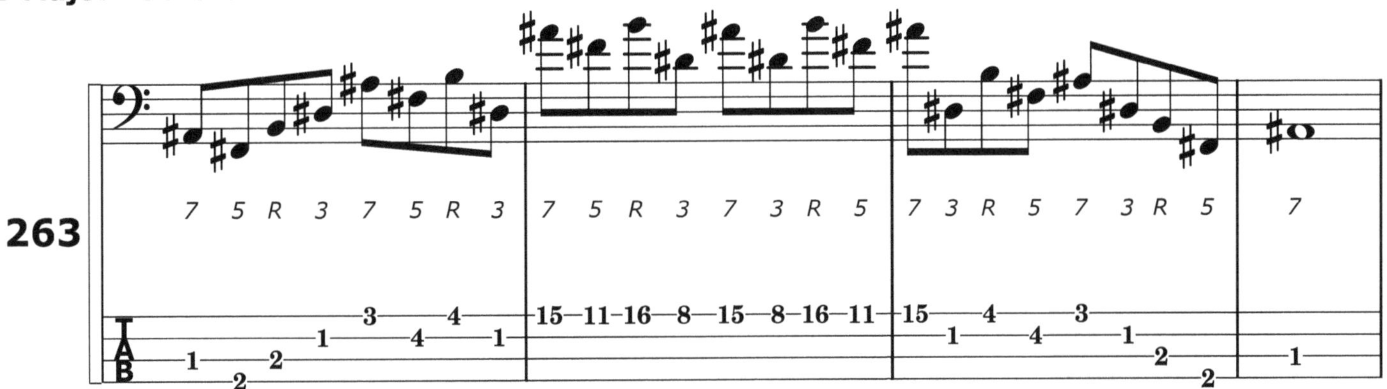

B Major - Seventh Pattern 6

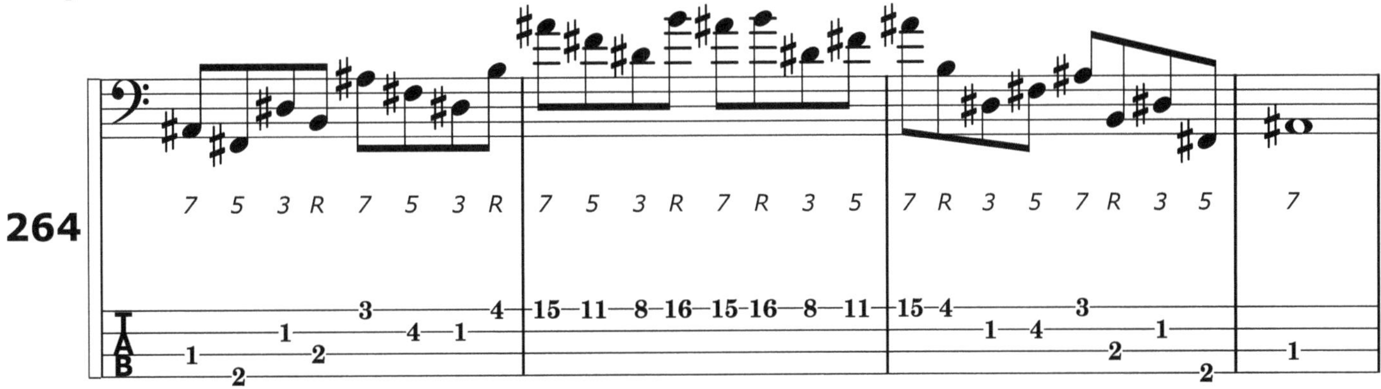

G♭ Major - Root Pattern 1

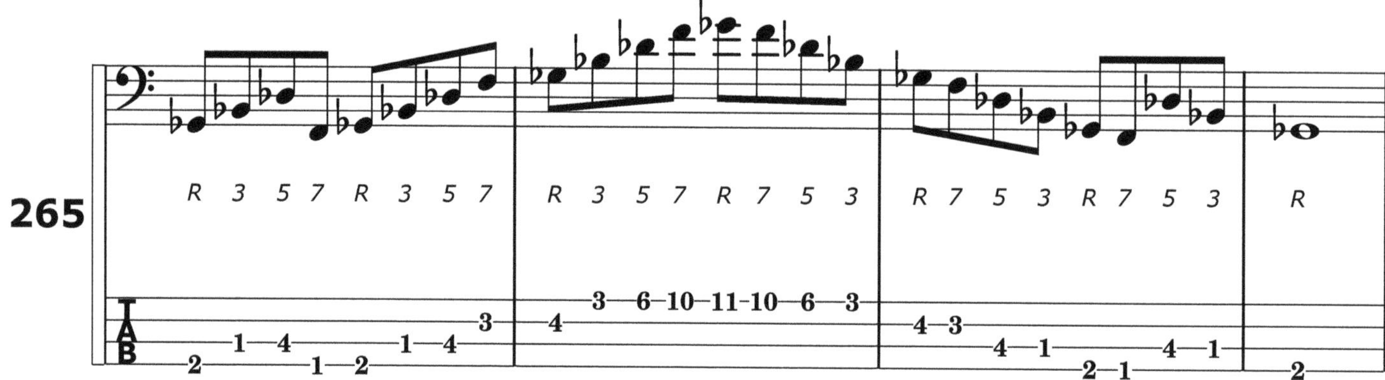

G♭ Major - Root Pattern 2

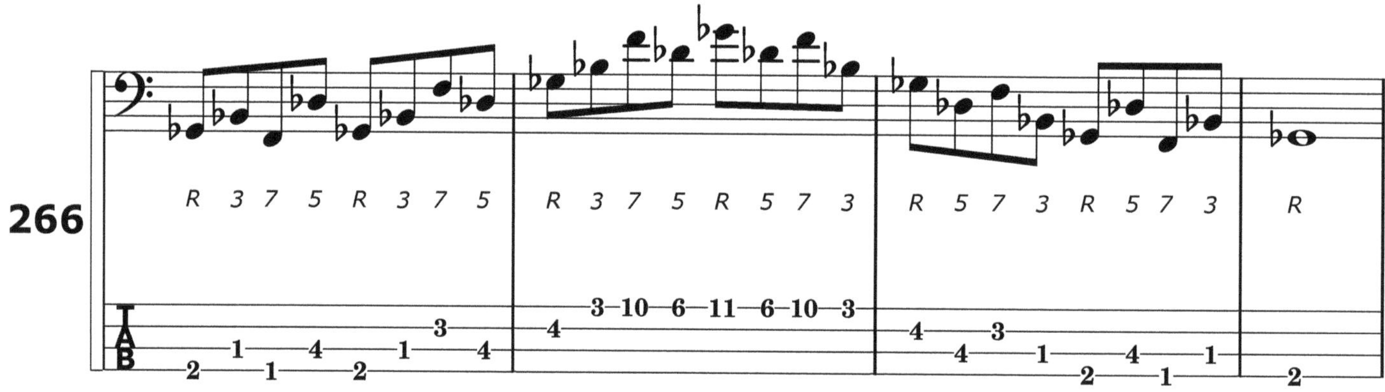

G♭ Major - Root Pattern 3

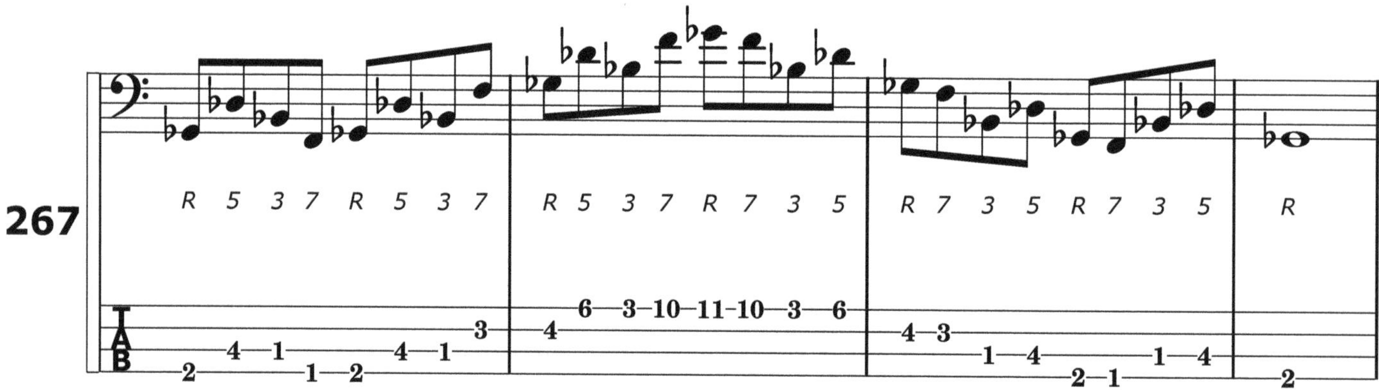

G♭ Major - Root Pattern 4

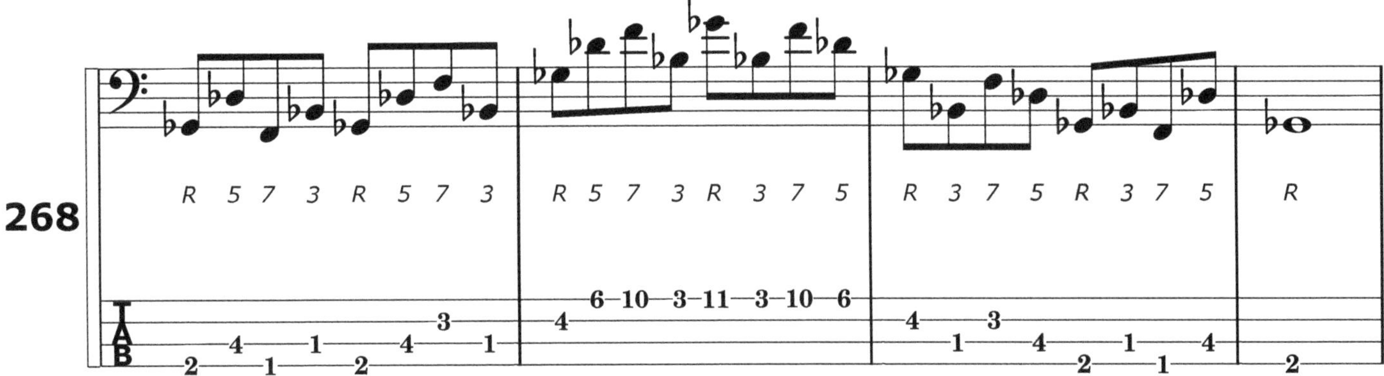

G♭ Major - Root Pattern 5

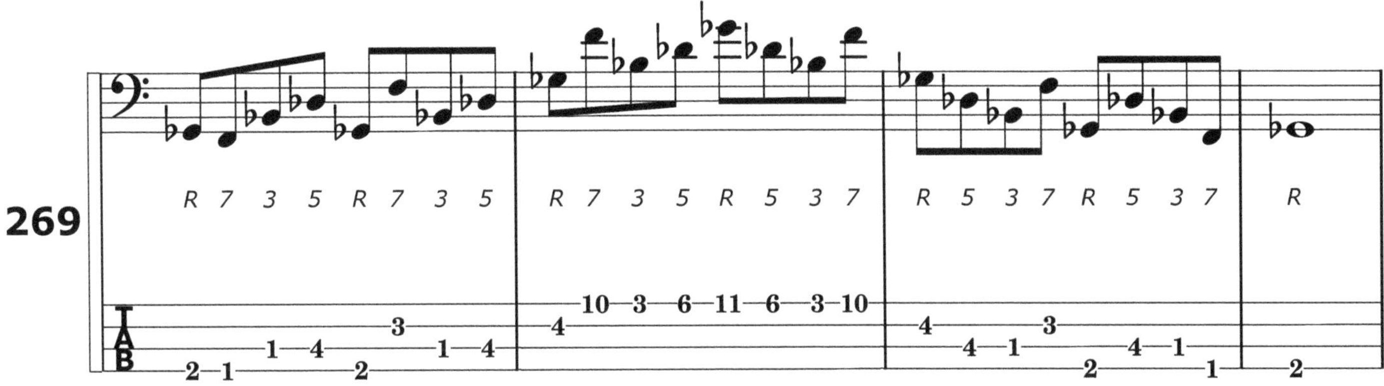

G♭ Major - Root Pattern 6

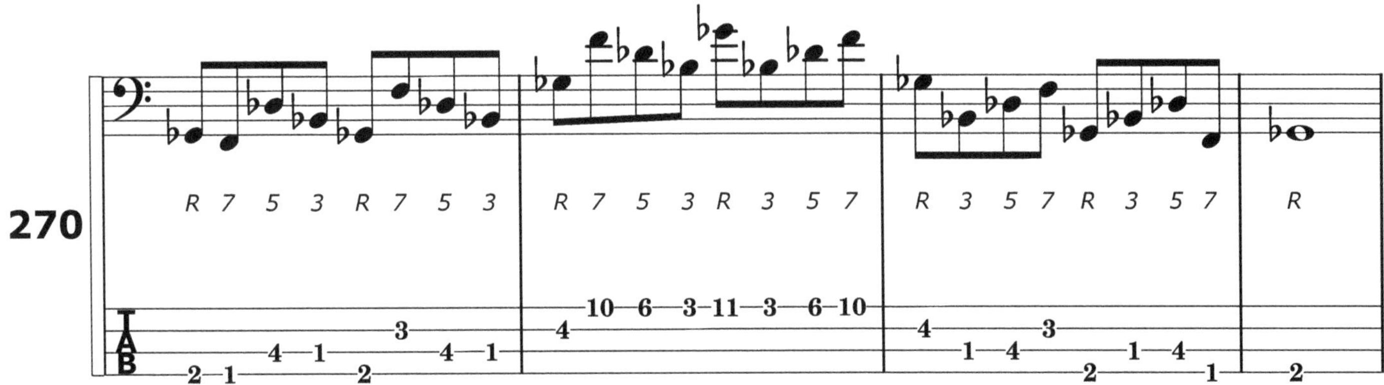

G♭ Major - Third Pattern 1

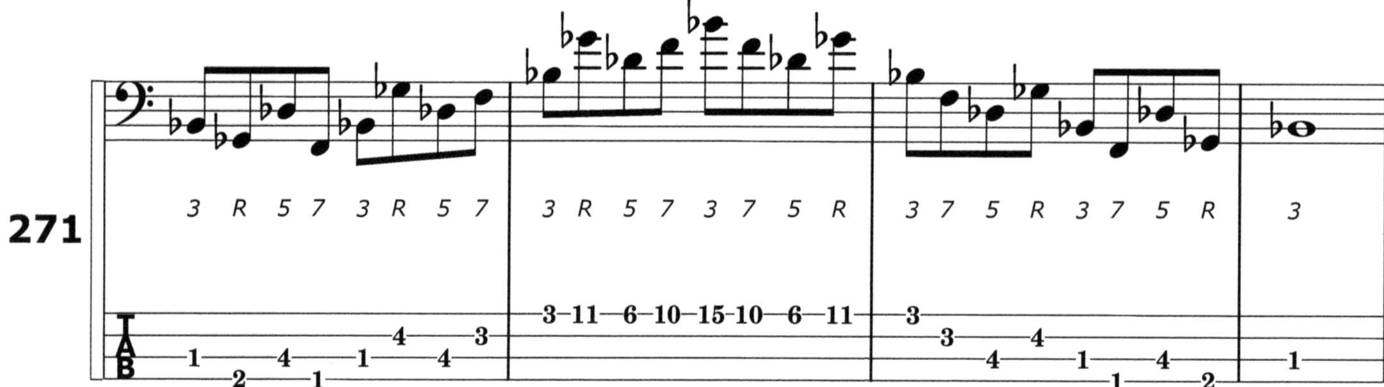

G♭ Major - Third Pattern 2

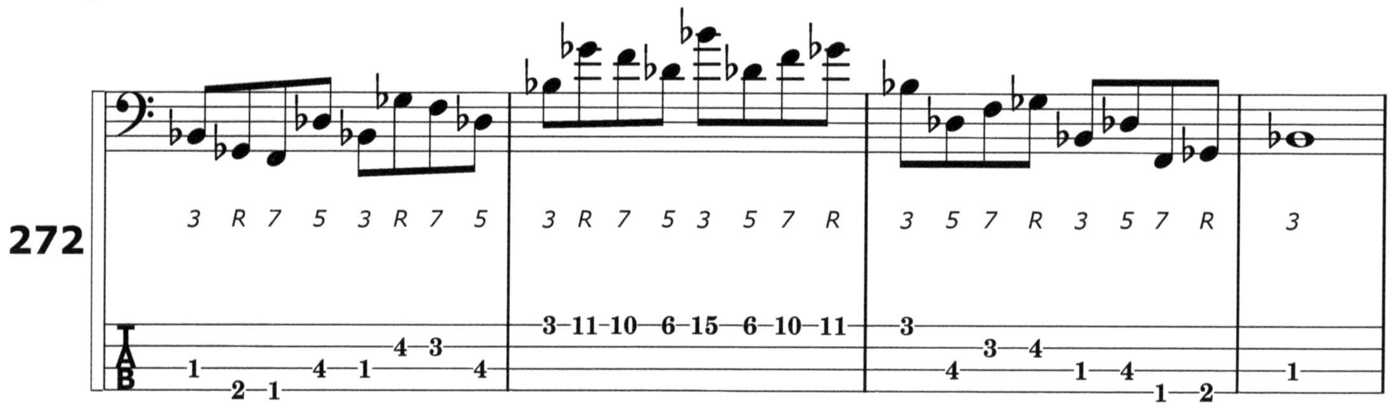

G♭ Major - Third Pattern 3

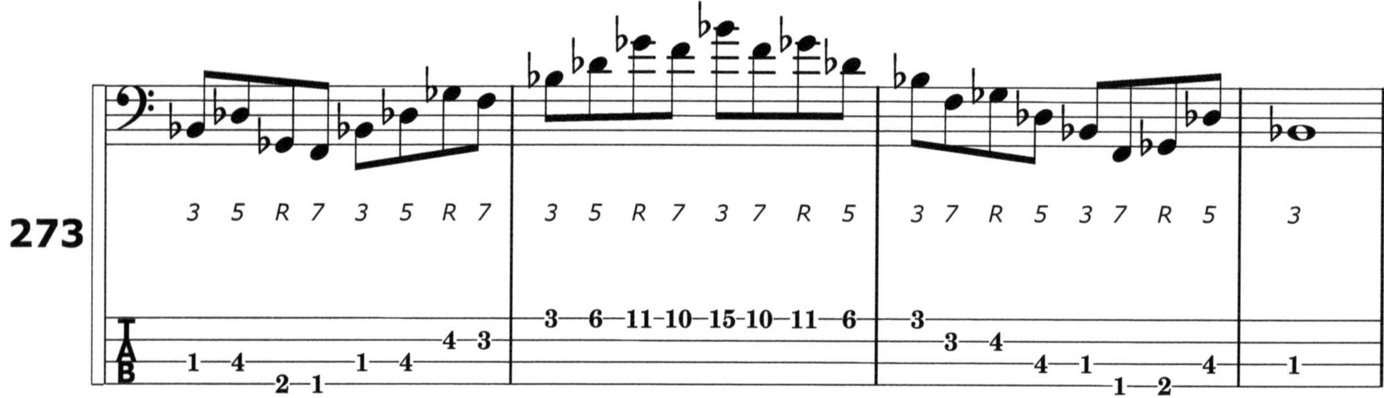

G♭ Major - Third Pattern 4

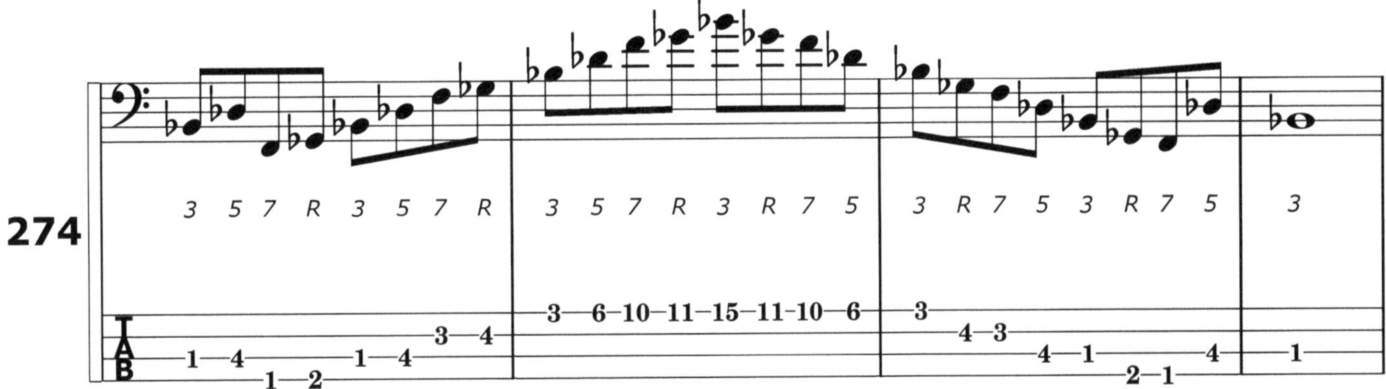

G♭ Major - Third Pattern 5

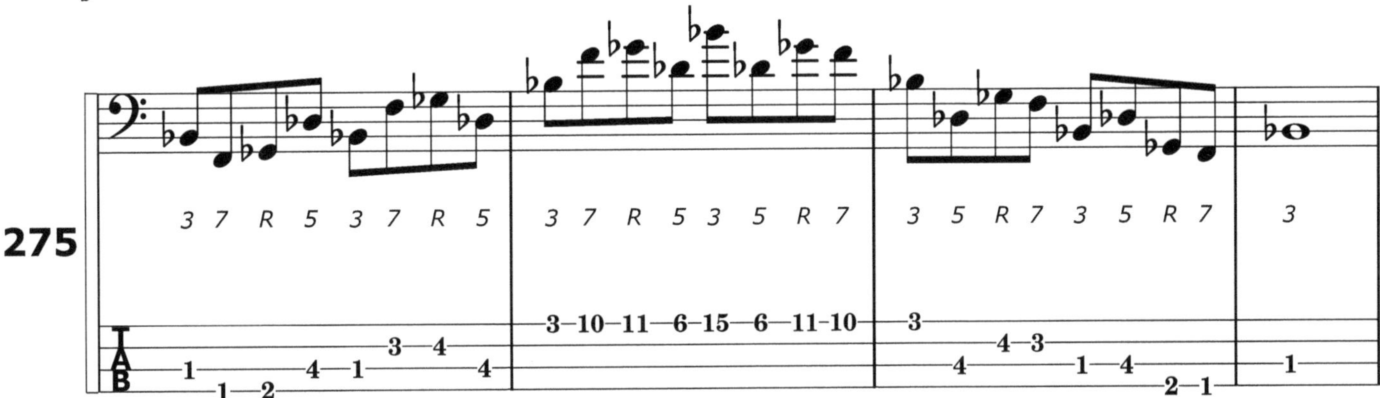

G♭ Major - Third Pattern 6

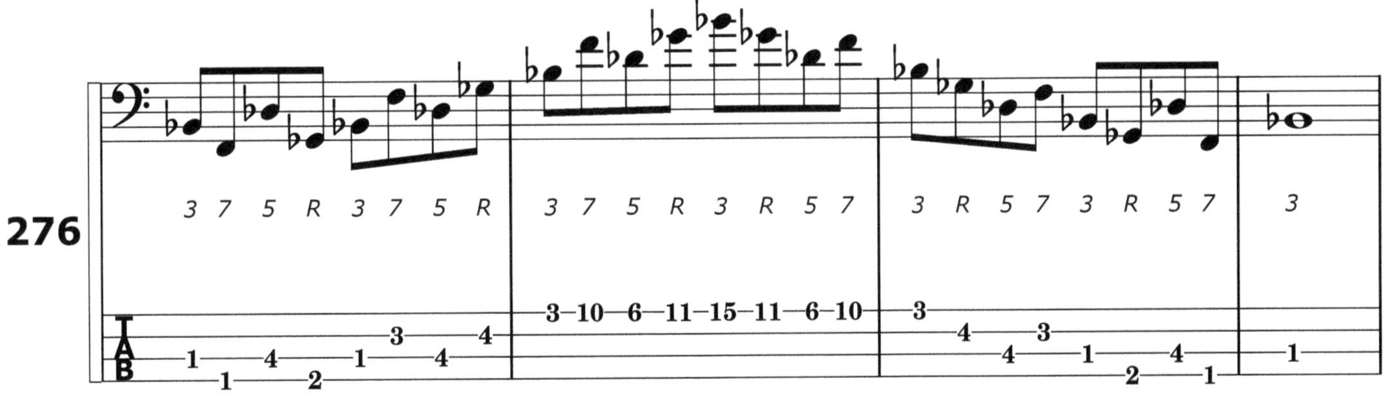

G♭ Major - Fifth Pattern 1

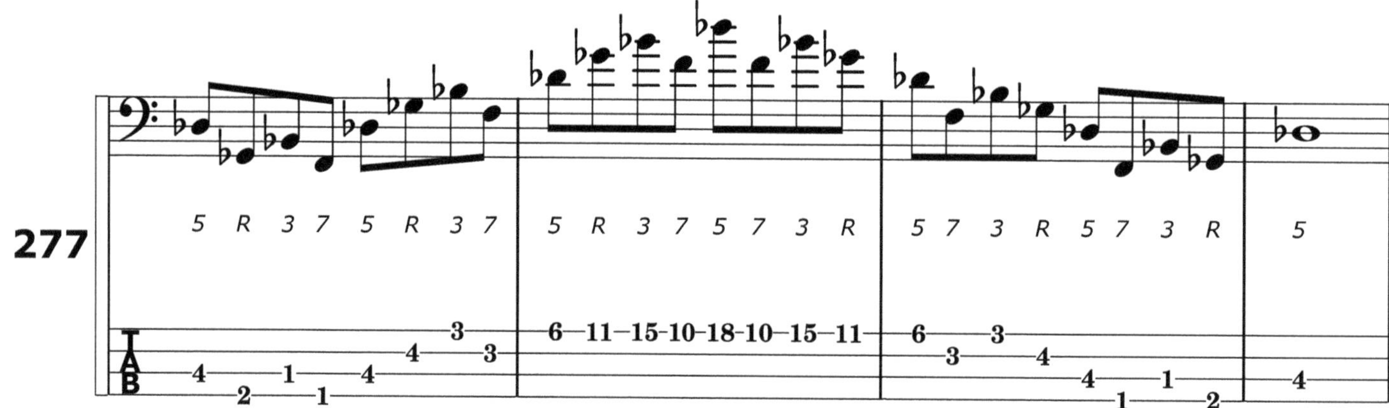

G♭ Major - Fifth Pattern 2

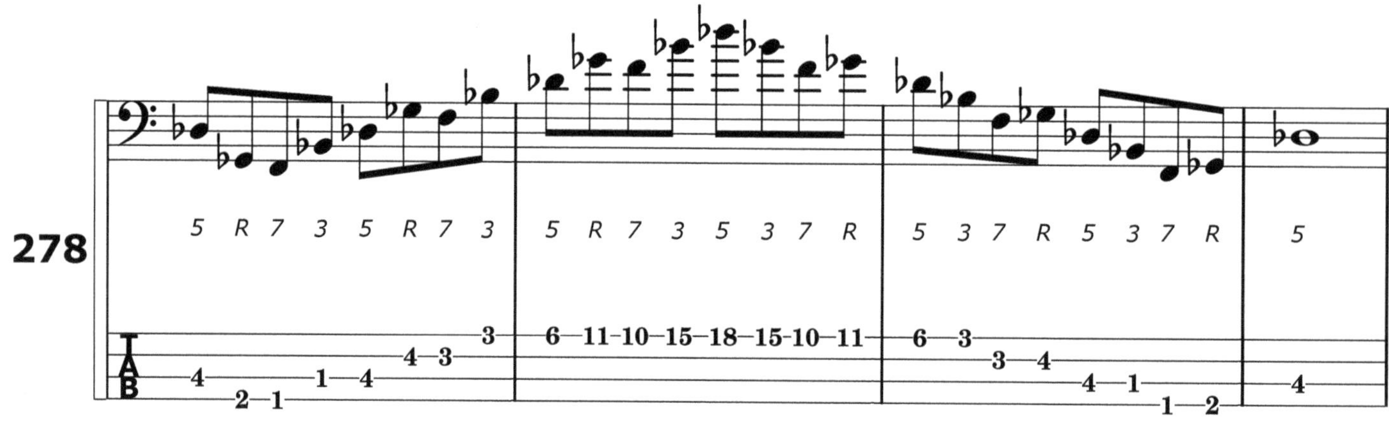

G♭ Major - Fifth Pattern 3

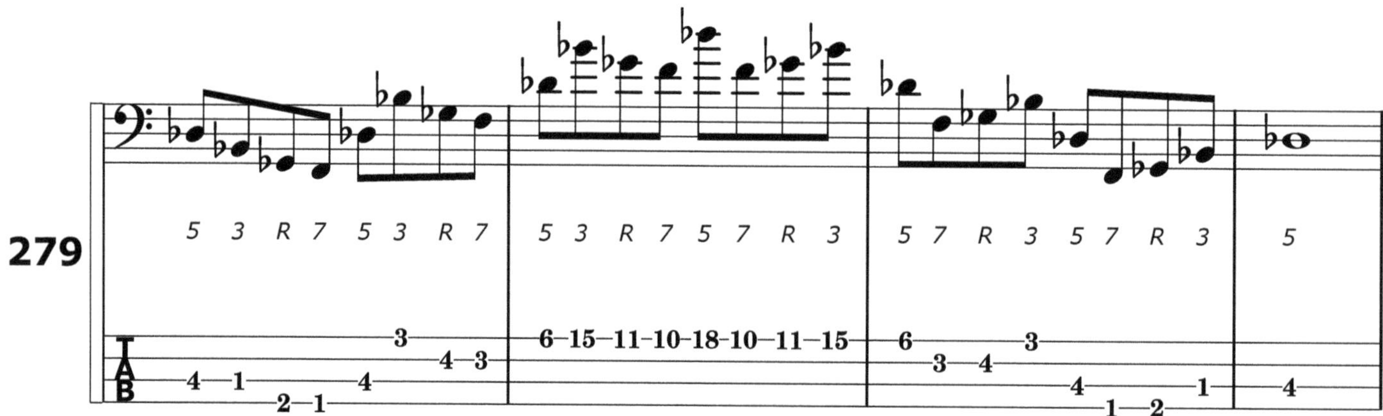

G♭ Major - Fifth Pattern 4

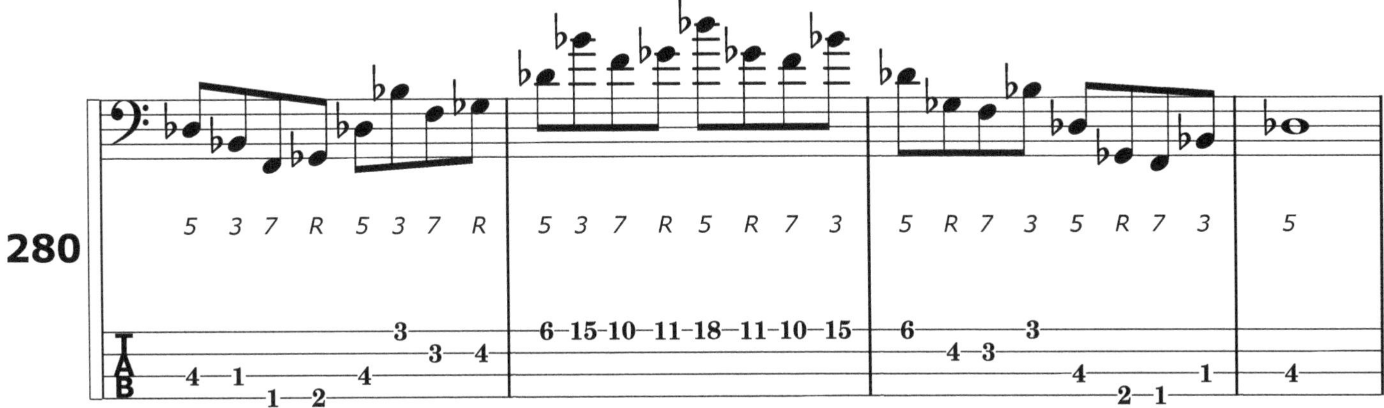

G♭ Major - Fifth Pattern 5

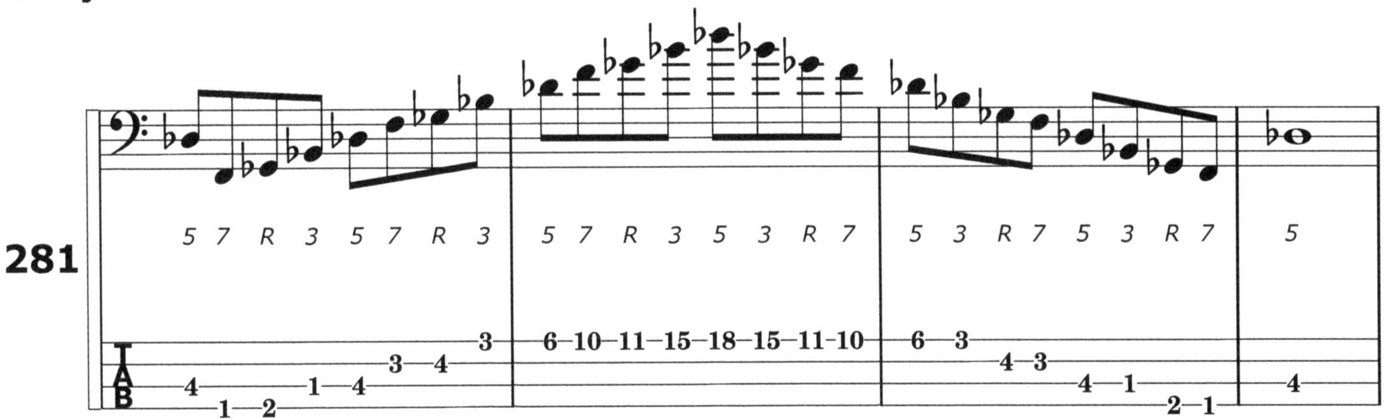

G♭ Major - Fifth Pattern 6

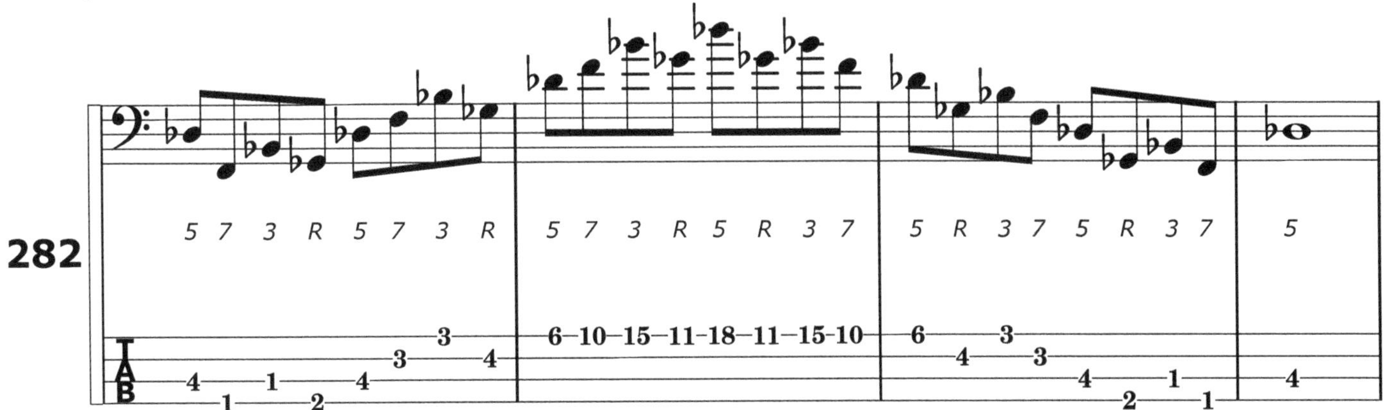

G♭ Major - Seventh Pattern 1

283

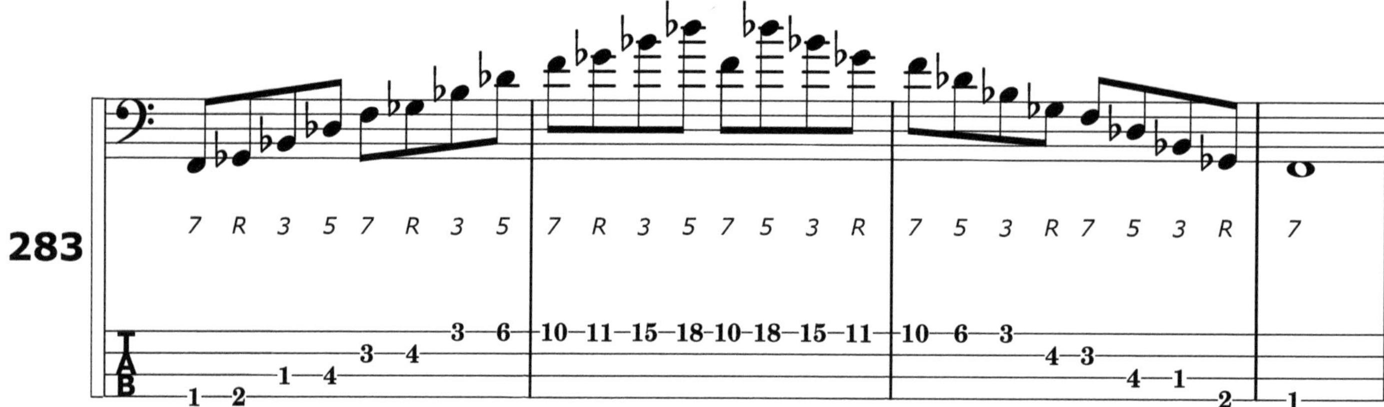

G♭ Major - Seventh Pattern 2

284

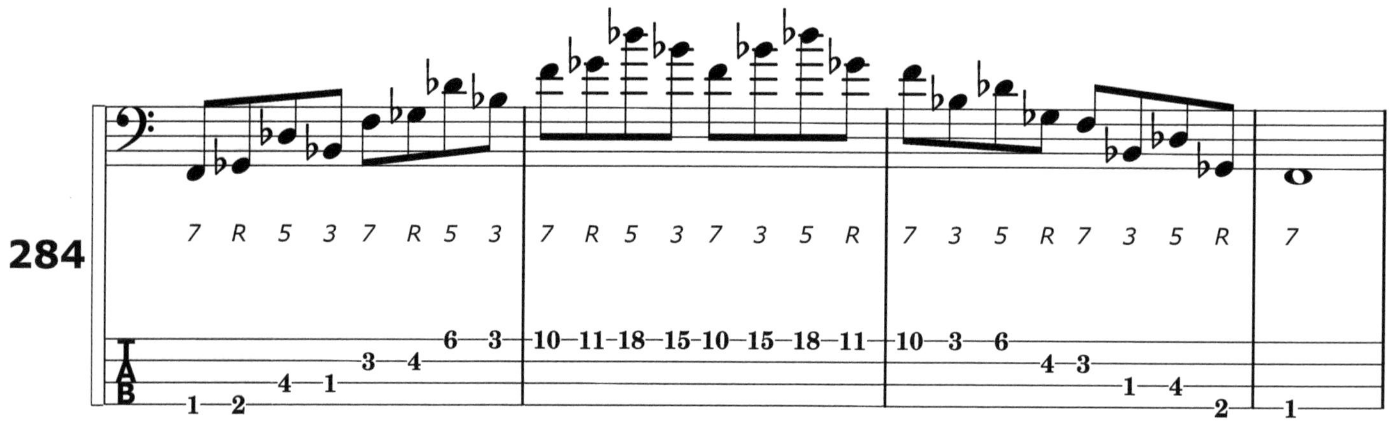

G♭ Major - Seventh Pattern 3

285

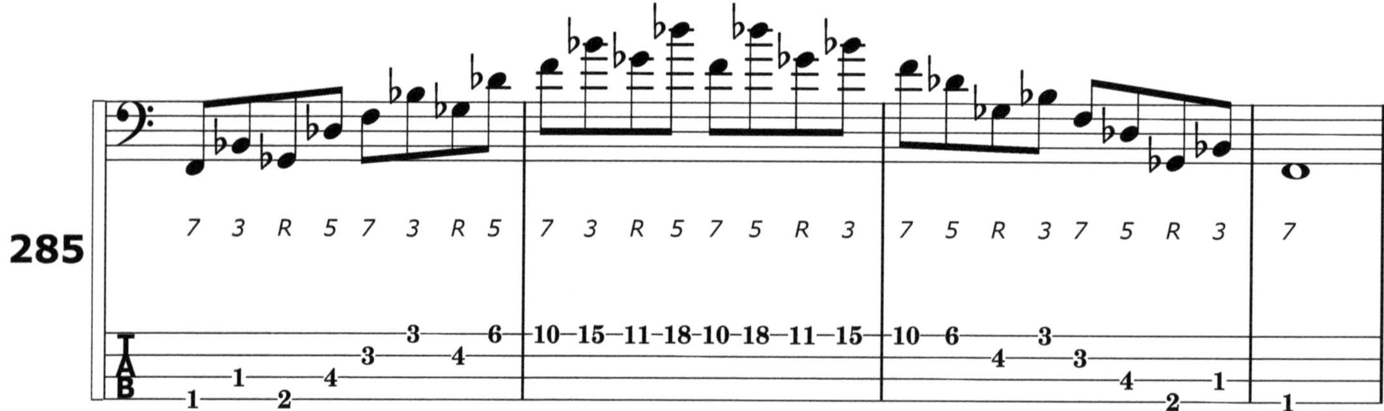

G♭ Major - Seventh Pattern 4

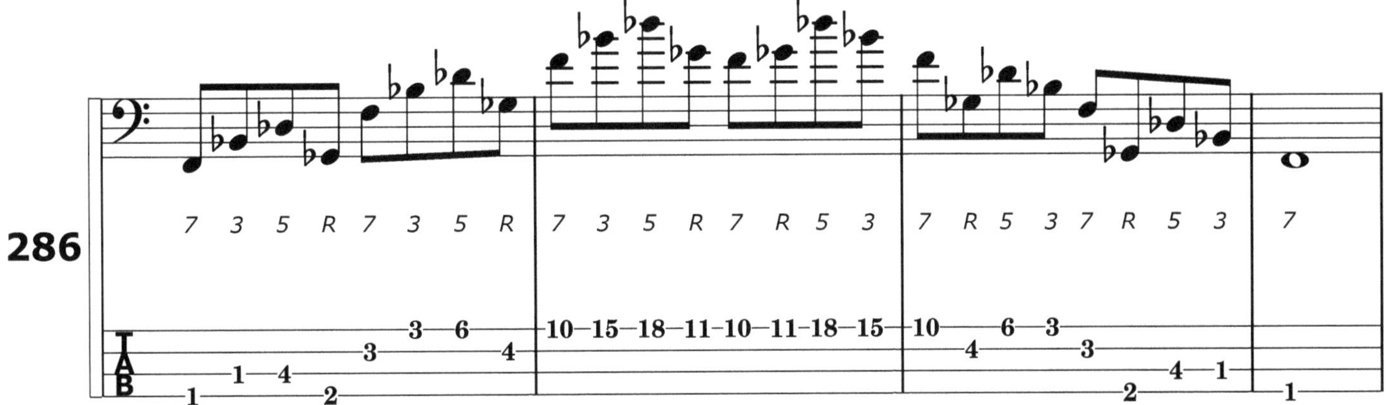

G♭ Major - Seventh Pattern 5

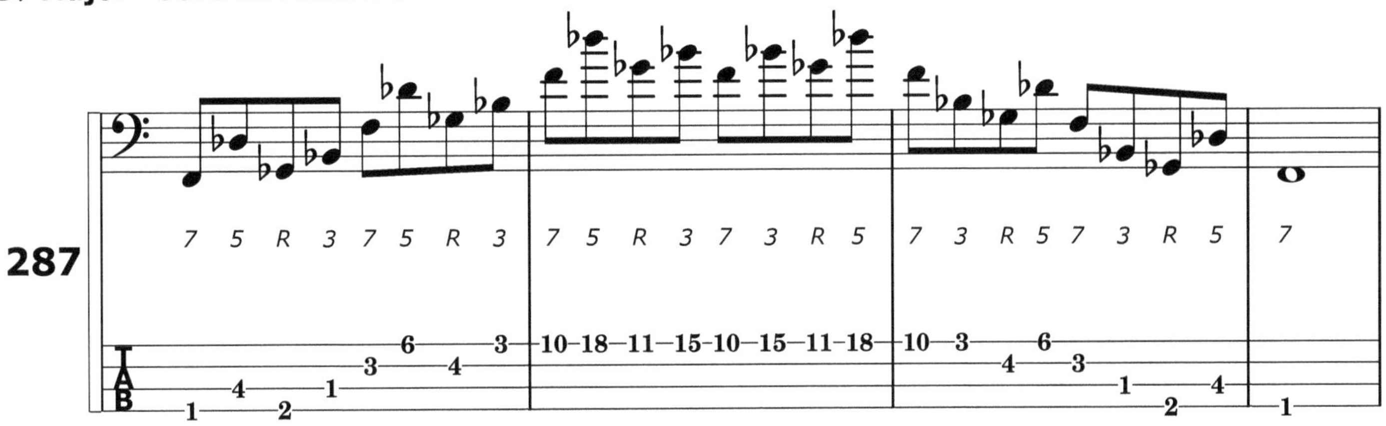

G♭ Major - Seventh Pattern 6

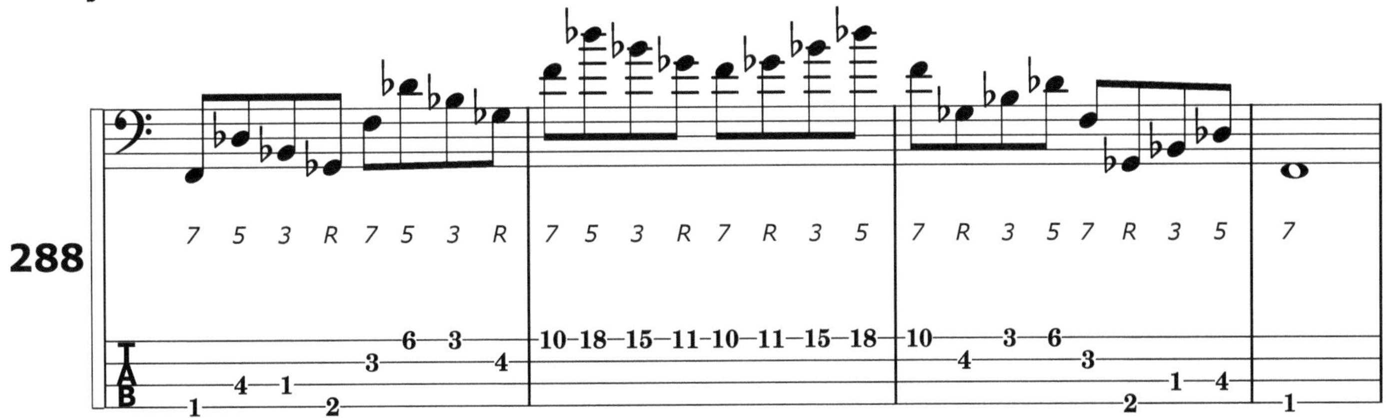

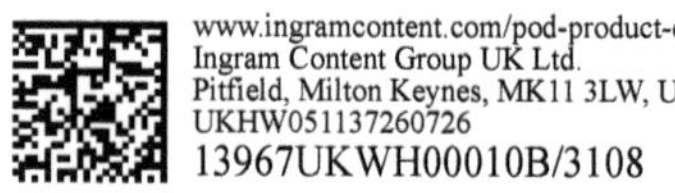
www.ingramcontent.com/pod-product-compliance
Ingram Content Group UK Ltd.
Pitfield, Milton Keynes, MK11 3LW, UK
UKHW051137260726
13967UKWH00010B/3108

9 781105 016790